CONQUEROR OF THE SEAS

THE STORY OF MAGELLAN

Stefan Zweig

MCMXXXVIII · THE LITERARY GUILD OF AMERICA, INC · NEW YORK

Translated by Eden and Cedar Paul

ACKNOWLEDGMENTS

While this book was still on the presses, there began to appear in Lisbon the documentary work on Magellan in the Portuguese language which had been for years in preparation. Only the first portions could be examined, but I must thank the honoured writer, the Visconde de Lagõa, for the information about it which he was so kind as to give me personally. I am equally indebted to the Visconde Carnaxide in Buenos Aires for special stimulation. Active assistance was rendered me by Dr. Leo Bagrow in the selection of illustrations, by Dr. Christine Rohr in the translation of the documents to be found in the Appendix, and not least by Professor Eugen Oberhummer of Vienna, leading expert on the age of discovery, who took an active interest in this work even before the final preparations for printing it.

—S. Z.

CONTENTS

viii   CONTENTS

ILLUSTRATIONS

INTRODUCTION

Books originate under the spur of the most diversified feelings. Some may write books owing to the stimulus of enthusiasm or through the promptings of gratitude; on the other hand, bitterness, anger, or annoyance may kindle the requisite spiritual passion. Often curiosity supplies the motive force, the psychological pleasure derived from the way in which writing about men or their doings explains these to oneself. Frequently it is less creditable factors, such as vanity, cupidity, or delight in self-portraiture, that arouse the itch for writing. It would be well for every author to analyse what urge, what desire for personal gratification, has led him to commit his thoughts to paper. For my part I have no doubt as to the internal causes that led me to pen the present work. I did so under stress of a comparatively unusual but very powerful sentiment—that of shame.

This is how it came to pass. Last year I was able to undertake a long-desired journey to South America. I knew that in Brazil some of the finest landscapes in the world would be disclosed to me, and that in Argentina I should have an incomparable encounter with many of my spiritual comrades. This anticipation alone would have sufficed to make the voyage memorable, but there were many other circum-

stances calculated to please. The sea was calm; I had opportunities for complete relaxation on the swift and roomy liner,
where I was freed from ties and daily vexations. Greatly, at
first, did I enjoy these paradisaical conditions. Then, on the
seventh or eighth day, I became aware of a froward impatience. The sky was so unfailingly blue, and the blue
waters were so unfailingly smooth. In my mood of exas-
peration the hours seemed to pass too slowly. I yearned for
the arrival in port; was eager to note every day how much
the clock had been put back; and was irked by being expected to enjoy such utter idleness. The continual sight of
the same faces wearied me, and the monotony of the ship's
routine had become insufferable. On, on; quicker, quicker.
This fine, comfortable, swift steamer was steaming far too
slowly for my taste.

Yet I was thoroughly ashamed of myself in the very moment when I realized my impatience. "Here you are," I said
to myself reproachfully, "travelling in the safest of ships
upon the loveliest voyage imaginable, with all the luxuries
in the world at your disposal. If you find it chilly in your
cabin after sunset, you need merely turn a switch and the air
is warmed. If the equatorial sun is too hot for you at noon,
in two or three strides you can go to the cool, shady room
where the electric fans are kept working, and a little farther
on you can plunge into a swimming-pool. At dinner you can
choose at will from the food and the drinks provided in this
most sumptuous of hotels; whatever you want—and more
than you can want—is brought to you as if by magic. You
can be alone to read when you like; should you prefer company, you can join in the games on deck, or listen to good

music. You are given both ease and safety. You know your destination; to the hour, almost to the minute, you know when you will get there; and your coming is eagerly awaited. So, likewise, in London, Paris, Buenos Aires, and New York, anyone who wishes can discover from moment to moment exactly where you are. If you trouble to mount a few steps to the wireless room, an obedient spark will carry a question or a greeting to almost any spot on the world's surface, and within the hour you will have an answer. Remember, impatient and ungrateful as you are, what voyages were like in the old days. Compare your present experiences with those of the valiant navigators who were the first to cross this ocean, and to make the world known to us. Are you not ashamed of yourself when you think of them? Try to picture how they set forth, on ships little larger than fishing-smacks, to explore the unknown, to sail they knew not whither, lost in the infinite, ceaselessly in peril, exposed to all the vicissitudes of storm, to every kind of privation. No light when darkness had fallen; nothing to drink but the brackish, lukewarm water stored in butts, supplemented by occasional rainfall; nothing to eat but biscuit that was often mouldy, and pickled pork that was often rancid—and not always a sufficiency of these unpalatable viands. No beds, no rest-room; stifling heat or pitiless cold, made worse for the mariners by the consciousness that they were alone in the unending desert of waters. For months, for years, no one at home knew what had become of them, any more than they themselves knew where they were going. Want was their fellow-passenger; death in myriad forms environed them by sea or on land, danger from man and from the elements.

Month after month and year after year in their poor little craft they had to endure the unspeakable torments of isolation. There was no one to come to their help. In the untravelled waters, months would pass without their catching sight of a sail. No one could save them from the hazards they had to encounter; and should they go down to destruction, it was likely enough that no one would record their fate."

Yes, as soon as I began to recall the early voyages of the conquistadors of the sea, I was thoroughly ashamed of my impatience.

Once this sense of shame had been aroused, it did not leave me for the remainder of the voyage. Not for a moment could I free myself from the thought of these nameless heroes. It made me long to learn more about those who had first dared to struggle against the elements, and to read more of the first voyages into unexplored oceans, voyages the description of which had fascinated me in boyhood. Going to the library, I chose a few volumes haphazard. As I studied them, it seemed to me that the deed worthiest of admiration was that of the man who made the most wonderful of all voyages of discovery—Ferdinand Magellan, who started from Seville with five little ships to circumnavigate the globe. Was not this the most glorious Odyssey in the history of mankind, the departure of two hundred and sixty-five resolute men of whom only eighteen got back to Spain on a crumbling vessel, but with the flag of triumph flying at the masthead?

There was not much about Magellan in these books, certainly not enough to satisfy me. As soon as I got home, therefore, I continued my researches, and noted with increasing astonishment how little trustworthy information there was concerning this astounding exploit. As had happened to me several times before, I found that to tell the story to others would be the best way of explaining the inexplicable to myself. Such was the origin of my book, which, I can frankly say, has come into being to my own surprise. For, in recounting this Odyssey as faithfully as I could after the examination of all the documents available, I have been animated throughout by the strange feeling that I must be painting a fanciful picture, must be relating one of the great wish-dreams, one of the hallowed fairy tales of mankind. Yet what can be better than a truth which seems utterly improbable? There is always something inconceivable about man's supreme deeds, for the simple reason that they greatly transcend average human powers; but it is by performing the incredible that man regains faith in his own self.

—STEFAN ZWEIG

Chapter One

NAVIGARE NECESSE EST

.

The name of the first man who undertook to circumnavigate the globe has come down to us in various forms. In Portuguese documents the great navigator is sometimes spoken of as FERNÃO DE MAGALHÃIS, sometimes as FERNÃO DE MAGALHÃES; after entering the Spanish service, he signed documents alternately MAGHALLANES and MAGHELLANES, while the cartographers latinized this Spanish form as MAGELLANUS. Not wishing to perplex my readers with needless variations, I have decided to use throughout the semi-latinized form, MAGELLAN, which has long had international currency. We have the precedent of COLUMBUS, who is rarely spoken of as CRISTOFORO COLOMBO or as CRISTÓBAL COLÓN. Almost invariably, too, I describe by the more familiar name of CHARLES V the Habsburg ruler who made MAGELLAN's voyage possible, although during the opening years of my narrative he had not yet been crowned Holy Roman Emperor, and was merely KING CHARLES I of Spain.

Navigare Necesse Est

THE quest for spices began it. From the days when the Romans, in their journeys and their wars, first acquired a taste for the hot or aromatic, the pungent or intoxicating dietetic adjuvants of the East, the Western World found it impossible to get on without a supply of Indian spices in cellar and storeroom. Lacking spices, the food of Northern Europe was unspeakably monotonous and insipid, and thus it remained far into the Middle Ages. Centuries were to elapse before the fruits, the tubers, and the other products which now seem commonplaces were to be used or acclimatized in Europe. Potatoes, tomatoes, and corn were unknown. There were no lemons to prepare acid drinks, there was no sugar for sweetening, the cheering tea and coffee were still lacking; even at the tables of the rich and the powerful, there was naught to relieve the sameness of perpetual gluttony—until, wonderful to relate, it was found that a touch of spice from the Orient, a dash of pepper, a minute addition of ground nutmeg, the mingling of a little ginger or cinnamon with the coarsest of dishes, would give an unwonted and wholesome stimulus to the jaded palate. Precious culinary overtones were interspersed between the crude treble and bass of sour and sweet, of sapid and vapid; and the still barbaric medieval gustatory nerves speedily found it impossible to dispense with these exotic flavourings. More and more of them was demanded. A dish was not properly prepared unless it had been pricked up with so gross an excess of pepper that it bit the eater's tongue immoderately. Even beer was strongly seasoned with ginger, and mulled wine was so laden with spices that it tasted like liquid fire.

The West, however, needed spices and kindred Oriental products not for the kitchen alone. The women of Europe made an increasing demand for the sweet-scented products of Araby: wanton musk, fragrant ambergris, heavy-smelling attar of roses. They asked weavers and dyers to provide them with Chinese silks and Indian damasks, goldsmiths and jewellers to supply them with lustrous pearls from Ceylon and glittering diamonds from Hindustan. Paradoxically enough, the spread of the Catholic faith promoted the use of Oriental products, for not one of the myriad censers swung in the countless churches of Europe drew its supply from European soil, each of them being provided with the materials for its fragrant smoke by sea or by land from the Arabian Peninsula. No less did the apothecaries have to vaunt Indian or Levantine specifics, such as opium, camphor, and the costly gum-resin, experience having taught them that their customers would not believe any balsam or other drug to be truly efficacious unless upon the porcelain vessel which contained it there was to be read in blue letters the magic word "Arabian" or "Indian." The rarity, the exotic character, and doubtless the high price of any Oriental medicament sufficed to enhance its suggestive working in the West. Throughout the Middle Ages, the terms Arabian, Persian, and Indian were, to European ears, almost synonymous with select, exquisite, distinguished, precious, and expensive—much as was the attribute "French" during the eighteenth century, elsewhere than in France. No other article of commerce was so much coveted as were Oriental spices, until it seemed that the mysteriously foreign aroma of these products of the distant East must have intoxicated the European mind.

For the very reason that they were so fashionable, Indian goods were dear, and grew steadily dearer. It is difficult, nowadays, to calculate the febrile rise in their prices, for, as is well known, historical accounts of such matters are vague and fabulous. Perhaps the best idea of the crazy cost of spices can be formed by recalling that in the eleventh century of our era pepper, which today stands unguarded on every restaurant table and is scattered almost as freely as sand, was counted out corn by corn, and was certainly worth its weight in silver. A "pepper-corn rent" is now a nominal rent, but this was not always so. Many States and towns kept their accounts in pepper as if it had been silver or gold. With pepper you could buy land, pay dowries, purchase the freedom of the city. Many princes assessed their taxes in weights of pepper. When, in the Middle Ages, you wished to describe a man as a bloated Crœsus, you spoke of him as a "pepper-sack."

Nor was pepper the only product of this sort. Ginger and cinnamon and camphor were weighed upon apothecaries' scales, the windows being carefully closed during the operation lest a draught should blow away the minutest fragment of the costly dust. But however absurd this over-valuation of spices may seem to a modern mind, it becomes comprehensible enough when we recall the difficulties and the risks of transport. In those days the East lay at an immeasurable distance from the West. The trade routes by land were perpetually threatened by robbers, and pirates abounded at sea. Great were the difficulties of travel, immense the risks to which caravans and ships were exposed.

What an Odyssey every pepper-corn, every dried blossom, had to traverse from the green plant in the Malay Archipelago to reach its last strand on the counter of a European shopkeeper. In the place of origin, not one of these spices was a rarity. On the other side of the earth, the cinnamon-laurel grew in Ceylon, the clove in Amboina, the nutmeg in Banda, the pepper plant in Malabar—as lavishly there as do thistles in our own land. In Malaysia, a hundredweight of one of these products was worth no more than a teaspoonful here in the West. But trade goods passed from hand to hand; the owner of each pair of hands demanded his recompense; and the goods we are now considering had to pass through many hands before they reached those of the last purchaser, the consumer, across deserts and seas. The first hand in the series was, as a rule, the most poorly recompensed—that of the Malayan slave who plucked the fresh blossoms, carrying them to market upon his brown-skinned back and receiving little more than his own sweat for his reward. It was his master who reaped the profit, the master from whom a Mohammedan merchant bought the load, paddling it in his lightly built prahu beneath the tropical sun from the Spice Islands to Malacca, not far from the modern Singapore. Here sat the first of the blood-sucking spiders, the lord of the harbour, the Sultan, demanding tribute from every dealer who wanted to tranship his goods. Not until the dues had been paid, could the aromatic freight be transferred to another and larger bottom in which, by sail or oar, it would be removed a farther stage on its journey, to one of the seaports of Hindustan. Months would be spent in such successive transhipments, for, in these latitudes, the sailing-boats were often becalmed week after week beneath cloudless skies, or must run before fierce hurricanes and escape from sea-robbers by headlong flight. Not only toilsome but fearfully dangerous was the voyage across two or three tropical seas, where, as a rule, at least one out of five ships was sunk by storm or plundered by pirates. With good luck, however, the Gulf of Cambay would at length be crossed, the southern coast of Arabia rounded, and Aden reached (if the destination should be the Red Sea and Egypt); or (if an earlier landfall were sought) Ormuz at the entrance to the Persian Gulf.

But the phase of land-travel that now followed was no less arduous and no less perilous. By thousands, in these seaports, waited the camels in long rows. Obediently, at a sign from the master, they kneeled for the bales of pepper or nutmeg or what not to be laden on their patient backs. Now the four-legged "ships of the desert" continued the north-westward trail. By the more easterly caravan route, which was the commoner, in journeys that lasted for months, the Arab caravans conveyed the Indian goods by way of Basra, Baghdad, and Damascus to Beirut or Trebizond; or, by the western route, to Jidda and Cairo. Extremely ancient are these paths across the desert, well known to caravan leaders since the times of the Pharaohs and the Bactrians. But if known to the itinerant traders, they were known equally well to the bedouins, the pirates of the desert. One bold raid would often carry off the fruit of laborious months. Besides, what escaped the sand-storms and the bedouins could not escape other robbers who regarded themselves as legitimate. The emirs of El Hejaz, the sultans of Egypt, and the rulers of Syria demanded tribute (and no small one) on every sack that passed through their territories. Egypt alone, it has been estimated, secured an annual revenue of hundreds of thousands of ducats from the transit trade in spices. Suppose that Alexandria had been safely reached, here there would be fresh octopuses awaiting their chance, who would prove neither the last nor the least—the ships of the Venetian fleet. Since its perfidious overthrow of its Byzantine rival, the maritime republic had secured a monopoly of the spice trade across the Mediterranean. The goods, instead of being shipped direct to their destination, had now to be brought to the Rialto, where the German, the Flemish, and the British factors would compete with one another for the wares. Then, in broad-wheeled wagons, through the snow and ice of the Alpine passes, would roll onward the precious goods which had come into existence in the tropics at least two years before. At last, at last, they would reach the Western retailers, who, having exacted a fresh profit, would pass them on to the consumer.

We learn from Martin Behaim's famous Nuremberg globe, constructed by that celebrated navigator and cosmographer when, in 1492, he was revisiting the city of his birth, that Indian spices had to pass through at least twelve hands before they reached the consumer. But, though so many had to share in the gains, each succeeded in squeezing a sufficiency of golden sap out of the India trade. Despite all its perils and hardships, the traffic in spices remained by far the most lucrative of the Middle Ages, because the bulk of the commodity was so small and the margin of profit so large. Even though, out of five vessels, four should go to the bottom, carrying their stored riches into the depths (in the case of Magellan's expedition, only one ship circumnavigated the world), and even though of two hundred and sixty-five men who set sail, more than two hundred should never get home, still it was only sailors and captains who lost their lives, while the trader would harvest his gains just the same. Did but one petty ship out of five reach home, after three years, well freighted with spices, its cargo would bring in a handsome profit. In the fifteenth century, a sack of pepper was worth more than a human life; and since, in those times, as always, there was an ample supply of lives, since lives were cheap and spices were dear, we need not be surprised that the merchants usually made good; that the palaces of Venice and those of the Fuggers and the Welsers were strongly built out of the rewards of the Indian spice traffic.

But as inevitably as iron rusts, does covetousness fester the souls of profiteers. Every trading advantage, every monopoly, is considered unjust by would-be rivals. The Genoese, the French, and the Spaniards looked askance at the success of the Venetians in diverting the golden Gulf Stream into the Grand Canal. With even more rancour did these trade rivals contemplate Egypt and Syria, where Islam interposed an impenetrable barrier between India and Europe. No Christian ship was allowed to sail the Red Sea, nor was any Christian trader allowed to travel by the land routes to the Indies. The use of Turkish and Arabian intermediaries was inexorably enforced upon the giaours. The upshot of this regulation was not merely a needless increase of cost to European consumers, but also a great withdrawal of profit from Christian merchants. An additional consequence was a steady flow of the precious metals to the Orient, inasmuch as European wares did not move eastward to an extent that could compensate for the exchange value of Indian luxuries. Were it only because of the unfavourable balance of trade, the Western World grew more and more eager to escape from this ruinous and degrading control, until at length forcible measures were taken to bring it to an end. The Crusades were not exclusively or mainly (as romanticists are apt to believe) the outcome of an endeavour to liberate the Holy City from the grip of unbelievers. The primary object of the first military coalition of Christian Europe was to break through the Mohammedan barrier across the Red Sea and thus free the trade routes to the East. Since the attempt failed, since Egypt could not be torn from the Moslem grasp and Islam continued to bar the way to the Indies, there necessarily arose an urgent desire to discover a new route to Hindustan, which would be delivered from the menace of the followers of the Prophet.

The boldness which inspired Columbus's voyages to the west, Bartholomeu Dias's and Vasco da Gama's expeditions to the south, and John Cabot's voyage from Bristol to Labrador, was, above all, the outcome of the long-repressed yearning to free the West from Mohammedan arrogance and to discover an unhampered route to the Indies on which Christian trade would no longer be shamefully subject to Islam. Always when important discoveries or inventions are made, those who make them believe that they do so under stress of moral impulsion, whereas often at bottom material motives are at work. No doubt kings and their counsellors would have been impressed by the ideas of Columbus and Magellan, would have been friendly to these explorers' schemes for ideal reasons. But they would never have opened their purse-strings freely, nor would merchant adventurers have backed the hazards to the extent of equipping fleets, had there not been good prospects of discovering a new trade route to the Indies, the land of gold and spices. Throughout that age of amazing discoveries and explorations, the driving force was the mercantile spirit. Behind the hero stood the trader. Alexander apart, the first impulse to the European invasion of India was thoroughly mundane. The quest for spices began it.

Wonderful things happen in history when the genius of an individual coincides with the genius of the times, when one man perspicaciously grasps the creative yearning of his age. Among the countries of Europe, Portugal, while in prolonged and splendid struggles she had thrown off the Moorish yoke, had not yet found an opportunity of fulfilling her part in Europe's mission. Though her victory had definitively established her independence, the fine energies of a young and passionate nation lay fallow; the natural will to expansion proper to every rising people had found no outlet. Possibilities of landward extension were restricted by the Spaniards, friends and brothers though these were; so that for a small and poor country the exclusive possibility of enlargement and colonization lay on the sea.

At first sight, Portugal's situation seemed most unfavourable. According to the Ptolemaic system of geography (dominant throughout Europe from the end of the second century until the close of the Middle Ages), the Atlantic Ocean, whose rollers broke unceasingly on the Portuguese coast, was an endless and non-navigable waste of waters. No less unnavigable, declared Ptolemy in his map of the world, was the southern route along the African coast. It was impossible, taught the Alexandrian geographer whose authority was supreme at all the universities, to live at or near the Equator. Neither animal nor plant could endure the vertical rays of the sun. Uninhabitable sandy deserts extended to the South Pole. There was no possibility of circumnavigation, since Africa continued without a breach into the Terra Australis. In the view of medieval geographers, Portugal, lying beyond the Mediterranean, the only navigable sea, was in the worst possible position among the maritime nations of Europe.

It became the life purpose of a prince of Portugal to prove the possibility of what had been declared impossible, to attempt, in accordance with the words of the Bible, to make the last first. What if Ptolemy, though a leading geographical authority, had been mistaken? What if this Atlantic Ocean, whose mighty waves brought to Portugal's coast strange woods which must have grown somewhere, was not endless after all, but led to new and unknown lands? What if Africa were habitable south of the Equator? What if the Alexandrian sage had blundered when he declared there could be no seaward route to the south of this unknown continent, that there was no marine means of communication with the Indian Ocean? If Ptolemy had been wrong, Portugal, precisely because situated in the extreme west of Europe, would be the predestined starting-point of all voyages of discovery. Portugal would command the nearest route to the Indies; was not excluded from possibilities of successful navigation, but was privileged in that respect above all the nations of Europe.

This wish-dream, this determination to transform little Portugal into a sea power and to make of the Atlantic Ocean (hitherto regarded as an impassable barrier) a new trade route, became the leading idea of the Infante Enrique, whom history both rightly and unrightly has called Prince Henry the Navigator. Unrightly because, apart from a short voyage on a warship to Ceuta, Henry of Portugal never set foot upon a ship; and no book, no nautical treatise, no map penned by him has come down to us. Yet he is justly styled the Navigator, for he devoted all his wealth to furthering navigation. Having won his spurs in early youth in the Moorish wars during the siege of Ceuta (1415), one of the richest men in the country, son of John I of Portugal (surnamed the Great) and grandson of John of Gaunt, he could have indulged his ambition by aspiring to the most brilliant posts, for he would have been made welcome at any of the courts of Europe, and England offered him high military command. Being, however, an eccentric and an enthusiast, he preferred a life of creative solitude. Establishing his headquarters at Sagres, a small seaport at the south-western extremity of Portugal, near Cape St. Vincent, he erected there an observatory, and directed thence his exploring expeditions. For the rest of his life, which lasted wellnigh half a century more, since he did not die until 1460, he commanded from Sagres the great offensive against the unknown seas.

Perhaps we shall never know what gave this bold dreamer the courage to defy the greatest geographical authorities of his time, to disbelieve the contention of Ptolemy and those who accepted Ptolemy's dictum as incontrovertible, that Africa was a continent extending to the South Pole. Still, we can guess why Prince Henry the Navigator believed it would be possible to sail round Africa into the Indian Ocean. There had always been a rumour, recorded by Herodotus among others, that in the time of the Pharaohs a Phœnician fleet journeyed southward down the Red Sea and, two years later, unexpectedly returned by way of the Pillars of Hercules. It is possible, too, that the Infante had learned from Moorish slave-traders how, beyond Libya Deserta, beyond the sands of the Sahara, was a land of wealth, termed by the Moors "bilat ghana." There is still extant a map prepared in the year 1150 for Roger II, the Norman king of Sicily, by an Arabian cosmographer in which the region we now call Guinea is correctly inscribed under the designation of "bilat ghana." (The modern name "guinea," both the place and the coin, is probably derived from this Moorish word "ghana," wealth.) Furthermore, it is likely that Prince Henry was better informed than the traditional geographers of his day, who swore by Ptolemy and therefore rejected the writings of Marco Polo and his Arab contemporary Ibn Batuta as "travellers' tales."

The essential greatness of Prince Henry the Navigator lies in this, that, knowing the vastness of his aims, he knew also the difficulty of attaining them; that he was resigned to the belief it would be impossible for him to see their realization, since the preparation for fulfilment would need more than one generation. How would it be possible to undertake a voyage from Portugal to the Indies without a knowledge of the seas that would have to be traversed, and without ships for the journey? At the time when Prince Henry set to work, both the geographical and the nautical knowledge of Europe were absurdly primitive. In the Dark Ages which followed the break-up of the West Roman Empire, the cosmography of the Greeks, the Phœnicians, and the Latins had been forgotten. It seemed incredible and to belong to the domain of fable that Alexander had once reached the frontiers of Afghanistan and advanced far into India. Lost were the excellent maps of the Romans; ruined were their military roads, extending into Britain in the North-West and Bithynia in the South-East; vanished was the facility of travel; destroyed was their excellent news-service, which had been geographical as well as political; dead the lust for discovery; pitifully decayed the art of navigation. Lacking bold and distant aims, without compasses or charts, little ships hugged the coast from port to port, in perpetual terror of storms or no less dangerous pirates. Such was the wretched condition of cosmography and so small were the ships, that the conquest of the ocean and of overseas lands seemed out of the question—and this can only enhance the greatness of Prince Henry the Navigator. A generation of labour and sacrifice was requisite to compensate for the neglect of centuries. Prince Henry was determined to devote the whole of his life to the task.

Nothing more than a few ruined walls remains of the castle at Sagres built by Prince Henry and shattered by Sir Francis Drake, the heir of his discoveries. Through the mists of legend it is difficult, at this date, to discern in what fashion

Prince Henry elaborated his plans of world conquest for Portugal. According to the accounts of Portuguese chroniclers, which may be in great measure romantic, he collected books and maps from all quarters of the world, summoned Arabian and Jewish sages, and commanded them to prepare better instruments and charts. Every ship's captain who put into the port was questioned; what information could be gathered was recorded and tabulated; and numerous expeditions were equipped. The art of shipbuilding was greatly improved. Within a few years, the primitive "barcas," small undecked fishing-smacks to carry eighteen men, had grown into "naos," broad-beamed cutters with a draught ranging from eighty to one hundred tons, which could keep afloat on the open sea even in bad weather. These new and more seaworthy boats needed a new type of captain. Associated with the captain was a "master of astronomy," a navigating expert, who could understand the sailing directions, and could make such rough determinations of latitude and longitude as were then possible. Gradually, by theoretical and practical training, those who had been mere fishermen were systematically transformed into navigators and discoverers. Even as King Philip of Macedon bequeathed to his son Alexander the irresistible phalanx with which Alexander conquered the world, so did Prince Henry the Navigator bequeath to Portugal the best and most modern ships of his time, and the excellent seamen who were to conquer the ocean.

It is, however, a part of the tragic fate of forerunners that they should die without catching more than a distant glimpse of the Promised Land. Prince Henry the Navigator did not survive to see any one of the great discoveries that were to make his country memorable in the history of geographical discovery. When he died at Sagres, on November 13, 1460, scarcely anything of geographical importance had been achieved. The widely trumpeted discovery of the Azores and of Madeira was only a rediscovery, for the existence of the islands was known to Laurentino in 1351. The new "naos" had timidly sailed down the west coast of Africa, but in the course of half a century they had not yet reached the Equator. A petty trade had begun, partly in white ivory and still more in what was called "black ivory"—the latter term meaning that raids were made on the coast of Senegal to carry off Negroes for sale in the Lisbon slave-market. A little gold, too, was brought back from Africa. Such were the inglorious results of Henry's glorious dreams.

Nevertheless, a decisive success had already been achieved. The immense gain to Portuguese navigation lay, not in the distance covered, but in the moral sphere: in the increasing spirit of enterprise, and in the destruction of a paralysing legend. For centuries mariners had whispered one to another that there was a place on the West African coast beyond which it was impossible to sail. On the farther side of this began "Cape Non," "the green sea of darkness," and destruction awaited the ship that dared venture into these perilous regions.

What would happen there? The boiling waters would melt the pitch and oakum out of the seams; planks and sails would catch fire in the scorching sun; every Christian who tried to enter the "land of Satan," which was as hot as the crater of a volcano, would be burned as black as a Negro. Thanks to this fable, so overwhelming was the dread of any

voyage along the African coast that the Pope, to enable
Prince Henry to secure seamen for his first expeditions, had
to give every man jack of them a preliminary absolution.
Thus only did it become possible to secure a few resolutes for
the initial voyages of discovery.

What a triumph it was, therefore, when Gil Yanez first
rounded the reputedly impassable Cape Non, and came back
to report of Guinea that the famous Ptolemy had been proved
a humbug, "for it is as easy to sail on this coast as on our own,
while the country is extraordinarily rich and beautiful." The
dead point had been passed. Portugal no longer needed to
press men into the service, for adventurous spirits flocked
from all lands. Every new successful voyage made the mariners bolder. A brood of young and hardy fellows sprang to
life, persons who were no longer inclined to count the risks
or reckon up the cost. As always when a new generation is
inspired with zeal for new work, the world became transformed.

The death of Prince Henry meant no more than a momen-
tary pause, the drawing of a deep breath before the next great
leap. Hardly had the energetic King John II ascended the
throne in the year 1481, when there ensued an impetus ex-
ceeding every expectation. What had proceeded at a snail's
pace, now went with the rush of a charging lion. Hitherto,
explorers had crept along the coast, but now they advanced
with giant strides, exploring as much as a hundred or even
five hundred miles a year. Perhaps only our own generation,
which is witnessing the conquest of the air, only we, who
little more than thirty years ago were willing to rejoice at the
tidings of the flight of an aeroplane which was able to sustain

itself in the air for five or ten miles beyond its starting-point at the Champ-de-Mars; who were wildly excited when, in 1909, Blériot flew across the English Channel, and then, only eighteen years later, were told of the first flight across the Atlantic and of the successful aerial voyage from England to Australia—only we are perhaps in a position to understand the excitement that ran through Europe when, towards the close of the fifteenth century, it heard of the triumphs of Portugal. In 1471 the Equator was reached; in 1483 Diogo Cam landed at the mouth of the Congo; and at length, in 1486, Prince Henry's prophetic dream was fulfilled. A Portuguese navigator, Bartholomeu Dias, rounded the southern point of Africa, now known as the Cape of Good Hope, but by him, for adequate reasons, christened Cabo Tormentoso— the Cape of Storms. Though his sails were torn to rags and his ship was partly dismasted, the bold adventurer kept on his course to where the east coast of Africa begins at Algoa Bay. Here Mohammedan pilots could have been taken aboard to guide him across the Indian Ocean, but his men mutinied, refusing to go any farther. For the moment he had done all that he could. Sad at heart he returned, deprived by the cowardice of his crew of the fame of being the first European to reach the Indies by sea. It was left to another Portuguese, Vasco da Gama, to do this great deed; for, as so often, the beginner, the luckless initiator, is almost forgotten amid the glories of the successful finisher. No matter, the decisive deed had been done. For the first time the geographical shape of Africa had been determined, and, in defiance of Ptolemy's authority, it had been proved that there existed a sea route to the Indies. The disciples and the heirs of Prince Henry the

Navigator had fulfilled their master's wish-dream a generation after their master's death.

The gaze of the Western World was now directed with
astonishment and envy at this small and hitherto unconsid-
ered nation of sailors established upon the south-western corner of Europe. While the great powers—France, Germany,
and Italy—were wasting their strength and their substance in
senseless wars, Portugal, regarded as a Cinderella, had enor-
mously enlarged her territories, so that it seemed as if no
limits could be imposed upon her ambitions. Betwixt night
and morning she had become the sensation of the world, winning new realms vaster by far than any mere provinces.
Within a decade, she, least among European nations, was
claiming the ownership of more lands than had belonged to
the Roman Empire in the days of its greatest expansion.

The attempt to enforce such extravagant imperialist claims
could not fail to result in a speedy exhaustion of the energies
of Portugal. Any child might have foreseen that so tiny a
land, which contained no more than one and a half million
inhabitants, could not, in the long run, occupy, colonize, administer, or merely monopolize the trade of all Africa, India,
and Brazil; and still less defend these vast possessions against
the jealousies of other nations. One drop of oil cannot calm
the waters of a stormy sea, nor can a country the size of a pin-
head permanently subjugate enormous territories. Thus from
a reasonable point of view the boundless expansion of Portugal was an absurdity, a dangerous form of quixotry. But it is
part of the irrational nature of heroism that whenever a man
or a people undertakes a task that exceeds the bounds of possibility, the energies grow to an unexpected degree. Never

COLUMBUS
Painting in the Portrait Collection of Archduke Ferdinand of Tirol

PRINCE HENRY THE NAVIGATOR
Detail from the triptych in the Museum of Early Art, Lisbon

perhaps did any nation concentrate its forces more splendidly than did Portugal at the close of the fifteenth century. Not only did she find her Alexander and her Argonauts in Albuquerque, Vasco da Gama, and Magellan, but she discovered her Homer in Camoens and her Livy in Barros. Men of learning, architects, and noted merchants seemed to crop up on all sides. As in Hellas under Pericles, in England under Elizabeth, in France under Napoleon, so, at this date, Portugal realized her ideal and made it materially manifest before the world. Even though in her heroic struggle she was bled white and rendered exsanguine for centuries; though almost everything which, at such cost, she now got possession of, was subsequently torn from her grasp—undeniably her glories were proved in word and deed. For a brief space in history, Portugal was the leading nation of Europe, the advance guard of mankind.

Now whatever great deed is done by one nation is done for all the nations. They feel, one and all, that a bold thrust forward into the unknown has made an end of the hitherto prevailing measures, concepts, distances. Thus, with the utmost impatience, at all the courts and all the universities, people awaited the latest tidings from Lisbon. With remarkable clarity, Europe recognized that navigation and discovery were about to cause more decisive changes in the world than wars or heavy artillery; that the thousand years of the Middle Ages had drawn decisively to a close; and that there had begun a new age, the "modern age," which would think and act upon an entirely new scale. With fine historical foresight, Politian, the Florentine humanist, an apostle of peaceful reason, raised his voice to celebrate the glories of Portugal, and the thankfulness of the whole of cultivated Europe is conveyed by his inspired words:

"Not only has this country left far behind the Pillars of Hercules and tamed a raging ocean, but it has re-established the hitherto interrupted unity of the habitable world. What new possibilities and economic advances, what an enlargement of knowledge, what confirmation of old science hitherto rejected as incredible, can now be expected! New countries, new seas, new worlds (alii mundi), have emerged from the darkness of the centuries. Portugal has become the guardian of a second universe."

But an amazing incident was to interrupt the triumphal campaign. Already had this "second universe" been won in the East, already had the crowns and the treasures of the Indies been secured for King John II. It seemed that after the rounding of the Cape of Good Hope no other country could get ahead of Portugal, or do more than limp painfully in the rear. Prince Henry the Navigator had been careful to secure from the Pope a charter to the effect that all the lands, seas, and islands that lay beyond Cape Bojador on the West African coast, three hundred leagues from Cape St. Vincent, should belong exclusively to Portugal. Three other Popes had confirmed this remarkable donation, which, with a stroke of the pen, made the unknown East with its hundreds of millions of inhabitants the lawful property of the Portuguese Crown.

Those who have indisputable security in their hands are not much inclined for further speculation. It is not surprising, therefore, that King John II should show little interest in the vague schemes of an obscure Genoese who demanded from the monarch a whole fleet "wherewith it may be found possible to reach the Indies from the west." Christopher Columbus was, indeed, given friendly audience at Lisbon. He was not rudely rebuffed. But the court remembered that all previous expeditions for the discovery of the fabled island Antilia, which was said to lie to the west between Europe and India, had lamentably failed. Furthermore, why risk good Portuguese ducats for an uncertain western route to the Indies when, after years of arduous labour, the right path had so recently been discovered, and in the shipyards on the Tagus men were working overtime to construct the great fleet which, within the next few years, was to sail round the Cape of Good Hope to India?

Like thunder from a clear sky, therefore, was the news which reached Lisbon that this Genoese adventurer, under the Spanish flag, had actually crossed the "Oceano Tenebroso," and in a few weeks had discovered land in the west. A miracle had been worked. Fulfilled had been the mystical prophecy of Seneca's tragedy *Medea*, which for long long years had fascinated the imagination of navigators.

> Venient annis
> Saecula seris, quibus Oceanus
> Vincula rerum laxet et ingens
> Pateat tellus, Typhisque novos
> Detegat orbes, nec sit terris
> Ultima Thula.

In very truth they seemed to have come, "the days when, after centuries, the ocean discloses its secrets, and an unknown land appears, for the pilot of the Argonauts discovers new spheres and Thule is no longer the most distant country in the world."

Columbus, indeed, had no idea that he had discovered a new continent. Down to the day of his death he continued stubbornly to believe that he had reached the continent of Asia, and that by steering westward from his "Hispaniola" he would, within a few days, be able to reach the mouth of the Ganges. But that was why Portugal was so terribly alarmed. Of what use would be the papal charter conferring a right to all lands reached from the east, if Spain could steal a march upon her by reaching the Indies from the west? The labours of Prince Henry the Navigator for fifty years, and the labours of his successors during the thirty years since his death, had at one stroke been rendered futile. The Indies had been lost through the foolhardy venture of this wretched Genoese. If Portugal wished to retain her advantages and her privileges in the Indies, her only chance was to take up arms against these unexpectedly successful rivals.

Fortunately the Pope was able to avert the threatening peril. Portugal and Spain were his favourite children, because their kings never tried to resist his will. They had fought the Moors and had expelled the infidels; with fire and sword they rooted out heresy; no other governments were so ready as the Portuguese and the Spanish to help the Holy Inquisition to deal roundly with Moors and Jews. His beloved children must not quarrel. His Holiness therefore decided to divide all as yet unknown parts of the world between Spain and Portugal—not, in the hypocritical terminology of modern

diplomacy, as "spheres of influence," but bestowed upon
them out and out as peoples, lands, islands, and seas, in virtue
of his authority as Christ's vicegerent on earth. Taking the
globe as if it had been an apple, by the Bull of May 4, 1493,
he sliced it in twain. The line of section started a hundred
leagues from the Cape Verde Islands. All undiscovered countries westward of this line were to belong to his dear child
Spain; all that lay eastward, to his dear child Portugal. To
begin with, the two children expressed themselves grateful
for this gift. Soon, however, Portugal grew uneasy, and
begged that the boundary should be thrust a little to the west.
This was arranged by the Treaty or Convention of Tordesil-
las, on June 7, 1494, whereby the line was transferred two
hundred and seventy leagues to the west. Thanks to this re-
adjustment, Portugal would receive the still undiscovered
Brazil.

However grotesque, at first sight, may appear a generosity
which thus bestowed the greater part of the world upon two
nations, regardless of the claims of the others, we cannot but
admire this pacific solution as one of the rare reasonable
actions of history, inasmuch as a potential dispute was settled
by a peaceful understanding instead of by force. For years,
nay for decades, possible conflicts between Spain and Portugal were actually avoided thanks to the Convention of Tor-
desillas, even though the settlement was necessarily pro-
visional. For if we cut an apple in twain with a knife, the
line of section shows upon the surface. Within which half
would the much desired, the precious Spice Islands lie?
Where the meridian traversed the other hemisphere, would
they be to the east or to the west of the line of division?

Would they be on the side of Portugal or on the side of Spain? At the date of the settlement, neither the Pope nor the kings nor the sages knew, for the globe had not yet been measured. Meanwhile, pending the final decision, the rival nations had plenty to do in swallowing the huge morsel which fate had assigned them: on the one hand, little Spain had to swallow the huge area of the Americas; and on the other, little Portugal had to swallow the whole of India and Africa.

Columbus's successful voyage aroused measureless astonishment in Europe. Immediately thereafter came a frenzy for adventure and discovery such as the Old World had never before known. The achievement of one courageous man will awaken the courage of an entire generation. Everyone in Europe who was discontented with his means and his position, everyone who felt himself thrust into the background and was too impatient to wait; younger sons, unemployed officers, bastards of the nobles, fugitives from justice—one and all wanted to go to the New World. The princes, the merchants, the speculators hastened to get together whatever ships were available; and it was necessary to hold aloof at the pike's point the adventurers and swashbucklers who were all-too-eager to be recruited. Whereas Prince Henry the Navigator had had to induce the Pope to grant plenary absolution to participators in the voyages he planned, for otherwise he could not have secured crews, now whole villages flocked to the seaports, pestered the captains, and the recruiting-agents were hardly able to defend themselves from the press-gang of would-be sailors. One expedition followed in the wake of another. As if called into existence by magic, there were discovered, north, south, east, and west, new islands, new territories, some of them embedded in the ice, others luxuriant with palms. Within two or three decades, the few hundred little ships which set forth from Cadiz, Palos, and Lisbon discovered more previously unknown regions than had been discovered by all mankind in tens of thousands, nay hundreds of thousands of years.

Here is a brief catalogue of the incomparable results of these voyages of discovery. In 1498, Vasco de Gama, having rounded the Cape of Good Hope in the previous November, reached Calicut on the Malabar coast. The same year, Cabot (an Italian navigator in the English service) reached Newfoundland and the mainland of North America. In 1500, independently of one another, Pinzón under the Spanish flag and Cabral under the Portuguese discovered Brazil, while Gaspar Cortereal, a Portuguese successor of the Vikings, reached Labrador.

During the first years of the sixteenth century, there was a further quick succession of wonderful discoveries. Two Portuguese expeditions, in one of which Amerigo Vespucci participated, followed down the South American coast as far as the Rio de la Plata. In 1500 the Portuguese discovered Madagascar; in 1505, Mauritius; in 1509 they reached Malacca, thus having the key of the Malay Archipelago in their hands. In 1513, Ponce de León discovered Florida; also in 1513, from the peak of Darien, Núñez de Balboa, first of all Europeans, caught sight of the Pacific Ocean.

Thenceforward there were no unknown seas. Within the brief space of a century, European navigators had increased their achievements, not a hundredfold, but a thousandfold. Whereas in 1418, under Prince Henry the Navigator, it had aroused astonishment when the first barcas reached Madeira, in 1518 Portuguese ships sailed as far as Canton. Soon a voyage to India was regarded as less venturesome than, not long before, had been the voyage to Cape Bojador. At such a winged tempo, the picture of the world was altered and extended from year to year, nay from month to month. By day and by night the cartographers were hard at work in Augsburg, but could not keep up with the unceasing demand for revised maps. These were snatched from their hands damp and still uncoloured. There was a like impetuous demand for stories of travel and for globes, now that everyone wanted news about the "mundus novus." Hardly had the cosmographers revised their maps in accordance with the latest intelligence, when new reports arrived. The old representations had to be thrown aside, and fresh ones made, for what had been an island was now known to be a continent, a continent in which new rivers, new mountains had to be depicted; and the etchers had scarcely finished a new map when yet further news came to hand demanding further revision.

Never before and never since have geography, cosmography, and cartography known such frenzied advances as during these fifty years, when, after ages of ignorance, the shape and size of the world were at length definitively established, the globular form of our revolving planet being now proved beyond dispute. This was the work of little more than one generation, whose navigators faced unknown dangers for all coming times, whose conquistadors vanquished lands and seas, whose heroes performed many of the tasks which an inert world had previously left undone. Only one thing remained to do—the last, the finest, and the most diffi-

VASCO DA GAMA
Miniature in the British Museum, London

ALBUQUERQUE
Pen-and-ink miniature in the British Museum, London

cult—to circumnavigate the world on one and the same vessel, thus giving absolutely incontrovertible proof, in defiance of the cosmologists and theologians of the past, that the world is quasi-spherical in form. This was to be the life work of Ferdinand Magellan.

Chapter Two

MAGELLAN IN THE EAST INDIES

March 1505 – June 1512

Magellan in the East Indies

THE first fleet that sailed from Lisbon down the estuary of the Tagus into the unknown distance was on a voyage of discovery; the second fleet was dispatched for the purposes of peaceful trade with the newly annexed territories; the third fleet was armed and equipped for war. On this March 25, 1505, came the next stage of that inexorable rhythm which was to prevail throughout the colonial epoch now opening. For centuries the same process would be repeated: first a "factory" (as trading-stations were then called) would be established; next would be built a fortress for its alleged protection. The native rulers were, to begin with, deluded by prospects of pacific trade; then, when enough soldiers had been sent to the "factory," the local potentates would be forcibly deprived of their land and their other possessions. A decade had scarcely elapsed before Portugal, dizzy with success, had forgotten that her primary aim had been nothing more than to secure a modest share of the spice trade. The fortunate gamester soon forgets his good intentions. From the day when Vasco da Gama landed in the Indies, Portugal's main task became to thrust other nations from the groaning board. For she now regarded all Africa, India, and Brazil as her exclusive domain. From Gibraltar to Singapore and China no ships were to trade

upon half the globe unless they belonged to the smallest
country in Europe.

It was made a spectacular occasion, this March 25, 1505,
when Portugal's first war fleet, which was to inaugurate the
conquest of the New Empire, left the port of Lisbon. There
had been nothing comparable to it in history since the crossing of the Hellespont by Alexander the Great. The affair was
no less tremendous, seeing that the Portuguese fleet, likewise,
was setting forth to conquer a world. Twenty ships were
awaiting the king's order to upanchor and sail; no longer the
little open barcas of the early days of Prince Henry the
Navigator, but broad-beamed, heavy galleons, with several
decks, high in the bows and the stern, each ship having three
or four masts and being amply manned. In addition to the
hundreds of able seamen trained for war, there would be
on board such a galleon as many as fifteen hundred fully
equipped and armoured soldiers, as well as a couple of hundred bombardiers or gunners. Besides the ship's carpenters,
they carried other craftsmen to build ships and fortresses in
the Indies.

At the first glance, every one of the onlookers must realize
that so important a fleet had an important aim—the seizure
of the East. For good reasons had the title of Viceroy of the
Indies been bestowed upon Dom Francisco d'Almeida, the
admiral of the fleet. Nor was it by chance that Vasco da
Gama, "Admiral of the Indian Ocean," the first hero and
navigator of Portugal, was entrusted with the fitting out of
the expedition. Almeida's military task had been made perfectly clear. He was to dismantle and demolish all the Mohammedan trading-stations in India and Africa, to build

fortresses at all important strategic points, and to garrison them adequately. In anticipation of England's political ideas, he was to occupy the places of ingress to and egress from all inland seas; block the chief straits from Gibraltar to Malacca; close the southern inlets from the Red Sea and the Persian Gulf into the Indian Ocean, which was to be made impracticable for any maritime traffic other than that of Portugal. He had also received instructions to annihilate the sea power of the Sultan of Egypt and of the Indian rajahs; was to keep the Eastern ports under such strict control that from the year of Our Lord 1505 no ship unprovided with a Portuguese licence could take on board so much as a pepper-corn. In pursuance of these military and naval schemes, he was to spread Christianity in the countries he would conquer—this plan giving his expedition the character of a crusade. With his own hand, in Lisbon Cathedral, the King gave Dom Francisco d'Almeida a new banner of white damask bearing in crimson satin the Cross of Christ, and this banner was to wave victoriously over the lands of the Moors and other pagans. The admiral kneeled to receive the sublime emblem, and there kneeled with him fifteen hundred of his men who had confessed their sins and received the Host, taking oath of fidelity to their earthly lord, the King of Portugal, as well as to their heavenly master, whose realm was to overcome that of the foreign unbelievers. From the cathedral they marched in solemn procession to the harbour. The guns thundered farewell. Magnificently, then, the ships sailed down the Tagus into the open sea which the admiral had vowed to conquer for Portugal as far as the ends of the earth.

Among the fifteen hundred who, with bowed heads, had kneeled before the altar, and with uplifted hands had taken the oath of loyalty, was a man of twenty-four, Ferdinand Magellan, who had not as yet made a name in the world. Of his origin little more is known than that he was born about the year 1480, his very birthplace being open to dispute. Chroniclers have spoken of Sabrosa, in the province of Traz-os-Montes, but this is now known to be erroneous, recent researches having disclosed as a forgery the will in which that birthplace is mentioned. It seems most probable that Magellan was born in Oporto. About his family nothing more is known than that it was noble, though only in the fourth grade of nobility, that of the "fidalgos de cota de armas." Still, this sufficed to make him an armiger, and to give him entry at court. It seems probable that in early youth he had served Queen Elinor as one of her pages, though there is no evidence of his ever having held an important position at court. When, at the age of twenty-four, he became a member of the expeditionary force to the East, it was only as a plain "sobresaliente," one of the fifteen hundred supernumeraries who took their meals with the crew and the cabin boys, and shared the sleeping accommodation of these; no more than one of the "unknown soldiers" who set forth by thousands in this war for the conquest of the world—thousands of them to perish, a dozen or so to survive—but the only one upon whom was to devolve the immortal fame of their common deed.

Magellan was merely one among fifteen hundred. There is scant mention of his name in the chronicles of the wars in the Indies; nor, to be honest, can one say about him during these years more than that they must have been years of invaluable experience. A sobresaliente is not likely to be coddled; he will be treated as roughly as a maid of all work, will have to do his share in reefing sails during a storm, to take his turn at the pumps, to stand in the forefront of the battle, to dig trenches under fire and beneath the burning sun. In the "factory," he will have, alternately, to play the part of shopkeeper and sentry; will have to fight among the common soldiers and sailors by land and at sea; will have to heave the lead and use the sword, to obey orders as well as issue them. By thus participating in all risks and all tasks, he learns every trick of the trades of war and of commerce, becoming at one and the same time soldier, sailor, merchant, acquiring knowledge of men, lands, seas, and the movements of the stars. In due course, Destiny, having in view for him a lofty task, will have initiated him into those supreme concerns by which the station of his country and man's knowledge of the globe will be decided for decades and for centuries. Thus it came to pass that, after a few minor skirmishes, which were plunder-raids rather than genuine warfare, Magellan received his true baptism of fire in the naval action of Cannanore on March 16, 1506.

This battle of Cannanore marked a turning-point in the history of Portuguese conquests in the Indies. In 1498, at the time of Vasco da Gama's first arrival on the Malabar coast, the Zamorin of Calicut had given him a friendly reception, being fully prepared to trade with the representatives of this unknown people. Eight years later, however, when the Portuguese reappeared with a fleet of larger and better-armed ships, the Indian ruler was quick to realize that the strangers from the West had come for conquest as well as for trade. With alarm the Hindu and Mohammedan traders became aware that a fearsome pike had invaded their trout-stream, that the strangers intended to make themselves masters both by land and by sea. Dread of the Western pirates kept the Eastern ships in port; the spice trade was brought to a standstill; the supplies of overland commerce by the desert route to the Mediterranean were withheld; and at Venice, on the Rialto, it grew plain that the customary channels of a lucrative traffic had been forcibly blocked.

The Sultan of Egypt, whose transit dues were thus cut off, began by trying whether a remedy could be found in threats. He wrote to the Pope that if the Portuguese continued their robber campaign in the Indian Ocean, he would, as a reprisal, destroy the Holy Sepulchre in Jerusalem. But neither the Pope nor any other European emperor or king could control the imperialistic will of Portugal. Nothing but force could put restraint upon these conquerors, so that the sole resource of the injured parties was to get together in an attempt to destroy the Portuguese in the Indies before they had established their power. The attack was prepared by the Zamorin of Calicut, privily supported by the Sultan of Egypt, and doubtless by the Venetians, who (gold being thicker than blood) under the rose sent gun-founders to Calicut. At one blow, the Portuguese navy was to be attacked and destroyed.

Often enough, however, the presence of mind and the energy of a minor personality, the intervention of someone who would seem to have been cast for a trifling part, will turn the course of history. The Portuguese were saved by a lucky chance. Wandering hither and thither through the world in those days was an Italian adventurer named Ludovico Vartema, a bold fellow whose vigour makes him no less attractive than his courage. The young man had been driven forth on his travels, not by ambition, but by a native lust for vagrancy. He says of himself, without any false pride, that, "being disinclined to learn only from books," he had determined "to see with his own eyes the various places in the world, since the reports of an eye-witness are of more value than all hearsay evidence." He was the first giaour to enter the forbidden city of Mecca, his description of which is still the standard one. After numerous vicissitudes and with much hazard to his life, he not only made his way to the Indies, to Sumatra and Borneo (which had already been visited by Marco Polo), but was the first European to set foot upon the greatly coveted Spice Islands—a fact which was to have much influence upon Magellan's subsequent adventures. On his way home through Calicut, disguised as a Mohammedan monk, Vartema learned from two Christian renegades of the Zamorin's intended attack upon the Portuguese. Moved by a sense of Christian solidarity, at grave risk to his life he made his way to Cannanore, where he had a private interview with Dom Lourenço, son of Viceroy Almeida. Vartema's information was of the utmost importance to the Portuguese. Whereas, on March 16, 1506, the Zamorin, with two hundred ships, had hoped to take the eleven of the Portuguese by surprise, these were in battle array when the Indian forces appeared on the scene. This was the most serious attack that Portugal had as yet had to repel; but with the loss of eighty dead and two hundred wounded (a huge number for the first colonial wars) they won a victory which, for the time being, made them supreme in the Indian Ocean.

Among the wounded was Magellan, it being his fate during these years to be wounded again and again without securing distinction. He was sent with the other wounded to Africa, where we lose track of him, for who troubles to report the life or death of a supernumerary? No doubt he was shipped on one of the transports; and it is possible (accounts vary) that, in the summer of 1507, on the same ship he accompanied Vartema to Lisbon. But he had already become inspired with a craving for far horizons. Portugal seemed a humdrum place, and his brief home leave was nothing more than an impatient waiting for the departure of the next Indian fleet, which brought him back to his true home—adventure.

A special task had been assigned to this new fleet, with which Magellan got back to the Indies. Indubitably his illustrious companion, Ludovico Vartema, had informed the Portuguese court about the wealth of Malacca and had given precise details concerning the position of the Spice Islands. Thus it had become plain to the Portuguese authorities that the conquest of the Indies would be incomplete, and that the sources of wealth would not have been fully tapped, until the primary spring of the riches of the Indies, the original home of these much-desired spices, was in Portuguese hands. The first step to this end must be to gain control of the Strait of Malacca, which was the key to the Malay Archipelago. In accordance with the hypocritical system that was already becoming traditional, the first expedition to Malacca was not a warlike one. The ruler of Portugal began by sending Lopez de Sequeira to Malacca with only five ships, to spy out the land while presenting himself as nothing more than a peaceful trader.

The little fleet reached Hindustan without incident in April 1509. The voyage to Calicut, which no more than ten years earlier, when Vasco da Gama first made it, had been proclaimed in song and story as a deed of incomparable heroism, was by this time within the capacity of every Portuguese merchant captain. From Lisbon to Mombasa, and from Mombasa to Hindustan, was a journey now possible to every deep-sea ship. The ports of call had become familiar; no pilot was needed, nor any "master of astronomy." It was not until, on August 19, 1509, Sequeira set forth from Cochin to continue his eastward voyage, that the Portuguese ships sailed into unknown waters.

In three weeks and two days, on September 11, 1509, the small armada anchored in the port of Malacca. From afar those on board the fleet could see that Vartema had not exaggerated when he said that in this harbour "there are more ships than in any other place in the world." Barks, junks, and prahus of Malay, Chinese, and Siamese origin thronged the roads. Thanks to its position, this strait, of which the Golden Chersonese forms the eastern boundary, had become the great place of assembly in the Eastern seas. Malacca was the Gibraltar of the East, commanding the route to the Malay Archipelago, the South Seas in general, China, and Japan. It was natural, therefore, that it should be a great emporium for goods of all sorts: spices from the Moluccas; cloves and

rubies from Ceylon; porcelain from China and ivory from
Siam; cashmeres from Hindustan and sandal-wood from Timor; damascened swords and pepper from the Malabar coast;
slaves from Borneo. The place was a babel of tongues, and
one where men of all tints of skin rubbed shoulders, with
a population estimated (perhaps by exaggeration) at two
hundred thousand, where the Sultan's splendid palace and a
huge stone mosque towered above the wooden huts of the
common folk.

The Portuguese stared open-mouthed at the huge city,
this jewel of the worshippers of the Prophet, sparkling in the
tropical sunshine, and destined, so they thought, to become
the brightest jewel in the crown of their King, who was to
be the Portuguese Emperor of the East. The Malay Sultan,
in his turn, contemplated the new arrivals in ships of an unfamiliar type with no less amazement and with much disquiet.
He and his viziers had good reason for being uneasy. There
they were, then, at last, the uncircumcised bandits, the accursed giaours who had found their way to Malacca. Tidings
of the disaster to the forces of the Zamorin of Calicut had
spread long ere this across the wide Bay of Bengal. The ruler
of Malacca knew full well that these terrible foreigners did
not really come (as did the Siamese, the Japanese, and the
Chinese in their junks) merely for the purposes of peaceful
trade, but would await a favourable opportunity to establish
themselves upon a firm footing and pursue their essential
purpose of plunder. The counsel of prudence was to keep
the Portuguese ships out of Malacca harbour, for once
the invaders had gained entry it would be too late. However,
the Sultan had also heard of the disastrous powers of the

heavy artillery with which they were armed, the big guns whose threatening, black, but silent mouths could be seen plainly enough from the shore. He knew that these white robbers could fight like devils, and were in fact irresistible. The best course would be, then, to encounter lies with lies, to meet false friendliness with feigned pleasure, to counter deceit with deceit, and to await the chance of striking a shrewd blow before they had gathered their forces for the assault.

With high-flown protestations of delight, therefore, did the Sultan of Malacca receive the envoys of Sequeira, and with exuberant gratitude accept their presents. They were heartily welcome, he declared, and his markets were open for them to trade as they pleased. Within a few days he would get together as much pepper and other spices as they could carry home with them. Hospitably he invited the captains to a banquet in his palace, and though this courteous invitation was refused (the Portuguese having been warned of the danger of acceptance), the soldiers and the sailors were given shore leave, and rejoiced to stretch their legs once more on firm ground, where they could find plenty of those women who are always ready to greet Jack ashore. What a comfort to escape from the stinking cabins of the ships! They sat chattering in the tea-houses, bought what they wanted in the markets, delighted in the tart Malayan drinks and in the flavour of fresh fruit. Never, since leaving Lisbon, had they secured so cordial a reception. The Malays, in their turn, paddled off by hundreds to the Portuguese ships in their crazy-looking catamarans; scrambled up the ropes as adroitly as monkeys; were amazed at the numerous foreign utensils they had never seen before. Brisk barter went on between the two parties, and the crew were not best pleased to learn that the Sultan had quickly got the promised freight together, that Sequeira could send his boats to fetch it next morning and would have it aboard before evening.

Sequeira, delighted to hear that matters were to be arranged so quickly, did actually send the boats of the four largest vessels, strongly manned, to collect the goods. He, being a Portuguese nobleman who regarded mercantile transactions as beneath his dignity, remained on board, to play chess with one of his comrades, as the most agreeable way of passing the long hours of a hot day on shipboard. The three other big galleons lay drowsily at anchor. But Garcia de Sousa, the captain of the little caravel which was the fifth ship of the Portuguese fleet, was struck by the fact that, from the increasing number of Malay prahus which were surrounding the four galleons, ostensibly to bring goods on board, more and more of the naked, brown-skinned fellows were climbing up the ships' ropes. His suspicions were aroused. Perhaps the Sultan was less friendly than he seemed, and was preparing a treacherous onslaught by land and by sea.

Luckily the little caravel had not sent her own boat ashore, and de Sousa ordered the trustiest of his men to pull over quickly to the flag-ship and warn the captain. De Sousa chose his messenger well, for he was Ferdinand Magellan. With sturdy strokes he pulled across, to find Captain Sequeira tranquilly playing chess, but he was quick to note that several Malays stood behind each of the players, ostensibly watching the game, but each of them with a kris ready to hand. Inconspicuously he whispered a warning to Sequeira. The latter, not wishing to disclose uneasiness, quietly continued his game, but he commanded one of the seamen to take an outlook from the masthead, and kept his own sword-hand ready.

Magellan's warning had come at the last moment, and indeed too late. At this precise instant a column of smoke rose from the Sultan's palace, the prearranged signal for a simultaneous assault on the Portuguese by land and sea. On the flag-ship, the sailor at the masthead uttered a shout of alarm. Sequeira sprang to his feet, and struck down the Malays before they could use their krises. A signal was piped; on all the ships the Malays were thrust overboard, and those who regained their prahus made a joint attack upon the ships; Sequeira gave orders to slip the cables and bore down on the enemy, at whom his guns thundered. Thanks to the watchfulness of de Sousa and the promptness of Magellan, the surprise attempt to seize the fleet failed.

Less fortunate was the fate of the shore party, a handful of men taken by surprise, scattered through the streets among thousands of foes. Most of the Portuguese were mercilessly cut down when the signal was given; some were taken prisoners; and only a few succeeded in making their way to the strand. Even so, it was too late, for the Malays had seized the boats, thus making return to the ships impossible, so that one after another the Europeans fell into their hands. One only among them, the most valiant of them all, Francisco Serrão, close friend of Magellan, made good his escape. He was surrounded, wounded, and might have been thought already doomed. Magellan, however, rowed to land accompanied by one of the soldiers, the pair of them venturing their lives to save their companion. Coming to the rescue of Serrão, who was outnumbered ten to one, his friend brought him off alive. In this disastrous attack, the Portuguese lost their boats and more than a third of their strength. But Magellan won a blood-brother, whose friendship and trust were to be decisive in his future career.

For the first time one of Magellan's most conspicuous character traits became manifest in his obscure personality. I refer to his hardihood, his formidable resolution. There was nothing emotional about him, nor anything to attract attention, and this explains why he remained so long in the background, for throughout life he was a man of the shadows. He had no talent for making himself conspicuous or for inspiring affection. Yet whenever a task was set him and, even more, when he set himself a task, the obscure and secretive adventurer acted with a dazzling combination of shrewdness and courage. All the same, he never pushed himself into the foreground or boasted of his achievements. Having done some such deed as the rescue of Serrão, he quietly and patiently returned into the shadows. Since he had the gift of silence, he knew also how to wait, as if aware that, for the peculiar mission he was destined to fulfil, fate would continue to school him and to try him in various ways. Indeed, there was speedily to come a new trial. Almost immediately after arriving at Cannanore he had taken part in one of the greatest victories of the Portuguese fleet; then, in Malacca, he had participated in a great disaster. Now came a third test of courage, one of the hardest tests to which a mariner can be put—shipwreck.

Magellan had already determined to return home on one of

the regular transports with the next monsoon, but the ship ran at night upon a shoal of the Great Padua Bank (also known as the Pedro Reef) in the Laccadive Islands. No lives were lost, but the ship was broken up, and since there was not accommodation for all the crew in the boats, some of them had to be left on the sand-bank, while the others returned to the Malabar coast for help. Of course the captain, the officers, and the men of rank demanded for themselves the privilege of going with the boats, but this angered the "grumetes," the common seamen. A furious dispute was imminent, when Magellan voluntarily declared himself willing to renounce the privileges of station and to stay with the men who were to be left behind, provided the officers and fidalgos gave their word of honour to send back a ship as soon as they got to land.

This valiant demeanour seems to have attracted the notice of his superiors, for, a little later, in October 1510, when Albuquerque, the new Viceroy, had occasion to ask the advice of the "capitanos del Rey," Magellan was among those questioned. At length, after five years' service, the sobresaliente was promoted from the rank of simple soldier and sailor and was given a commission as officer of the fleet which was about to be dispatched in order to make good the disastrous reverse Sequeira had sustained at Malacca.

Two years had elapsed since Magellan's last voyage to the Far East, to the Golden Chersonese. Nineteen ships, a choice war squadron, arrived off Malacca on July 1, 1511, and a fierce struggle began. This lasted six weeks before Albuquerque succeeded in overcoming the Sultan's resistance. Then, however, the plunderers got possession of a booty richer than they had ever dreamed of; and, with their grip upon Malacca, they secured for Portugal access to all the islands of the East. At length the main artery of Mohammedan trade had been severed, and within a few weeks that trade had bled to death. Far onward into China and Japan and far back into Europe rolled the formidable tidings of the most decisive blow sustained by Islam for centuries. Before the assembled faithful, the Pope offered up solemn thanksgivings for the splendid achievements of the Portuguese, who had got possession of half the world for Christendom. Rome witnessed a triumph such as had not been known there since the days of the Cæsars. An embassy led by Tristan da Cunha brought to the Eternal City the booty of the conquered Indies: costly steeds, leopards, and other beasts, the most precious specimen being an elephant, which was led in the procession and, amid the acclamations of the Roman populace, kneeled thrice before the Holy Father.

But while the Western World was thus celebrating the triumph of Christendom, Portugal did not rest upon her laurels. History relates no instance in which a conqueror has been surfeited with conquests, and Malacca was regarded as nothing more than the entry to the treasure house of the Spice Islands. The anterooms having been forced, the Sunda Islands and the Moluccas had become the goal of ambition; above all, the almost legendary Amboina, Banda, Ternate, and Tidore. Three ships were fitted out to sail for their discovery and occupation, under the command of Antonio d'Abreu, and several contemporary chroniclers mention Magellan as one of the participators in this voyage to the easternmost limits of the world. In reality, however, Magellan's

FERDIN·MAGELLANVS·SVPERATIS
ANTARTICI   FRETI·ANGVS
TIIS·   CLARISS·

MAGELLAN
Painting in the Portrait Collection of Archduke Ferdinand of Tirol

FERDINAND CORTEZ
Painting in the Portrait Collection of Archduke Ferdinand of Tirol

voyage to the Indies was now drawing to a close. "Enough!"
said Destiny to him. "You are keen enough, experienced
enough, in the East! New paths are opening for you!" Never
was he to set eyes upon the semi-fabulous Spice Islands of
which he had dreamed all his life. Although they would continue to loom before his inner vision, he would never be permitted to see them in actuality, "por vista de ojos." This particular El Dorado was to remain a vision of the mind, a
creative dream. But, by a remarkable conjuncture of circumstances, Magellan was, through his friendship with Francisco
Serrão, to learn more about the Spice Islands than almost any
other man of that day; and his friend's adventures among
them were to lure him into the greatest and boldest adventure of his time.

Francisco Serrão's remarkable private enterprise, which
was to prove so decisive in Magellan's career, forms an agreeable and tranquillizing episode in the bloody chronicle of
Portuguese battles and massacres. Among the conquistadors
who were both heroic and brutal, the figure of this voluntary
Crusoe assumes a most congenial aspect. After bidding farewell in Malacca to Magellan, who was about to return home,
Francisco Serrão set sail for the Moluccas with the other captains. They reached their destination without incident, and
secured a friendly welcome. The fierce culture of the warlike
Mohammedans had not made its way to these distant shores.
The indigenes of the Spice Islands, naked and pacific, lived
in a state of nature. They had no coined money, nor did they
set much store by lucre. For two or three bells or bracelets,
the simple-minded islanders would barter spices by the hun-

dredweight, so that at the first two islands the Portuguese touched, Banda and Amboina, they could fill the holds of their ships to bursting. Impatient to bring his precious freight into safe-keeping, Antonio d'Abreu decided not to visit the other Spice Islands, but to make with all speed for Malacca.

Perhaps in his greed he had overloaded his ships. Anyhow, one of them, the one commanded by Francisco Serrão, struck a rock and split. The disaster was irreparable, and the mariners were lucky to get off with their lives. The forsaken men wandered hither and thither on the reef for a few days until at length Serrão, by a cunning device, got possession of a pirate craft on which he returned to Amboina. Here the chief gave the wanderers a no less friendly reception than when they had come as great lords ("fueron recibidos y hospedados con amor, veneración y magnificencia"). It was now the plain duty of Captain Francisco Serrão to return forthwith to Malacca on board one of the many junks which made the voyage month after month, and to place himself once more under the orders of his master the King of Portugal, to whom he had sworn fealty.

But the paradisaical landscape, the warm balsamic climate, had seriously undermined his sense of military discipline. He no longer cared a fig or a pepper-corn whether, ten or twelve thousand miles away in Europe, a monarch might be grumbling. He felt he had done more than enough for Portugal, had carried his skin to market too often. Now he was going to seize his chance of enjoying his own life after the manner of the naked and carefree inhabitants of these fortunate islands. Let other mariners and other captains continue to plough the seas, gathering cinnamon and ginger and what not for alien traders at the cost of their own blood and sweat. Let them, if they were fools enough and loyal enough, continue to play the robot amid dangers and hard knocks, in order that the alfanda of Lisbon should be able to pouch more taxes. He, Francisco Serrão, sometime captain in the Portuguese navy, had had enough of war and adventure and the spice trade. Without more ado, he leapt from the heroic world into an idyllic one, having determined to adopt the wholly primitive, splendidly slothful manner of life of these friendly savages. The dignity of captain-general, bestowed on him by the King of Ternate, was not burdensome. The only service he was called upon to perform was to act as military adviser in case of war. In return, he received a house of his own with a sufficiency of slaves and a pretty brown-skinned wife, by whom he had several whity-brown children.

For years this new Odysseus continued to enjoy the embraces of his dusky Calypso, with no demon of ambition to expel him from a dolce far niente Eden. Down to the day of his death, nine years later, the refugee from Western civilization never quitted the Sunda Islands, being not perhaps the most heroic, but probably the wisest and the happiest of the conquistadors and capitanos of the Great Age of Portugal.

To begin with, Francisco Serrão's renunciation of the world seemed to have no bearing upon the life and exploits of Magellan. In reality, however, the epicurean choice of his friend exerted a decisive influence upon Magellan's life, and therewith upon the history of maritime discovery. Across the vast oceanic distances the pair, connected by ties of close friendship, remained in unceasing contact. Whenever op-

portunity offered of sending a missive to Malacca and thence
to Portugal, Serrão wrote in great detail to Magellan, giving
enthusiastic descriptions of the wealth and the amenities of
his new home.

"I have found here a new world, richer and greater than
that of Vasco da Gama," declared Serrão, who had suc-
cumbed to the charm of the tropics, and begged his friend
to leave ill-paid service in Europe and join him in the Spice
Islands as soon as possible. Because of Serrão's letters, Magellan was better primed than any other European with precise
geographical and statistical data about the Sunda Islands. We
can hardly doubt that it was through his keeping in touch
with Francisco Serrão that Magellan must have happened
upon the inquiry whether these islands that lay so far to the
east might not be more readily approachable by Columbus's
route, from the west, than by Vasco da Gama's, from the
east.

How far negotiations between the two friends went, we
do not know. Beyond question the pair must have concerted
some sort of plan, for after Serrão's death there was found
among his papers a letter from Magellan wherein the latter
promised to come to Ternate as soon as possible, "if not by
Portugal, by another way." Thanks to the lures of Serrão,
an idea and a mystery gained power over a man, and this idea
determined the man's destiny.

The leading idea, a few scars on his sunburned frame, and
a Malay slave whom he bought in Malacca—these were all
that Magellan brought home after seven years' service on the
Indian front. The battle-scarred soldier must have been filled

with astonishment when, in 1512, he at length set eyes upon a very different Lisbon, a very different Portugal, from those he had quitted seven years before. There was something new and strange to look at as soon as he reached Belem. The lowly little church, which aforetime had blessed Vasco da Gama's voyage, had been replaced by a glorious and mighty cathedral, the first visible sign of the immense wealth with which the Indian spice trade was endowing Portugal. But there were changes everywhere.

Seven years ago there had been but little shipping in the Tagus estuary. Now there were sails on all sides. Hammers of shipwrights resounded in the yards, for craftsmen were busily equipping new and greater fleets. The port was thronged with masts flying the flags of every nation in Europe. The warehouses on the quays were full. Thousands of persons hurried to and fro along the streets which led between rows of newly erected palaces. Every workshop hummed with talk about the conquest of the Indies. Lisbon, which had been a petty provincial city, had become one of the great capitals of the world, and the home of luxury. Ladies driving in open carriages flaunted their Indian pearls; richly dressed courtiers hastened to the King's palace; and the returned soldier was quick to recognize that he and his comrades in the East had shed their blood so that, by some marvellous alchemy, it might here be transmuted into gold. While they, beneath the fierce tropical sun, had been fighting and suffering, enduring privations and despair, Lisbon, through their deeds, had been made the heiress of Alexandria and Venice, while King Emanuel, "el fortunado," was now the richest monarch in Europe. Everything was changed. Everything was more luxurious, more inclined to promote enjoyment and spend thrift ease; as if the conquest of spices had given wings to th gold it brought. Yet he himself, Ferdinand Magellan, ha returned as he had left, an "unknown soldier," in soiled, torn blood-stained clothing; expected by no one, thanked by n one, greeted by no one. As a stranger, Magellan came hom after seven years' service in the Indies.

Chapter Three

HE RENOUNCES ALLEGIANCE TO PORTUGAL

June 1512 - October 1517

He Renounces
Allegiance to Portugal

HEROIC eras are never sentimental. Little gratitude did the kings of Spain and Portugal show to those bold conquistadors who added whole worlds to their dominions. Columbus was brought back to Seville in chains; Cortez fell into disgrace; Pizarro was murdered; Núñez de Balboa, the discoverer of the Pacific, was beheaded; Camoens, Portuguese warrior and poet, spent, like Cervantes, months and years in a jail which was little better than a dungheap. Amazing was the unthankfulness of the age of discovery. The soldiers and the sailors who had fought to secure the jewels of Montezuma and the treasures of the Incas for the Emperor wandered as beggars and cripples, lousy and neglected, in the alleys of Cadiz, Lisbon, and other seaports—the few of them, that is to say, who did not leave their bones in the colonies, but returned home to be kicked hither and thither like mangy dogs. What interest in such achievements had the courtiers who never left the safe shelter of their palaces, where they lived as drones, where they spent the time in gambling until they could secure appointments as adelantados, the governors of the new provinces? Then they filled their moneybags, thrusting aside as vexatious intruders the colonial fighters, the frontier officers of those days who, after years of sacrifice and exhaustion, were fools enough to return.

It counted for nothing that Magellan had fought at Cannanore, at Malacca, and in many other battles; that he had dozens of times risked life and health for Portugal's victory. When he got back home, he was not more esteemed for his exertions. Only to the chance that he was of noble blood and had in youth been attached to the King's Household ("criaçao do Rey") did he owe the favour of being re-enrolled as a pensioner or almoner, at first in the lowest grade as "mozo fidalgo," with the beggarly allowance of one thousand reis a month. A little later, presumably after making a good deal of fuss, he was promoted a stage to become "fidalgo escudeiro," with a stipend of eighteen hundred and fifty reis (or, according to another story, as "cavalleiro fidalgo," at twelve hundred and fifty reis). This pompous designation gave him neither rights nor duties, beyond entitling him to become a loafer in the royal anterooms. Impossible that an honourable and ambitious man should long content himself with such a pittance for such "work." It was only to be expected that Magellan would seize the first opportunity of renewed war service.

Even for this he had to wait nigh on a year. But then, as soon as, in the summer of 1513, King Emanuel began to equip a great military expedition against Morocco, hoping to make an end of the Moorish pirates, the fighter of the Indies was prompt to report for service, a decision which could be explained only as the outcome of discontent with his enforced idleness. For Magellan, who had hitherto done almost all his fighting by sea, and had become one of the most experienced navigators of his time, could find little scope for his talents in land warfare. Besides, in the army that was sent to Azimur he was merely a subordinate officer without independent command. As had been the case in the Indies, his name did not appear in the front line of the dispatches, although, as in India, his person was always in the forefront of danger. On this occasion, too, Magellan was wounded—for the third time —in hand-to-hand fights, and seriously. A lance-thrust in the left knee divided an important sinew, and the injured leg remained permanently damaged.

A man with a limp, who can neither advance nor retreat swiftly, has lost his value in the front line. Magellan might well have retired to the rear, and have drawn a good pension. He was, however, determined to go on serving his country in some active capacity, so he and another officer were given joint positions as quartermasters ("quadrileiros des preses"). They were assigned the responsible task of looking after the large quantity of horses and cattle which had been taken from the Moors, and while they were thus engaged an unfortunate incident occurred. A dozen sheep vanished during the night from the huge flock, and it was bruited abroad that Magellan and his comrade had secretly resold some of the spoils to the Moors, or had negligently allowed the enemy access to the pen. By a strange chance this pitiful accusation of having defrauded the State was the same as that which the Portuguese Colonial Office brought against the other greatest Portuguese of his time, Camoens the poet. Both of them, after having served for years in the Indies where, if inclined to plunder and peculation, they had ample opportunities, but who had

returned home from El Dorado as poor as church mice, had
their honour tainted by the same disgraceful and unfounded
suspicions.

Magellan, however, was of tougher fibre than the gentle
Camoens, and was therefore by no means inclined to be vic-
timized, or to allow himself to be imprisoned for months. Not
as did the writer of the *Lusiads*, would Magellan pusillani-
mously turn his back upon his enemies. Directly he heard of
the intention to bring a public charge against him, he left the
army and returned to Portugal to defend himself.

Magellan did not come back as a penitent, as a man ready
to acknowledge guilt. This is shown by the fact that, as soon
as he reached Lisbon, he demanded audience of the King,
not in order to justify himself, but, being fully aware of his
own merits, to ask for worthier employment and better pay.
Once more he had wasted two years; once again, in open
fight, he had been wounded and on this occasion crippled.
Emanuel did not give him time to make his demand. The
King had already been informed by the High Command in
Africa that this presumptuous captain had left the Moroccan
army without leave. King Emanuel, therefore, declining to
receive Magellan in audience, sent him blunt orders to return
to the colours in Africa and place himself at the disposal of
the High Command. For the sake of discipline, Magellan
complied. By the next boat he went back to Azimur. When
he got there, no investigation was made and no charge was
brought against him. No one ventured to accuse this trusty
soldier; so, with the express permission of the High Command, with all the honours of war, and supplied with docu-

ments that would prove his innocence and his excellent services, Magellan made his way home once more to Lisbon—this
time, naturally, much embittered. Instead of earning distinction, he had earned nothing but suspicion; instead of gaining
rewards, he had gained only scars; long had he kept silence,
and remained in the background. But now, when he was
thirty-five years of age, he had grown weary of petitioning
for things that were his plain right.

It would certainly have been more prudent of Magellan
to refrain from reporting to King Emanuel immediately on
returning, and from reiterating the demand which so recently
had been contemptuously refused. He would have done well
to keep his own counsel for a while, seek allies in court
circles, try to ingratiate himself. But adroitness and subtlety
of that sort were foreign to Magellan's nature. Little as we
know of his personality, this much is certain, that, small, obscure, inconspicuous, and silent as he was, he was utterly
devoid of the arts which would have enabled him to woo the
favour of the mighty or to make himself liked by his subordinates. We know not why, but King Emanuel was always
hostile to him ("sempre teve hum entejo"); and even the
leal Pigafetta has to admit that his officers detested him ("li
capitani sui lo odiavano"). He did not know how to smile,
how to make himself amiable, how to be obliging, or how to
advocate his ideas eloquently. Taciturn and reserved, always
enwrapped in a cloud of loneliness, this perpetual solitary was
environed with rime, ungraciousness, and mistrust. Half un-
consciously his comrades were aware that in the silent depths
of his being there lurked a strange and obscure ambition,
which made his aims incomprehensible to them, and there-

fore rendered him far more suspect than are persons who hotly and frankly try to secure advantageous positions. There was always something hidden behind his hard, deep-set eyes, behind his hirsute mouth—a mystery that could not be pierced. A sinister impression is invariably produced by men who are able, year after year, to veil themselves in mystery, to refrain from the natural disclosures of frankness. From the first, Magellan created obstacles for himself through the obscurity of his nature. It was not easy for anyone to espouse his cause and march joyfully onward at his side; and perhaps it was harder still for this tragic solitary that his disposition compelled him to be so incessantly alone.

Yet it was utterly alone, without protector or patron, that the fidalgo escudeiro Fernão de Magalhãis sought audience of his king, thus choosing the most unlucky path a man can choose at court—the honest and direct route. King Emanuel received him in the same throne-room, perhaps sitting on the same throne as that in which his predecessor John II had refused Columbus's proposal. In the identical spot was renewed an identical scene. For the short, stocky, broad-shouldered, black-bearded Portuguese, the man with veiled glances who now made obeisance before King Emanuel—to be no less contemptuously dismissed—cherished thoughts as remarkable as had been those of the Genoese foreigner. Indeed, as regards boldness, resoluteness, and experience, Magellan probably excelled his more famous predecessor, Columbus.

This momentous interview had no witnesses; but the unanimous descriptions of contemporary chroniclers enable us to see into the throne-room across the mists of time. We can picture the lame Magellan limping up to the King and, with a bow, handing His Majesty the documents which showed irrefutably that a false and malicious charge had been brought. Then he put his first request, begging the monarch, in view of a further wound which made him unfit for active service, to increase his monthly pension by the amount of half a crusado (a coin having the approximate value of an English shilling today). This was a ludicrously small demand, and it was unseemly that a proud, hard-bitten, ambitious man should have to bend the knee for such a trifle. Magellan, of course, was concerned, not for the silver coin, the half-crusado, but for rank and honour. At this royal court, where everyone was struggling for place and power, the amount of a nobleman's pension, his "moradia," was emblematic of his position in the Royal Household. Magellan, now thirty-five years of age, a veteran of the Indian and Moroccan wars, had no mind to occupy a position inferior to that of lads on whose cheeks the down had scarcely grown, and whose business it was to hand Emanuel a finger-bowl or to open the door of His Majesty's coach. He had never thrust himself forward from pride; still, pride forbade him to let younger and lesser men than himself take precedence.

The King, nevertheless, knitted his brows as he stared at the impatient petitioner. No more than Magellan, was the wealthy Emanuel concerned about a trifling silver coin. What annoyed him was the manner of the man who, instead of humbly begging a favour, impetuously demanded a right; the man who, unwilling to wait until the monarch spontaneously conceded an increase of pension as an act of grace, stiffly reminded King Emanuel of his alleged claims. Well, the stubborn fellow should be kept waiting until he learned how to ask more obsequiously. In an evil hour, the King of Portugal, though generally known as "el fortunado," rejected Magellan's demand, without foreseeing how many thousand golden ducats this half-crusado he was now saving would in the end cost him.

It was time for the suitor to withdraw, since the King's angry countenance did not bode the sunshine of courtly favour. But instead of making a servile obeisance and quitting the throne-room, Magellan, fortified by pride, stood his ground before King Emanuel to put his second request, which was the one he had most at heart. He asked whether the monarch could not offer him some worthy post in the royal service, since he felt too young and vigorous to spend his life as a court pensioner and recipient of alms. Ships set sail to the Indies, to Africa, or to Brazil, month after month, and almost week after week. Nothing could seem more reasonable than to give the command of one of these to a man who knew the eastern sailing-routes perhaps better than any other then alive. Except for Vasco da Gama, certainly no one in Lisbon, no one in Portugal, could boast of being better informed upon these matters than Magellan. King Emanuel, however, had by now begun to find the hard, challenging glances of his would-be servitor intolerable. He coldly refused, and would not even hold out any hope for the future. There was no position in the Portuguese service for Ferdinand Magellan.

That was over and done with. The importunate suitor endured a second rebuff. But Magellan had something else to request, a third petition which was rather an inquiry than a petition. He asked whether His Majesty would have any ob-

AMERIGO VESPUCCI
Engraving by Crispin de Passe

EMANUEL I, KING OF PORTUGAL
Copper engraving, c. 1700

jection to Magellan's taking service in some other country, where he might find chances of promotion. With mortifying indifference, Emanuel replied that there could be no objection whatever. This was tantamount to saying that Magellan would do well to renounce every prospect of activity at the Portuguese court; his pittance would still be paid, but nothing would please King Emanuel better than that he should shake the dust of Portugal from his feet.

Since no third party was present at this interview, we do not know whether then, or later, or perhaps earlier, Magellan disclosed to the monarch the plans he had in mind. Perhaps he was given no opportunity for expounding his schemes; or perhaps he did expound them, and received no encouragement. Anyhow, Magellan had unquestionably shown his goodwill towards the land of his birth, had proved his desire to serve Portugal with his blood and his life. It was the King's contumelious refusal which forced on him a decision such as must be made once at least by every person of creative temperament.

When, a rejected beggar, he left the palace, Magellan knew that he must wait, must hesitate, no longer. At thirty-five he had enjoyed all the experiences open to a warrior on land or to a mariner at sea. Four times he had doubled the Cape, twice from the west and twice from the east. Again and again he had risked his life; thrice he had been seriously wounded. He had seen an enormous amount of the world, knowing more of the East than did the most famous geographers and cartographers of his day. For nearly ten years he had been tried and tested in the technique of war. He had learned how to handle both sword and arquebus, tiller and compass, sails and artillery, spade and lance. He had studied navigation and knew how to keep a ship's reckoning; was as good a leadsman as the most experienced of pilots; and was as precise a manipulator of the forerunners of quadrant and sextant as any "master of astronomy." What others·learn timidly from books, he had learned boldly by repeated experience of calm and storm, battles by land and sea, rapine and siege, onslaught and shipwreck. During these ten years, upon thousands of nights and days, he had learned to await the will of the boundless ocean, ever ready to seize the skirts of happy chance. He had made acquaintance with men of all kinds and colours; yellow and white, black and brown, Hindus and Negroes, Malays and Chinese, Tamils and Turks. In all forms of service, by water and on land, at all seasons of the year and in every zone, in frost and under the burning sun, he had faithfully done his duty to king and country. But service is a matter for youth, and now, when his thirty-sixth year was approaching, Magellan decided that he had sacrificed enough for strangers' interests and strangers' glory. Like every man of creative temperament who is half-way through his career, he felt the desire for a responsible post and for self-realization. His native country had left him in the lurch; his ties with office and duty had been severed. So much the better; now he was free. As so often when a man seems to be at the mercy of the winds, he is in reality being blown back upon his own self.

When Magellan formed a resolution, he never acted on it impulsively. Although contemporary descriptions have thrown little light on his character, it is plain that his remarkable gift for silence was displayed as a supreme virtue throughout his career. He was neither impatient nor loquacious, being able to hold inconspicuously aloof even amid the tumult of an army, and always able to think out his plans as a solitary. Looking far ahead, quietly reckoning with every possibility, he never disclosed a scheme or a resolve until his ideas were ripe, well thought out, and incontrovertible.

On the present occasion, Magellan turned his talent for silence to admirable use. Any other man, after being treated so contemptuously by King Emanuel, would probably have hastened to leave the country and offer his services to another sovereign. But Magellan stayed quietly in Portugal for a year, without informing anyone as to his schemes. There was nothing conspicuous about his manner of life. All that anyone could notice—insofar as such conduct was noticeable in one who had been a famous navigator to the Indies—was that he had a good many interviews with pilots and captains, and especially with those who had made voyages to the South Seas. Still, what was there to wonder at in this? Men who are fond of shooting big game love to talk of their own and others' exploits, while seamen are fond of yarning about the sea and about newly discovered lands. Even when, in King Emanuel's private library, he gained access to all the charts, the sailing directions, and the log-books of the latest expeditions to Brazil (kept as secretissima in the Tesoraria), this could not arouse suspicion, for what should an unoccupied ship's captain study in his abundant leisure other than such documents?

Somewhat more striking was a new friendship entered into

by Magellan. Ruy Faleiro, with whom he became more and more closely associated, was an unstable, irritable, nervous intellectual, a talkative fellow, opinionated and quarrelsome, who might have seemed the last man in the world to please the reserved, self-controlled, inscrutable seaman and warrior. But it was the divergency of the two men's gifts, their polar oppositeness, that brought them, for the time being, into harmony. The harmony would be short-lived, but while it lasted they were continually together. Magellan loved marine adventure and the practical exploration of the world, whereas Faleiro had a passion for abstract geography and astronomy. Being a pure theoretician, a man of the study who had never been on board a ship or left the soil of Portugal, Ruy Faleiro knew what he knew about the heavens and the earth from calculations, reading, mathematical tables, and maps; but in this abstract sphere, as a cartographer and astronomer, he was accounted the greatest authority in Portugal. He could not hoist a sail or handle the tiller, but he had constructed his own system of longitude which, though fallacious, embraced the entire globe in its scope and did yeoman's service to Magellan during the latter's voyage of circumnavigation. Though he could not steer a ship, his charts, his sailing directions, his astrolabes and other instruments appear to have been the best nautical accessories of his time. To Magellan, the man of practice, whose only universities had been warfare and adventure, who knew no more of astronomy or geography than what he had learned upon his own voyages, the services of such an expert as Faleiro could not but be of the greatest value. Precisely because the two were so divergent in their talents and their tastes, they represented the happiest combination of the theoretical with the experimental, of thought with deed, of spirit and matter.

In this particular instance, such an association as that of Magellan and Faleiro had peculiarly important relationships to their time. Both of these exceptional Portuguese (who were exceptional in such different ways) had been profoundly mortified by King Emanuel's treatment, and both had been hindered in the development of a career. For years Ruy Faleiro had aspired to the appointment of astronomer royal, and beyond question no one in Portugal could put up a better claim. But even as Magellan had spoiled his chances by taciturnity and pride, so had Ruy Faleiro hindered his advancement at court by talkativeness and outbursts of temper. His enemies spoke of him as a fool, while jealous competitors, hoping that the Inquisition would rid them of him, spread abroad the suspicion that he was in league with the devil and made use of unnatural powers to gain his ends. The fact that they were both victims of hatred and mistrust brought them more and more closely together.

Magellan passed on to Faleiro what he had learned from Serrão concerning the far eastward situation of the Spice Islands, and mooted the possibility of reaching them from the western side by a new route. Faleiro, having studied Magellan's scheme, provided it with a scientific foundation. With precise calculations and with tables of figures, he was able to confirm what Magellan had reached by intuition. The more the theoretician and the practical man compared their suppositions, the more manifold the lights they threw upon their problem, the more zealous did they become, until a definite plan crystallized. Soon it was hardly possible to disentangle from this stupendous plan, which was to enrich and almost to terminate the great period of discovery, what had come from one mind and what from the other. The upshot was that they determined to realize jointly a design which had been jointly formed. They mutually pledged themselves to keep the details secret until achievement had crowned their efforts; they also decided, in case of need, without the aid of their country and perhaps against their country, to do a deed that was to benefit, not one land alone, but all mankind.

The moment has now come for asking what was the mysterious scheme hatched by Magellan and Faleiro in the shadow of the King's palace at Lisbon. In what respect were their plans so novel, unprecedented, and precious that the conspirators exacted mutual pledges of secrecy? What made the project so dangerous that it had to be hidden like a poisoned dagger? The answer seems disconcerting at the outset. The new scheme was nothing more than a determination to realize the idea which Magellan, fired by Serrão's encouragement, had brought back from the East Indies—the idea that the Spice Islands could be reached (as an alternative to sailing eastward round the Cape of Good Hope like the Portuguese) by sailing westward to the Americas. There seemed to be nothing really new about this notion. Columbus had set sail across the Atlantic, not for the still unknown America, but for the Indies. Although the world in general speedily recognized his error, down to the day of his death the Genoese navigator continued to believe that the land he had discovered must be an outlying territory of the Emperor of China.

Spain was by no means inclined, at first, to waste her strength in attempts upon this western route to the Indies. Columbus was discredited as a man whose imagination had outrun his wisdom. His announcement that gold was to be had for the gathering in Santo Domingo and Hispaniola had proved little better than a hoax. There was no gold; there were no spices; there was not even "black ivory," for the natives were of a weakly constitution, and died off like flies when the conquistadors made them do hard work as slaves. Although as far as moral gains were concerned the discovery of America had brought Spain wonderful renown, so far as material gains were concerned these proved illusory until, in the fifteen-twenties, Cortez conquered Mexico while Pizarro plundered the treasure houses of the Incas, and then, in 1546, the silver mines of Potosí were discovered. From the commercial outlook, the Americas were a blank. The gold-hungry Castilians did not want to colonize and administer these new territories. They wanted to leave America behind them, and find a quick road to the Indies, the paradise of jewels and spices. On the King's instructions, repeated efforts were made to discover a way through or round this new "terra firma," and to raid the treasuries of the East, the Spice Islands, in advance of the Portuguese.

One expedition followed in the wake of another. But in their search for a maritime route to the Indies of their hearts' desire, the Spaniards were disillusioned, as, before them, the Portuguese had been disillusioned by Africa. Prince Henry believed Africa to be much smaller than it was, and the way to the Indies far shorter. He hoped to find the Southern Cape at or near the Equator, and his mariners were alarmed to discover that the southward extent of Africa seemed boundless. The Spanish navigators had a similar experience with the Americas. Wherever, whether in the north or in the south, they tried to find a passage to the Indian Ocean, they encountered an impenetrable barrier of land. This long-extended continent continued to block their course. Surely there must be a way through somewhere, an "estrecho" or a "paso," a strait or a passage? During his last voyage to the west Columbus was still hoping to get back by way of India. When he coasted Brazil, it was not with a general purpose of discovery, but "con proposito di andare e scoprire un' isola verso Oriente che si dice Melacha"—in the expectation of reaching the Spice Islands, the Moluccas.

Cortez, in his fourth "relación," promised Charles V to do everything in his power to find the "paso," and he dispatched one of his officers to Panama for that purpose. Cortereal and Cabot steered northward into icebound seas upon the same quest. Juan de Solís, when he sailed up the Rio de la Plata at the turn of the year 1515–1516, was looking for the passage in the south.

But the search proved vain. Whether in the north or in the south, in frostbound zones or in tropical latitudes, the same impenetrable wall of earth and stone was encountered. Hope began to fade. Some of the cartographers now depicted South America as extending to the Pole. Others ceased to believe in the possibility of ever entering from the Atlantic Ocean that other ocean which Núñez de Balboa had seen from the peak in Darien, and which must unquestionably lead into the Indian Ocean. Too many ships had been lost upon what was disclosing itself as a fruitless quest; once again was it proving a dream, this Cabo Deseado, this longed-for cape.

But now, of a sudden, the almost unknown Ferdinand Magellan emerged from the anonymity of his inconspicuous existence, to declare: "There is a way through. I know it. I alone, I and Ruy Faleiro, know the place. Provide me with a fleet, and I will sail through, to circumnavigate the globe from east to west."

Here we approach a historical mystery about which sages and psychologists have for centuries cudgelled their brains, each after his own fashion. Let us unhesitatingly admit that Magellan's scheme was nowise new, being in the very air of his day. Magellan wished to do what Columbus had wanted, and Vespucci, and Cortereal, and Cortez, and Cabot. What was so strikingly new in Magellan's proposal was not the proposal itself, but the peremptoriness with which it was made. For, from the first, Magellan refrained from saying modestly, as those others had said: "I hope, somewhere, to find a paso, a way through." With the harsh accent of certitude he declared: "I shall find the paso. I know, I alone know, where to find it."

But how (here lies the riddle) could Magellan know beforehand in what parallel of latitude and in what meridian was to be found this passage which others had vainly sought? Neither he nor his partner Faleiro had ever been in America or even near the American coast. Neither he, therefore, nor Faleiro could be acquainted with the passage from direct observation. Since Magellan could not himself have set eyes on it, there remained as the only explanation that he must have been informed about its existence and its geographical position by someone else—by another navigator, another European, who had seen the passage with his own eyes and had actually sailed through it. In that case, we must infer by inexorable logic that Magellan was not the famous discoverer that history declares him to be, but a plagiarist and usurper who profited by another's achievements. In that case, the Strait of Magellan has been as wrongly called after Magellan as America has been called after Amerigo Vespucci.

The most important witness for the view that Magellan was not the discoverer of the Strait of Magellan is, strangely enough, Magellan's closest companion on his journey, his admirer and biographer Antonio Pigafetta. In set terms, honestly wishing to promote the renown of his beloved captain, Pigafetta informs us that when the fleet approached the strait all the others regarded the entrance as a closed bay, and wished to sail past it. Only Magellan knew beforehand that the entrance was masked, having seen as much in a secret map to which he had had access in the treasury of the King of Portugal. The map in question was the work of the distinguished cosmographer Martin Behaim. Here are Pigafetta's original words: "Il che aveva veduto descritto sopra una charta nella Thesoraria del Re di Portogallo, la qual charta fu fatta per un' eccellente uomo, detto Martin de Boemia."

Was then Martin Behaim, as was long maintained, this mysterious forerunner?

Not a bit of it. No doubt Martin Behaim, who for some years before his death in 1507 was court cartographer to the

King of Portugal, actually prepared maps for this monarch; and doubtless Magellan and Faleiro studied some of these maps. But during the decisive years from 1500, when Brazil was discovered, down to the year of his death, Behaim did not make any voyage to America. He himself, therefore, could not have been the discoverer, but at most could have incorporated in a map the results of what he had heard from mariners who had visited Patagonia. Who were these mariners? Did Portuguese ships, at a date previous to the drawing of Behaim's map, make their way into the passage leading from the Atlantic to the Pacific? Certainly there are documents which seem to show beyond dispute that in the opening years of the sixteenth century several Portuguese ships (one of them with Vespucci on board) explored the coast of Brazil and perhaps that of Argentina as well. One or more of these might have discovered the "paso."

But further questions arise. How far did these strange expeditions go? Did any of them reach the channel which was afterwards to bear the name of Magellan? For a long time this question was answered in the affirmative, upon the strength of the words already quoted from Pigafetta and upon that of the still extant globe by the famous cartographer Johann Schöner, a globe of the year 1515—published years before Magellan divulged his scheme—which plainly shows a southern passage (though in the wrong place). But this does not in itself explain where Behaim and the German professor got their information. In those days, nations and rulers guarded, like jealous merchants, against leakage of such intelligence, which might be used by commercial rivals for their own advantage. No foreigner had access to the Tesoraria, where the

pilots' log-books, sketches, and sailing directions were kept
under lock and key. By an edict under date of November 13,
1504, it was "forbidden on pain of death to give any information about navigation beyond the Congo River, lest foreigners should profit by the discoveries of Portugal."

Thus the question as to sources seemed unanswerable until
a fairly recent treasure-trove showed where Behaim, Schöner,
and ultimately Magellan got wind of the southern strait. This
was in a "Copia der Newen Zeytung aus Presillg Landt,"
which, somewhere about 1506, reported the result of one of
the before-mentioned Portuguese expeditions. The pamphlet
or Zeytung purports to be the translation of a business letter
from a Portuguese factor sent by him to the Welser family,
mercantile magnates in Augsburg. Here we read (in atro-
ciously bad German) that somewhere about the fortieth parallel of south latitude a Portuguese ship rounded a "cabo"
comparable with the Cape of Good Hope. Here was a strait
like the Strait of Gibraltar, a broad channel leading from east
to west into another ocean on whose waters it would be easy
to reach the Moluccas, the Spice Islands. Surely this was plain
demonstration that ships could sail from the Atlantic into the
Pacific?

Did not the proof seem complete? Was not the riddle
solved once for all? Must not Magellan have known as much
about the earlier Portuguese expeditions to "Presillg Landt"
as did the anonymous factor who penned the "Newe Zeytung" and thus acquainted the Augsburg geographer with
what was going on? In that case Magellan was no more than
a usurper and a plagiarist. His whole achievement shrinks to
his having translated a carefully guarded secret into dynamic

knowledge available to all mankind. He was no more than one of those who adroitly, swiftly, and unconscionably exploit the successes of others. But now comes another turn, the last turn, of the evidential screw. We know today what Magellan did not know, that the mariners of that early Portuguese expedition to South America never reached the Strait of Magellan; and that their reports, which Magellan no less than Behaim and Schöner regarded as trustworthy, were based upon a misunderstanding, a pardonable error. What did the pilots really find in the neighbourhood of the fortieth parallel of south latitude? What is the substantial significance of the eye-witnesses' report as related in the "Newe Zeytung"? Nothing more than that, somewhere near the fortieth parallel, the mariners had happened upon an indentation of the coast, had sailed into it for two days without coming to land, and that they had been driven back by a storm before finding the exit. They had, then, entered what they believed to be the eastern end of a channel leading through the Americas, but this had been a mere guess. The real strait of which they were in search lay, as the world has known since Magellan's voyage, near the fifty-second parallel.

What was it, then, that the navigators saw in south latitude 35–40? We have good reason to suppose that they were the first to make their way into the vast estuary of the Rio de la Plata, one of the world's most gigantic river mouths. How natural it was that they should mistake it for an arm of the sea leading to the "paso." No river with such dimensions was known to them from European experience, and readily, therefore, they jumped to the conclusion that it must be the greatly desired channel linking ocean with ocean. The maps and globes based on their reports make clear the nature of their mistake. If, in addition to the estuary of La Plata, they had, farther south, discovered the veritable Strait of Magellan, both arms of the sea would have been shown on the charts. But neither on Schöner's globe nor on any of the pre-Magellan representations is the Rio de la Plata depicted—only the mythical "estrecho" in the latitude where the estuary of that river actually exists.

This clears the matter up. Those upon whose reports the "Newe Zeytung's" story is based were self-deceived. They were the victims of an obvious and easily explicable delusion. Nor was Magellan a wilful impostor when he declared himself the recipient of authentic tidings of the existence of his strait. He was deceived by his forerunners' mistake when, upon the warrant of Behaim's chart, Schöner's globe, and the unnamed pilots' story, he formed his great design of circumnavigating the world. The enigma of Magellan is solved as soon as we recognize that he planned and acted in honest error.

Let us not underrate the importance of error. Through the promptings of genius, guided by luck, the most preposterous error may lead to the most fruitful of truths. In every branch of science, hundreds of highly important discoveries have been the outcome of erroneous hypotheses. Had it not been for Toscanelli's map, which absurdly underestimated the circumference of the earth and therefore deceived Columbus, that navigator would never have ventured into the unknown upon his attempt to discover a short route to the Indies. Nor would Magellan have been able to persuade a monarch to entrust him with a fleet, had he not firmly believed, with foolhardy assurance, in the accuracy of Behaim's inaccurate map, and in the soundness of the imaginative reports of the above-mentioned Portuguese pilots. Only because he had faith in a mystery, could Magellan unravel the greatest geographical mystery of his time—the exact size and shape of our planet. Only because, in the ardour of his heart, he surrendered to a sacred illusion, did he discover a wonderful truth.

Chapter Four

REALIZATION OF AN IDEA

October 20, 1517 - March 22, 1518

Realization of an Idea

MAGELLAN had now to make a momentous decision. He had conceived a bolder scheme than was entertained by any contemporary seaman, and he was convinced (rightly or wrongly) that the peculiar information at his disposal guaranteed success. But how could so costly and dangerous a scheme be carried out? His own king had contumeliously dismissed him, and he could not count on the support of even the most friendly among the Portuguese shipowners, for which of them would dare give a captaincy to a man who was out of favour at court? His only resource was to apply to Spain. There alone could he hope for furtherance. To the Spanish Crown he could look for help, since he brought most valuable information from the Lisbon Tesoraria, and also something of equal importance for the enterprise in view—a seemingly unchallengeable title. His partner Faleiro had calculated (the calculations being as erroneous as Magellan's information) that the Spice Islands lay within the Spanish zone as delimited by the Pope's assignment, and were therefore Spanish property, not Portuguese. The Portuguese captain was prepared to bestow upon Charles V the richest islands in the world and to show the monarch the shortest way thither, and he could therefore count on a good reception.

With Spanish aid he could realize his great idea, though at terrible cost. For if he should apply to Spain, he knew that he would risk, not merely his skin, but his knightly honour. He would have to forfeit his Portuguese name Magalhãis. His own king would despise him, and for centuries his fellow-countrymen would stigmatize him as a "traidor" and a turn-coat ("suo rege transfuga").

Was he really a traitor? Friendly historians obstinately refuse to admit the truth of this charge, and do their utmost to justify their hero. Magellan, they declare, did not commit a crime by entering foreign service, for this was the custom of the day. Columbus, Cabot, Cada Mosto, and Vespucci had all done the same thing. These comparisons, however, miss the point. Not only did Magellan leave his country, but he deliberately harmed his country. Well knowing that the Spice Islands were already Portuguese possessions, he determined to hand them over to Portugal's most formidable rival, Spain. He was more than bold, he was unpatriotic when he smuggled across the frontier naval secrets which he had learned through being given access to the Tesoraria in Lisbon. To put the matter in modern terminology, this man who was a Portuguese nobleman and had been a captain in the Portuguese fleet committed no less a crime than that which is committed by a modern officer who hands over to a rival power the secret maps of the General Staff and the plans for mobilization of his own country. Unquestionably he wronged his country, and did so in full awareness of the obloquy that would consequently attach to his name. If he turned his coat, as he did, we can find, not indeed an excuse, but greatness therein that he did so with his visor up and with such challenging boldness.

The man of creative temperament is guided by other and higher laws than those of nationality. One who has a task to perform, a discovery to make, or a deed to do on behalf of mankind, is not, truly, a citizen or subject of any country, for his loyalty is given to his work. To one authority alone will he bow, that which the task itself imposes on him; and he will find it permissible to ignore the interests of one State or one epoch, provided he be true to the obligations laid upon him by his destiny and his peculiar talents. After years of loyalty to Portugal, when entering middle life Magellan recognized the task that awaited him. Since the land of his birth refused to give him a chance of fulfilling that mission, he took his ideas to a new fatherland. Resolutely he tarnished his scutcheon and destroyed his civic honour—to rise again as devotee of an idea and the doer of an imperishable deed.

The season of patient planning was over. In the autumn of 1517 his bold resolve took active shape. Leaving his less determined partner in Portugal for the moment, Magellan, accompanied by the slave Enrique, crossed his Rubicon, the Spanish frontier, reaching Seville on October 20, 1517. At this juncture, Seville was not the residence of the young King of Spain, Charles I, whom the world knows better under his subsequent imperial title of Charles V. This young man in his eighteenth year had just arrived at Santander from Flanders, and was on his way to Valladolid, where he was to hold his court in the middle of November. Till then, Magellan could not have chosen a better place of sojourn than Seville which, in its commanding position on the Guadalquivir, was one of the largest and most important commercial cities of Spain, and had already become an important centre of trade with the Indies. So great was the afflux of merchants and captains, of brokers and factors, that the King had opened there his own trading-house, the famous Casa de Contratación, or India House. Here was collected and stored every document relating to the activities of the navigators and traders. ("Habet rex in ea urbe ad oceana tantum negotia domum erectam ad quam euntes, redeuntesque visitores confluunt.") It was at one and the same time a goods exchange and a shipping-centre, a mart for trade and navigation, a board of information and advice, where the business men who financed expeditions and the captains who commanded them could come to terms with one another under official supervision. Everyone who planned some new enterprise under the Spanish flag began by reporting at the Casa de Contratación.

It shows Magellan's extraordinary gift for silence, his remarkable genius for biding his time, that he did not take this essential step prematurely. Being no dreamer, no credulous optimist, no self-deceiver, but always a precise calculator, psychologist, and realist, Magellan had carefully reckoned up his chances and possibilities. He knew that he must not go to the Casa de Contratación until he had paved the way by enlisting others' support. Who in Spain had ever heard of him? The fact that he had spent seven years in the East Indies, had fought under Almeida and Albuquerque, would count for nothing in a city like Seville, where aventurados and desperadoes swarmed in all the taverns. It would not be any particular recommendation that he came from Portugal after failing to persuade his legitimate ruler of the value of his scheme; nor that he was, substantially, a refugee and a deserter. Even though he could produce evidence of having commanded ships in distant seas, this would count for little in a city where there lived captains who had sailed under Columbus, Cortereal, and Sebastian Cabot. The authorities at the Casa de Contratación would not be over-ready to trust him, an unknown, nay discredited man. That is why, for the present, Magellan kept away from the India House. He was sufficiently experienced to be aware of what was required in such cases as his. Like any other projector, like everyone who seeks support for problematic schemes, he must begin by finding introductions and recommendations.

Magellan would appear to have secured some such important introductions before leaving Portugal. However that may be, he was cordially received, on arrival in Seville, by Diego Barbosa, who had likewise renounced Portuguese nationality some time ago, for fourteen years had been highly respected in the important position of alcalde of the Seville arsenal, and was a Knight of the Order of Santiago. Various authorities declare that the Barbosas were kindred of the Magellans, but what made the two men draw closer together than cousinship could have done was the fact that a good while back Diego Barbosa had made a voyage to the Indies—before ever Magellan went there. His son Duarte Barbosa had inherited the father's adventurous spirit. He, too, had sailed the Indian, Persian, and Malayan seas, and was the author of a book of travel greatly prized in its day, *O livro de Duarte Barbosa*. The three men promptly became close friends. Seeing that, today, officers or soldiers who in the Great War were comrades on the same sector of the front tend to form a lifelong alliance, how much more must that have been so four centuries ago as regards the few dozen veterans who had safely returned from the perils of their voyages.

Barbosa hospitably invited Magellan to stay in his house; and, ere long, the energetic and imposing man of thirty-seven found favour in the eyes of Barbosa's daughter Beatriz. Magellan speedily became the alcalde's son-in-law, and this alliance gave him a strong footing in Seville. Having acquired Spanish nationality, he was no longer a nameless vagrant. Vouched for by his friendship and his marital alliance with the Barbosas, he could unhesitatingly approach the Casa de Contratación.

We have no trustworthy information regarding his reception at that institution, or the conversations he held there. We do not know how much of his scheme Magellan, bound as he was to Ruy Faleiro by the terms of their mutual oath, thought fit to disclose. It is probably an exaggeration to say that the people of the India House laughed his ideas to scorn, and the notion that they did so may well have been invented by analogy with what happened to Columbus. Probably they had neither the right nor the inclination to invest money in so nebulous a plan or to recommend its acceptance by the Crown. Nor did they offer Magellan any encouragement, since experts are proverbially suspicious of the unusual or the extraordinary. On this occasion, in accordance with precedent, one of the most decisive achievements of history came to pass, not with the aid of, but despite, the "competent authorities."

The India House refused to help Magellan. The very first door of the numerous doors that led into the King's audience chamber was slammed in his face. This must have been a black day for the projector. His journey, his recommendations, had been fruitless. In vain had been the eloquence, the passion, which had carried him away in his attempts to persuade those able to help him. His best arguments had not won over the three experts of the Casa de Contratación.

Often, however, in war, when a commander believes himself defeated and is preparing to retreat, a messenger brings tidings that the enemy has withdrawn, has evacuated the battlefield. Within a brief moment, in such circumstances, gloom changes into happiness. Such was now Magellan's experience. At the very time when he supposed that all three members of the commission were hopelessly adverse, it was announced to him that one of them had been greatly impressed by his ideas. Juan de Aranda, the factor, the business head of the Casa de Contratación, announced that he was desirous to hear—in private—fuller details of this extremely interesting and, as he fancied, practicable scheme, if Magellan would be good enough to get in touch with him.

What to the delighted Magellan must have seemed a boon from heaven was, in reality, an extremely mundane affair. Juan de Aranda (like the emperors and the kings, the captains and the merchants of his day) was by no means concerned— as the histories we read in our youth declare—with the discovery of unknown regions of the world or with bringing happiness to mankind. It was not for purely spiritual motives that he was disposed to help and protect Magellan. The factor of the India House was, above all, a man of business, and it seemed to him that Magellan might put him in the way of making a good deal of money. Magellan must have fascinated this worthy in some way. It may have been the Portuguese captain's exceedingly clear demonstration, or his manly, confident aspect, or perhaps his unshakable conviction. Anyhow, whether through the workings of reason or the promptings of instinct, Aranda had become convinced that here was no wild-cat scheme, that something genuine, important, and lucrative was at stake. He decided, therefore, although officially he had thought it expedient to reject Magellan's proposal as impracticable, to "come in on his own account," as business men say; or, at any rate, to undertake the financing of the enterprise as silent partner. We can hardly regard it as honourable, as correct, for anyone as an official of the Crown or of the court thus to reject a proposal, and immediately afterwards to accept it in his private capacity. No doubt there is scriptural warrant for not letting the left hand know what the right hand does; but in actual fact Juan de Aranda was prosecuted later for having financed Magellan's venture.

Magellan, of course, would have been a fool to bother about Aranda's moral position. All that mattered to him was to harness to his chariot anything or anyone that could advance it; and, in his critical situation, he seems to have revealed to the factor more of the "secret" than was accordant with his vow to Ruy Faleiro. To Magellan's delight, Aranda was completely won over. True, before providing money

and exerting influence on behalf of this dubious project put
before him by a man personally unknown to him, he did
what every sensible man of business in such a situation has
always done, and sought information in Portugal as to Magellan's and Faleiro's standing. The informant to whom he
turned was none other than Christopher de Haro, who had
equipped the first expedition to the south of Brazil and was
fully acquainted with the general trustworthiness of the two
persons in question. Haro's report was thoroughly satisfac-
tory. Magellan, he said, was an experienced, well-tried navigator; Faleiro was a noted cosmographer.

The last obstacle had been removed. Thenceforward the
factor of the Casa de Contratación, whose recommendation
in nautical matters was of decisive value at court, determined
to forward Magellan's affairs in the conviction that thereby
he would be forwarding his own. The original partnership
between Magellan and Faleiro was thus enlarged into a triumvirate, to which Magellan contributed practical experience,
Faleiro theoretical knowledge, and Juan, de Aranda capital and business acumen. Aranda did not waste time. He
promptly wrote a long letter to the Chancellor of Castile,
explaining the importance of the enterprise, and recommend-
ing Magellan as "one who might do a great service to His
Highness." He enlisted the interest of various privy councillors, thus ensuring a royal audience for Magellan. More, this
zealous intermediary declared his readiness, not only to accompany Magellan to Valladolid, but also to defray the expenses of the journey and of upkeep while at court. The wind
had changed. Magellan's boldest hopes had been more than
fulfilled. Within one month in Spain, though it was a for-

eign land, he had effected more than during ten years' self-sacrifice in his native country. Now, when the doors of the royal palace had been opened to him, he wrote to Faleiro to come with all speed to Seville.

One might have expected that the astrologer would have unhesitatingly welcomed the remarkable progress of the negotiations, and would have been eager to embrace his partner. But in Magellan's life, as we shall have abundant occasion to notice, there was no day without its storm. Thrust into the background by his partner's successful initiative, Ruy Faleiro—a difficult, choleric, and sensitive man—was angered. The astrologer, with his eyes fixed on the stars and with very little experience in practical matters, was furious when he learned that Aranda had not undertaken to introduce the pair of them at court for purely philanthropic motives, but had been influenced by the determination to enter into a business partnership which would reduce Faleiro's own gains.

There were distressing scenes between the two original associates. Faleiro accused Magellan of having broken faith, and of having unwarrantably betrayed their "secret" to a third party. Hysterical with wrath, he refused to go to court with Aranda, although the latter had offered to defray expenses. The success of the enterprise was still endangered by this fit of spleen, when Aranda received the welcome tidings that the king would give them audience at Valladolid. The dispute between Faleiro and Magellan continued to rage; Faleiro would not travel with Aranda, who took another route; and it was not until they met just outside Valladolid that the three partners became reconciled. Then the bear's skin was divided before the hunt had really begun. A deed of partnership was drawn up and signed, in accordance with which Aranda, for acting as broker, was to have one-eighth of the total profit of the venture (out of which neither Aranda nor Magellan nor Faleiro was ever destined to make any money). Certainly we cannot regard this share as an excessive payment for the services of the shrewd and energetic factor, who knew well enough that the young and infirm Habsburg ruler (though he hoped to become Holy Roman Emperor and lord of the New World as well as of the Old) was burdened rather than gratified by the splendours of his position, and that anyone who wished to influence him must begin by winning over his Privy Council.

In the Privy Council, the chances of the acceptance of Magellan's scheme did not seem very bright. The council consisted of four members, three of whom—Cardinal Adrian of Utrecht, friend of Erasmus, and afterwards Pope Adrian VI; Guillaume de Croix, the monarch's sometime tutor; and Sauvage Niederländer, the chancellor—had their gaze directed more towards Germany than towards the Indies; towards Germany where King Charles was, they hoped, to receive the imperial crown which would make the Habsburg ruler master of the world. They were feudal aristocrats, bibliophiles, and humanists, for whom an overseas project which might possibly in the end turn out to the advantage of Spain was far beyond their ken. The only Spanish member of the Privy Council, and the only one who (being chairman of the Casa de Contratación) was an expert in matters of navigation, was the famous or infamous Cardinal Fonseca, Bishop of Burgos. Magellan must unquestionably have been alarmed when

Aranda for the first time mentioned Fonseca's name, for every navigator knew that throughout life Columbus had had no fiercer enemy than this peppery cardinal, who had ever been suspicious of new schemes. Still, Magellan had nothing to lose, everything to gain; so with resolute heart and uplifted head he appeared before the Privy Council to defend his ideas and sustain his mission.

We have several divergent and therefore untrustworthy reports about what passed at this decisive session. The only thing of which we can be certain is that something in the behaviour and the words of the sinewy and sunburned seaman must, from the first, have created a powerful impression. The King's councillors saw at once that the Portuguese captain was not one of those windbags or dreamers whom the success of Columbus had induced to come in crowds bringing projects to the Spanish court. There were very few Europeans who had journeyed as far eastward as he; and when he spoke of the Spice Islands, of their geographical position, their climate, and the immeasurable riches they could supply, his acquaintance with Vartema and his friendship with Serrão made his statements seem more trustworthy than the words of those who had learned of the Far East only from books and maps. At a sign from Magellan the slave Enrique, whom he had brought with him from Malacca, stepped forward. The members of the Privy Council were naturally astonished at sight of this slender Malay, the first man of his race they had set eyes on. Magellan had also brought to the meeting a slave woman from Sumatra, and the pair of Orientals chattered to one another in an unknown tongue, much as if a pair of humming birds were twittering before the august assembly. At length Magellan read, as weighty evidence, a letter from his friend Francisco Serrão, now Grand Vizier of Ternate, in which it was stated that the country where he had settled was "a new world richer and greater than that of Vasco da Gama."

Having thus awakened the interest of his audience, Magellan proceeded to his inferences and demands. As he had just explained, the Spice Islands, whose wealth was incalculable, lay so far to the east of the Indies that it was needless to approach them as did the Portuguese by the eastern route after rounding the southernmost point of Africa, crossing the vast Indian Ocean, and then sailing through the Sunda Sea. There was a much shorter approach to them from the west, which was precisely the part of the world that the Holy Father had assigned to the Spaniards. No doubt there was a long barrier in the path, in the form of the newly discovered continent of America. But he, Ferdinand Magellan, had received sure intelligence that there was a way through, a "paso," an "estrecho." Its precise situation was his secret and that of his friend Ruy Faleiro. He was prepared to make the voyage by this passage in the service of the Spanish Crown if a fleet were placed at his disposal. Thus Spain would get ahead of Portugal, though the Portuguese were impatiently stretching out their hands towards the treasury of the world. His Majesty—and here Magellan made obeisance before the pale and delicate young man with the prominent lower lip of the Habsburgs—the mightiest monarch of the day, would become, also, by far the richest.

Perhaps, however, King Charles was hesitating to send an

expedition to the Moluccas for fear of intruding into the sphere allotted by the Pope to the Portuguese? This fear was groundless. Thanks to his precise knowledge of the situation of the Spice Islands, he, Magellan, was in a position to prove that they lay within the zone that His Holiness had allotted to Spain. It would, therefore, be a great mistake for the Spaniards to wait until, in defiance of King Charles's indubitable right, the Portuguese got their claws upon the royal Spanish domain.

Magellan ceased. Now that the affair was passing from the practical to the theoretical field, now when it remained to be proved by meridians and maps that the Spice Islands were actually in the Spanish sphere, he drew aside, leaving to his partner Ruy Faleiro the task of cosmographical demonstration. Faleiro, in his turn, made obeisance, and pointed to a great globe which he had brought with him. It was plain to all men's sight that the Spice Islands in the other hemisphere were on the Spanish side of the papal line of severance; and, at the same time, he indicated the route which he and Magellan proposed to take. True, it would subsequently transpire that Ruy Faleiro's calculations of longitude and latitude were completely fallacious, for this man of the study never dreamed of the vast width of the still undiscovered and unnavigated Pacific Ocean. Twenty years later it was to become plain that the Spice Islands were not within the Spanish but within the Portuguese domain. Everything which, at this meeting of the Spanish Privy Council, the distinguished astronomer was now demonstrating with much gesticulation was utterly incorrect. But people are always ready to believe what will bring them advantage; and since this geographical

MAGELLAN
Engraving by Crispin de Passe

THE HARBOUR OF LISBON
Copper engraving from de Bry's Travel Book (1592)

expert declared that the Spice Islands belonged to Spain, His Majesty King Charles's advisers were in no mood to contradict. When some of them, curiously examining the globe, looked for the southern way through, the "paso," the "estrecho," the future Strait of Magellan, they could not find any indication of it; but Faleiro explained the cartographical omission on the ground that he and Magellan considered it essential to preserve their secret as long as possible.

Charles and his councillors had listened, perhaps indifferently, perhaps with interest. Now the unexpected happened. It was not the humanists or the men of learning who showed most enthusiasm for this voyage round the world which was to establish once for all the circumference of our planet and to set at rest the fable of lost Atlantis; it was the expert, the dreaded sceptic Fonseca, Bishop of Burgos, who espoused the cause of Magellan. Perhaps he was secretly aware of having made a gross blunder in his persecution of Columbus, and did not wish to incur the risk of being censured a second time as enemy of a great idea. Anyhow, through his advocacy the scheme was approved on principle, Magellan and Faleiro being told to prepare for His Majesty a written statement of their proposals and their demands.

With this first audience, the game was substantially won. But to him that hath shall be given, and good fortune usually follows hard upon the heels of good fortune. Within a few weeks Magellan had gained more than in many previous years. He had found a wife who loved him, friends to back him, supporters to accept his ideas, and a king who trusted him; now a trump card was put into his hand. There came to Seville the leading shipowner Christopher de Haro, the wealthy speculator who worked hand in hand with the other great capitalists of his time, the Welsers, the Fuggers, and the Venetians; who had at his own cost already financed a large number of expeditions. Hitherto Lisbon had been the centre from which he mainly worked. He had, however, been embittered (like Magellan) by King Emanuel's avarice and ingratitude, so anything which could annoy that monarch was to his taste, and Magellan's scheme came in aptly. He knew the man and had confidence in him. From the business outlook, he regarded the undertaking as likely to pay well. He therefore informed Magellan that, should the Spanish court and the Casa de Contratación be unwilling to provide the necessary funds, he would, in conjunction with his business associates, equip the required fleet.

Thanks to this unexpected offer, Magellan had two irons in the fire. When he first knocked at the door of the Casa de Contratación he came as a needy suitor, an unknown projector, begging for a fleet; and even after his reception by the Privy Council the authorities were inclined to chaffer, and to abate his demands. But now, with Christopher de Haro's offer in his pocket, he need no longer cool his heels as a needy petitioner in the anterooms of the palace, but could present himself as a capitalist, as a man with the sinews of war in his hands. Should the court be disinclined to undertake the risk, that would not matter, since he could get the funds he needed from other sources, and required nothing but the honour of sailing under the Spanish flag. For the privilege, he generously declared, he was willing to pay the Spanish Crown one-fifth of the profits of the venture.

This new proposal, which admitted the Spanish authorities as partners without their incurring any risk, was so favourable that, paradoxically, or perhaps on sound arguments, the Privy Council decided against accepting it. For if (such must have been the calculations of the Spanish court) so shrewd a business man as Christopher de Haro was willing to invest money in a scheme, it must be what is nowadays called "gilt-edged." It would be better, therefore, to finance the voyage out of the royal treasury, and thus make sure of the bulk of the profits as well as of the renown. Magellan's and Ruy Faleiro's demands were conceded with a haste that was in marked contrast with ordinary governmental activities of those days, and everything was speedily put through. On March 22, 1518, King Charles, in his own name and in that of his (insane) mother Joanna, subscribed with the formal "Yo el Rey" the "capitulación," the binding agreement, with Magellan and Ruy Faleiro.

"Inasmuch as"—thus begins this verbose document—"Ferdinand Magellan, Knight, born in the kingdom of Portugal, and Alderman (bachelor) Ruy Faleiro, of the same kingdom, propose to do Us a great service within the limits of that part of the ocean which has been allotted to Us, We order that the following agreement shall be entered into with you for this purpose."

The first of the subsequent clauses assigns to Magellan and Faleiro exclusive rights within the specified area. "You have, with the favour of fortune, to proceed upon the discovery of that part of the ocean which lies within the limits of what has been assigned to Us; and, seeing that it would not be right for others to work injury to you by proceeding thither while you are engaged on this enterprise, it is My favour and My will, and I pledge Myself, that for the ten years next ensuing We shall grant to no one permission to proceed by the same route as that which you have chosen for your discoveries. Should anyone wish to undertake such journeys and should he ask Our permission, We, before granting such permission, shall inform you of the fact, that you may simultaneously provide yourself with the same equipment and have as many ships as the others who propose such discoveries as yourselves are undertaking."

In the financial clauses, Magellan and Faleiro, "in view of their goodwill and of their services," are assigned onetwentieth of all income which may accrue from the lands they will discover, in addition to a particular right to two islands, should they discover more than six new ones. Further, as in the agreement with Columbus, there is conferred on them the title of adelantado or governor of all seas, lands, and islands for themselves, their sons, and heirs, and also the title of captain-general with plenary powers during the voyage both by land and by sea. These rights are nowise to be diminished by the presence in the fleet of a royal factor (veedor), a treasurer (tesorero), and an accountant (contador).

In this document it is likewise expressly declared that the two Portuguese are to receive all possible rights, that the King pledges himself to equip five ships of a specified tonnage, providing them with crew, victuals, and artillery sufficient for two years. The noteworthy document concludes thus: "In respect of all this I pledge My honour and My royal word that everything shall be precisely arranged as is specified in the foregoing, and to that end I have commanded that the capitulación shall be drawn up and signed with My name."

Nor was this all. It was expressly agreed that every office and official in Spain from the highest to the lowest was to be informed about this agreement, that they might support Magellan and Faleiro in their undertakings, always and for all time. A full list of the princes and grandees and authorities who were to be made acquainted with the tenor of the document followed. Thus it was clearly proclaimed that thenceforward the whole Spanish realm was to be devoted to the service of two obscure refugees from Portugal.

In his boldest dreams, Magellan could not have expected more than this. But something still more wonderful and still more important ensued. King Charles, though in youth he was of a hesitating and reserved temperament, became the most impatient and passionate advocate of the voyage of these new Argonauts. Something in the virile demeanour of Magellan must have stirred the youthful monarch. For it was he who now continually urged on the work. Week after week he asked for reports upon the progress of the equipment. Whenever any obstacles were encountered, Magellan merely had to apply to His Majesty, and a royal letter would brush resistance out of the way. This was almost the only occasion in the course of his long reign on which the usually vacillating Emperor proved inviolably faithful to a great idea. To Magellan, the homeless outcast, the despised and rejected, it must have seemed a wonderful transformation to find himself, of a sudden, appointed Captain-General of a fleet,

Knight of the Order of Santiago, Governor-to-be of all new islands and lands, Lord of life and death, Master of an armada, and, for the first time, able, unhindered. to do his own will.

Chapter Five

WILL OVERCOMES OBSTACLES

March 22, 1518 – August 20, 1519

Will Overcomes Obstacles

WHEN we contemplate great achievements, we like to simplify our view by concentrating upon dramatic, picturesque moments, to think of Cæsar crossing the Rubicon, of Napoleon upon the bridge of Arcole. For the sake of this concentration, the no less creative years of preliminary work are left in the shadows—the period of preparation, the time of patient organization, the season when the deed was being incubated. In the case of Magellan, no less than in that of others, the painter and the imaginative writer may wish to depict him in the moment of triumph when he was on his way through the straits he discovered. In reality, however, it must have been a harder part of his achievement to get his fleet ready, to bring about its equipment in defiance of a thousand obstacles. Once that was done, to steer it to the goal of his dreams must have been comparatively easy. The man who had hitherto been nothing more than a sobresaliente, an unknown soldier, was confronted with enormous difficulties. One lacking experience in organization had to undertake an entirely new task: to get his five ships ready for a voyage of which he knew only the port of departure, and not the extent. No one could advise Magellan, for no one was acquainted with the untrodden paths into which he was to venture. No one could tell him how long the journey would last; into what lands, through what climates, among what people it would lead. He must provide for all conceivable possibilities; for arctic cold and tropical heat, for storm and calm, for one or two or three years, for war and for trade. Single-handed, and in defiance of unanticipated resistance, he made his calculations and conducted his struggle. It was now, when the magnitude of the enterprise became apparent, that the full energy of the man, which had so long been eclipsed by other reputations, was fully disclosed.

Whereas his famous rival Columbus, the "Don Quixote of the Seas," a visionary and a dreamer, left the practical details of preparation to the Pinzóns and other pilots, Magellan (who in this matter resembled Napoleon), being as precise and meticulous in execution as he was bold and untrammelled in conception, attended personally to the most subordinate matters. His genius was shown not only in his imagination but also in his infinite capacity for taking pains. Just as Napoleon, for many weeks before his speedy and tumultuous crossing of the Alps, carefully calculated how many pounds of powder and how many sacks of oats should be supplied at a particular place on a particular day, so did this conqueror of the globe, when outfitting his fleet, decide for two or three years in advance how to provide for every conceivable eventuality.

It was a tremendous undertaking for one solitary man, in the case of so far-reaching an enterprise, to overcome the hundred hindrances which the inertia of circumstances interposed everywhere against the transformation of idea into fact. No doubt Charles of Spain had pledged his royal word to provide whatever should be needed for the circumnavigation of the globe, and had commanded every one of his officials and officers to give unrestricted aid. But between a royal command, soon to be an imperial command, and its fulfilment there remains place for numerous delays and frustrations. Again and again, truly creative work must be done by the actual creator in person if it is to be done at all. When dealing, as he did, most straitly with the Casa de Contratación, the public offices, the dealers, the purveyors, and the craftsmen, Magellan's sense of intimate responsibility for those whose lives were to be entrusted to his care made him narrowly watch every circumstance. He personally examined the supplies; checked every account; inspected every rope, every plank, every weapon in his ships; from masthead to keel he knew each of them as well as he knew his own finger-nails. Furthermore, just as when rebuilding the walls of Jerusalem the builders worked with trowel in one hand and sword in the other, so Magellan, when getting his fleet ready for its voyage into the unknown, had to be ever on guard against the disfavour and the hostility of those who wanted by hook or by crook to hinder departure. This was a heroic struggle on three fronts by a lonely man, faced simultaneously with the resistance of adversaries abroad, adversaries at home, and adversaries who took the form of the obstacles imposed by material conditions against any enterprise which is out of the common. The preparation for his achievement, and not merely the achievement itself, was of heroic significance and required daimonic powers of self-sacrifice. It is the obstacles that have to be overcome which give the measure of a deed and of the man who performs it.

The first attack on Magellan's enterprise came from Portugal. It need hardly be said that King Emanuel was promptly
informed by his spies of the adventurer's agreement with the
Spanish Crown. More distasteful news could hardly have
reached the King's ears. The spice monopoly was already
bringing him a comfortable two hundred thousand ducats a
year, although his ships had just started their voyages to the
Moluccas, the original source of all this wealth. What a disaster if, in the twelfth hour, the Spaniards should forestall
him, and reach his Golconda by the western route! The risk
to Portugal's finances was so great that the monarch felt he
must hinder this dangerous expedition; so the Portuguese
ambassador to Spain, Alvaro da Costa, was instructed to do
his utmost to smash the cuckoo's egg before the bird hatched
out.

Alvaro da Costa approached the matter energetically, from
both sides. First of all he went to Magellan, trying simultaneously to bribe him and to intimidate him—sweetmeats and
the whip. Was Magellan not aware what a sin he was com-
mitting against God and his lawful king by thus serving the
interests of a foreign potentate? Did he not know that his
king, Dom Emanuel, wanted to marry Elinor, the sister of
King Charles of Spain, and that this propitious alliance would
be frustrated if any wrong were done to Emanuel by Charles?
The ambassador offered high reward if Magellan would think
better of his course, would renounce the capitulación, and
would return to Lisbon as a loyal subject. But Magellan,
aware that his sovereign had little love for him, and justly
suspecting that his return to Portugal would bring him, not a
fat bag of gold coins, but a dagger-thrust, replied that, to his

great regret, the time for accepting such friendly overtures was past. He had given his word to the King of Spain, and would keep it.

Since this unimportant Magellan, though he had seemed no more than a pawn in the diplomatic game of chess, was, after all, not so easy to defeat, Alvaro da Costa boldly tried a move of "check to the king." Having obtained an audience, he dealt roundly with the young monarch. We learn this from a letter he wrote to Emanuel. "As regards the affair of Ferdinand Magellan, God knows how much I have done and what a deal of trouble I have taken. I spoke very bluntly to His Majesty here about the affair . . . explaining to him what an ill-mannered and unusual thing it was for a monarch to take the subject of a friendly neighbour king into his service against the latter's express wishes. . . . I bade him also bear in mind that this was not a suitable hour at which to mortify Your Majesty, above all for so trifling and problematical a cause. He had plenty of subjects of his own who could make voyages of discovery at any time, and need not engage persons who were discontented with Your Majesty. . . . I explained to him how greatly it would annoy Your Highness to learn that these men had begged permission to return home and that he had refused it. Finally I implored him, for his own sake as well as for Your Majesty's, to do one of two things: either to allow the two men to return home, or else to postpone the enterprise till next year."

King Charles, eighteen years of age, who had ascended the throne only a few months before, was still inexperienced in diplomatic matters. He could not hide his astonishment at Alvaro's impudent falsehood when the ambassador declared that Magellan and Faleiro wished to return to Portugal and had been refused permission to do so by the Spanish court. "He was so greatly surprised," reported da Costa, "that I myself was dumbfounded." As for the Portuguese ambassador's other proposal, that the enterprise should be postponed for a year, this was obviously unacceptable. A year was all the time which Portugal would need for the equipment of a fleet and for the sending of it to the Spice Islands. In a coldly defensive manner, therefore, the young king said that the ambassador had better discuss the matter with Cardinal Adrian of Utrecht. The Cardinal, in his turn, referred the question to the Privy Council, whereupon the Privy Council declared that Fonseca, Bishop of Burgos, was the only person authorized to advise King Charles about such a matter. In this dilatory way, by sending Alvaro da Costa from pillar to post, and with repeated polite assurances that Charles had not the slightest intention of putting any difficulties in King Emanuel's way ("muy caro y muy amado tío y hermano"), Portugal's diplomatic protest was gently and inconspicuously shelved. Da Costa had achieved nothing. On the contrary, Portugal's eager intervention had unexpectedly helped to promote Magellan's cause. The caprices of those who sat in high places had become strangely intertwined with the destinies of a gentleman who till yesterday had been practically unknown. It was not until King Charles had entrusted to Magellan the command of a fleet, that King Emanuel's sometime subordinate officer became an important person to that monarch. On the other hand, from the time when King Emanuel wished to buy Magellan back at any cost, Magellan's value rose immensely in King Charles's eyes. And the more Spain tried to hasten the departure, the more keenly did Portugal endeavour to retard it.

The principal agent of this sabotage was Sebastian Alvarez, Portuguese consul in Seville. He continually prowled round the ships, watched everything that was taken on board, and urgently advised the seamen against undertaking a voyage with such uncertain prospects. He also struck up a close friendship with the naval captains who were to sail under Magellan's orders, probing with his fingers what these Castilian noblemen had already found a sore point, reminding them that they, Spanish dons and veterans, were to be at the beck and call of aliens, of Portuguese adventurers. Everyone knows that nationalism is a string which even the crudest hand can easily set vibrating. Ere long the smouldering jealousy of the mariners of Seville burst into flame against the Portuguese. Here were men who had never made even the shortest voyage in Spanish service, who had run away from their own country, and yet, through mere bounce, had secured appointments as admirals and Knights of the Order of Santiago. But Alvarez was not content with whispers and murmurs round the captains' tables and in the taverns. The consul's design was to bring about a popular rising that would cost Magellan his command, and, with better luck, even his life. Nor can it be denied that this clever spy and provocative agent staged his revolt in masterly fashion.

In every seaport there are to be found numerous loiterers who do not know how to kill the weary hours. One sunny day in October, since nothing can amuse an idler more than to watch others at work, a crowd of loafers gathered round

Magellan's flag-ship the "Trinidad," which had just been careened to have her bottom cleaned and caulked. Their hands in their pockets, some of them perhaps chewing a plug of the new West Indian weed, the Sevillian wharf-rats watched how cleverly the shipmen, with hammers and wedges, with pitch and oakum, were stopping every rift and cranny. Then one of the onlookers pointed at the mast.

"Look!" he exclaimed. "What a scandal! This man Magellan, coming from the devil knows where, has, in the royal Spanish port of Seville, impudently hoisted the Portuguese flag upon a Spanish ship."

This challenge was too much for the collection of rascals. As their zeal grew hot, they completely failed to notice that the Spanish patriot who was talking so emphatically about the insult to the national honour was not a Spaniard at all, but consul of the King of Portugal, was Sebastian Alvarez, who had adopted the role of instigator. There were angry cries, and the noise brought about an afflux of more patriots of the same kidney. Someone proposed that, without more ado, the foreign flag should be lowered, and therewith the mob rushed upon the ship.

Magellan, who since dawn had been supervising the work of his men, explained to the alcalde who hurried to the scene of the riot that it was only by chance the Spanish flag was not flying at the mainmast. The reason was that it had been sent that day to have its colours freshened up. Besides, the flag that was flying was not the Portuguese standard but his own admiral's flag, which he was fully entitled to hoist on his own flag-ship. Having thus explained the nature of the mistake in

EMPEROR CHARLES V IN 1520
Etching by Hieronymus Hopfer

FRANCIS DRAKE
Copper engraving of the eighteenth century

the most courteous way possible, Magellan begged the alcalde to clear the decks of the disturbers of the peace.

But it is always much easier to raise the passions of a mob or of an entire nation than to allay the storm. An excited crowd continues to seek enjoyment in its own peculiar way. Shouts were raised that unless the foreign flag was lowered, the rioters would do the job themselves. The dispute had become threatening when, by good luck, Dr. Matienzo, the chief official of the India House, turned up. A personal friend of Magellan, he begged the latter not to be a stickler for his rights, and Magellan was about to lower the flag. Meanwhile, however, the alcalde whose aid Magellan had invoked had, for patriotic reasons, summoned the captain of the port (teniente del amirante) and a posse of police. This official declared that Spain had been insulted by Magellan's arrogant behaviour, and instructed his alguacils to arrest the foreigner, the Portuguese, who had dared to hoist the flag of the King of Portugal in a Spanish harbour.

In vain did Matienzo once more intercede with the captain of the port, declaring it to be a gross usurpation of authority to arrest a royal official whom the King of Spain had chartered to his high office. It would be better, said the man from the India House, for the port official not to risk burning his fingers. But these well-meant representations came too late. Magellan's own men were already on the verge of coming to blows with the assailants. Swords were drawn, and nothing but the captain-general's presence of mind and inviolable calm prevented the open breach of the peace which the Portuguese agent had been working for. Magellan declared himself ready to leave the ship to the pleasure of the mob, which might do what it willed with the property of His Majesty King Charles. The King's port officials would be responsible for any damage that might ensue. The alcalde, however, though still greatly excited, was unwilling to face this responsibility. The rioters whose national honour had been offended angrily withdrew, and some of them were punished with a flogging a few days later. Magellan wrote at once to King Charles, explaining that an insult had been offered to His Majesty, whose servant he was, and the monarch gave him unqualified support. The port officials were likewise punished. Alvarez had rejoiced prematurely, and work on the ship continued.

These machinations were rendered futile and were ignominiously defeated by Magellan's masterly and dispassionate handling of the situation. But trouble broke out in another quarter. As soon as one quarrel was smoothed over, a new one would occur. Every day brought a fresh incident. To begin with, the Casa de Contratación adopted a policy of passive resistance. Magellan had to ask Charles's personal assistance against this obstruction. Not until a royal rescript had been issued was official stubbornness overcome. The first orders for the equipment were issued in March, but in July nothing had been done; then, the monarch having become insistent, the treasurer of the Casa de Contratación suddenly discovered that there were no funds available. For a moment it seemed as if the enterprise would be indefinitely postponed for lack of money. Nevertheless, Magellan's indomitable will overcame every resistance, and he persuaded the court to bring a number of wealthy burghers into the affair as participators. Of the eight million maravedis that were needed to defray the cost of the armada, two million were provided by a company hastily organized by Christopher de Haro, the guarantors of this sum receiving the right to take an equal share in subsequent expeditions.

Now that the financial kink had been straightened out, it was possible to pay for supplies and to get the ships ready for sea. They did not look particularly grand, the five galleons ordered by His Majesty, when they were at length got together in the inland port of Seville. "They are very old and much patched up," wrote Alvarez the spy. "I should be terribly alarmed if I had to sail on board one of them no farther than the Canaries, for their ribs are as soft as butter." But Magellan knew, being an experienced navigator to the Indies, that old horses are often safer to ride than young ones, and that able workmanship can make even old and worn-out vessels seaworthy. Let the shipwrights get on with the job, and, while they were freshening up and overhauling the weather-beaten tubs, his business was to find an experienced crew.

But here other difficulties loomed. Although criers were sent through the streets of Seville, and also through those of various other harbours as far away as Cadiz and Palos, the required two hundred and fifty men were not forthcoming. Somehow or other it must have leaked out that the voyage was more than a little uncanny. The recruiting-agents could not give plain information as to whither the ships were bound, and it seemed suspicious that men were being asked to sign on for as long as two years. It was not exactly a guard of honour that was ultimately sharked up. These tatterdemalions looked like Falstaff's contingent. They were of all races and nations: Spaniards, Negroes, Basques, Portuguese, Hollanders, Englishmen, Italians, men from Capri and Corfu; but at any rate they were hardy rogues, genuine desperadoes, ready to sell their souls to the devil, prepared to sail north, south, east, or west, provided only they were paid their advance.

Well, the men had signed on. But now Magellan struck a new snag. The Casa de Contratación declared that there were too many Portuguese among them, and that not a maravedi should be paid to these foreigners. But Magellan, in virtue of the royal cedula, had unrestricted right to choose his followers wherever he pleased ("que la gente de mar que se tomase fuese a su contento como persona que de ella tenía mucha experiencia"); and he stood by his guns. Another letter to the King, another request for aid. This time, however, Magellan had touched a sore spot. Ostensibly to avoid mortifying King Emanuel by providing a Spanish expedition with too large a number of Portuguese among the crew, but in reality from fear that Magellan and his Portuguese might form a clique, King Charles declared that no more than five of that nation should be enrolled.

Meanwhile other difficulties had arisen. The stores (to save expense, much of these had been ordered from distant provinces and even as far away as Germany) had not yet come to hand. While this delay was giving trouble, one of the Spanish captains refused to obey the admiral's orders and insulted him in face of the crew. Again the powers of the court had to be invoked; again royal oil had to be used to smooth matters over. One rescript followed another, the competence of the various officers having again to be strictly defined. Time after time it seemed as if the ships would never be able to get away from Seville harbour.

Repeatedly, however, Magellan's alertness and indefatigable energy overcame all difficulties. With sorrow, King Emanuel's busy agent was forced to recognize that the artifices with which he did his best to frustrate the expedition came to nothing because of his adversary's impenetrable defence. Work underground like a mole though Alvarez might, Magellan's tenacity was too much for him. The fleet was ready, the ships were newly rigged, were laden and manned; the five of them were merely awaiting orders to drop down the Guadalquivir. Once the fleet had put out to sea, Magellan would be master of the situation; neither king nor cabal could interfere with him any longer. But Alvarez had a last arrow, a poisoned one, in his quiver.

Concerning this last endeavour, we have accurate information in a letter which the consul wrote to King Emanuel. It refers to a meeting with Magellan. "Since I was of opinion," wrote the secret agent to his chief, "that the moment had come for doing what Your Majesty had commanded, I went to Magellan's house. I found him occupied in packing stores and other things in hampers and boxes. I inferred from this that he was fixed in his evil intentions, and that now was my last chance of talking to him. I reminded him, therefore, how often, as a good Portuguese and his friend, I had tried to restrain him from the gross blunder he was about to commit. I assured him that the course he proposed to follow was beset with as many perils as St. Catherine's wheel, and that he would be much better advised to return home and woo Your

Majesty's favour, since he could count on your magnanimity.
. . . He might rest assured that all Castilians of rank in this
city were wont to speak of him as a man of base origin and
no breeding . . . and that in general, having run counter to
the interests of Your Majesty's country, he was regarded as a
traitor."

Such conjurations and threats did not make the slightest
impression upon Magellan. What Alvarez communicated to
him under the mask of friendship was by no means new. Who
could know better than he that Seville and Spain were un-
friendly to him? Daily and hourly he had been aware of the
dull-witted but malicious opposition with which the court
officials encountered each of his demands; and only too
plainly had he read the hatred and anger of the hidalgos in
their cold, contemptuous glances. He knew that the Castilian
noblemen who were his captains obeyed his orders reluctantly, and that their haughty politeness towards him personally was but the outcome of their dread of King Charles.
No matter. Let the alcaldes of Seville hate him, let the envious snarl and the blue-bloods murmur—now that the fleet
was ready for departure neither emperor nor king, and still
less mere ill-will, could hinder him. Their power came to an
end with the walls of Seville. Once he had put out to sea, he
would be safe. There he would be lord of life and death, lord
of his ways, lord of his goals, would be no longer a servant
in Spain but a master in unknown and unconquered lands.

So far, however, Alvarez had not yet made use of his
poisoned arrow. Now he took it from the quiver. Once more,
he said hypocritically, he wanted to advise Magellan as a
"friend." He "honestly" warned this friend of his not to feel

too secure; that it would be better to renew allegiance to his rightful king; one letter to King Emanuel, and all would be forgotten and forgiven. Perhaps Magellan had been too ready to trust the promises of the Spanish court, but that court, Alvarez assured him, was not so straightforward as he fancied. Certainly the King of Spain had appointed him and Faleiro commanders-in-chief; had, by royal charter, made them admirals of the fleet. But was Magellan sure that secret counter-instructions had not been issued? Perhaps he had been too ready to believe the honeyed words of Bishop Fonseca. Besides, could he be sure of Faleiro? Was he not aware that Faleiro had publicly declared in Seville he (Faleiro) had no intention of obeying Magellan's orders during the voyage? Magellan had better not deceive himself or allow himself to be humbugged. Seal and charter notwithstanding, his admiral's rank and his supreme command were in a parlous state. There certainly existed (this was all he was able to disclose to his friend Magellan) a number of secret clauses and instructions for the captains of the King, "of which you will learn only when it is too late for you to save your honour."

"Too late for you to save your honour." At this Magellan fired up. The man who had hitherto been imperturbable, and had always been able to control his temper, showed that the poisoned arrow had wounded him, and the spy was able to report: "He was greatly astonished that I knew so much." Always the creator of a work is better acquainted than anyone else with its hidden defects, with its weak points. For a long time Magellan had been aware of a certain ambiguity in the attitude of the Spanish court, and numerous signs had led him to believe that all was not above board. King Charles had appointed three Spanish noblemen as "controllers" of his actions. True, they were actually called no more than veedor, tesorero, and cortador, whose ostensible function was to keep accounts with a view to the ultimate distribution of the profits of the venture; and, in accordance with the capitulación, his own supreme command was guaranteed independently of the King's treasurer.

But suppose what this rascal said were true. Suppose that other cedulas had been issued without a word to him. Suppose that Juan de Cartagena, Luis de Mendoza, and Gaspar Quesada really had secret instructions. Had not King Charles, once at least, acted in defiance of the wording of the capitulación when forbidding him to take more than five Portuguese on board? Did the Spanish court actually believe him to be a secret agent of Portugal? There could be no doubt that the four Spanish captains, whose hostility to him was evident, were secretly working against him. Would they not, in any case, as soon as the fleet was out of reach of King Charles, his protector, openly take sides against him, standing together, four against one? Would they not, perhaps under cover of secret orders, demand the right of the majority in defiance of his sealed charter? In that case Alvarez's warning was genuine, and it would be "too late to save his honour."

Magellan could not deny that there might be some substance behind the insinuations of this well-informed spy. Was it true? Had King Charles been secretly working against him? He was defenceless, he who had made such precise calculations for the voyage, in face of a danger which was itself as incalculable as the uncertain invariably is. This was a most disagreeable feeling for a man who could not but have the impression that he was like a card-player who sits down at the card-table and before he touches a card becomes aware that all the others are cheats who have entered into a conspiracy against him.

What Magellan had to endure in this hour was the tragedy of Coriolanus, as immortalized by Shakespeare, the tragedy of the man whom mortified honour has led to turn his coat. Coriolanus, like Magellan, was a patriot who for years had devotedly served his country, and then, unjustly treated by his country, had placed his powers at the service of an adversary. The purest sentiments cannot help a turncoat, whether in Rome or in Seville. Like a shadow there clings to him the suspicion that he who has abandoned one flag can betray another; he who has renounced allegiance to one king can be unfaithful to another. The turncoat is lost when he conquers and is equally lost when he is conquered, for he is hated by both sides; everywhere he is alone, alone against all. A tragedy really begins when its hero becomes conscious of the tragedy of his position; and perhaps at this moment Magellan for the first time foreboded disaster.

But one who is a hero is one who will fight against an overwhelmingly powerful destiny. Resolutely Magellan refused the spy's overtures. No, he would not come to terms with King Emanuel. He would be true to his oath, to his office. Disconsolately Alvarez had to withdraw, seeing that naught but death could break the will of this man of iron, so his report to King Emanuel concludes with the pious wish: "May it be pleasing to Almighty God that they will make such a voyage as that of the Cortereals," which voiced the hope that

Magellan and his fleet should disappear in unknown seas as completely as did the brothers Cortereal, whose fate remains a mystery to this day. Should this pious wish be fulfilled, then "Your Majesty need have no further care, and will remain envied by all the princes of this world."

The arrow had hit its mark. It had not laid Magellan low, or made him weaken in his purpose. Yet its poison, the burning venom of mistrust, rankled henceforward in his mind. From this moment, Magellan knew or believed that he was surrounded by enemies upon his own ships. Still, the sense of insecurity did not weaken him in any way, but hardened his will, and emboldened a man who was already bold, making him more venturesome than ever. One who sees an impending storm knows that nothing can save ship and crew but the firm hand of the captain, with none to dispute his orders.

Away, then, with anything that would hamper the free fulfilment of his will. He must rid himself of hindrances. Precisely because veedors and contadors had been appointed to control his actions, he would break these shackles. There should be only one commander. If Magellan was to be alone against all, he would remain truly alone. One will must lead and command in the decisive hour; there should no longer be two captains-general, two admirals, in the fleet. One must stand above all, and if necessary against all. The last difficulty among the countless difficulties he had already overcome compelled Magellan to relieve his partner Ruy Faleiro of the joint command. He would not have his undertaking burdened by the coequal authority of a hysterical and quarrelsome fool. Before the squadron left harbour, this ballast must be flung overboard. For a long time the astronomer had been a superfluous load. He had done nothing all these months, for it is not an astrologer's job to rule seamen, have ships caulked, choose stores, test firearms, and lay down rules. Magellan knew that on the voyage, likewise, Faleiro would be more of a hindrance than a help, would be a stone tied round his neck. With dangers confronting him and conspiracy at his back, he must be able to work untrammelled.

We do not know how Magellan achieved the diplomatic masterstroke of getting rid of Faleiro. Probably Faleiro had cast his own horoscope, and had discovered that he would not return from the voyage, this making him willing to be dissuaded. Outwardly the enforced renunciation was disguised as a rise in rank. An imperial edict appointed Faleiro sole commander of a second fleet (whose ships and sails existed only on paper), which was to follow Magellan at some later date—the Greek calends. In return, Faleiro handed over to Magellan his maps and astronomical tables. Now the last and greatest difficulty had been overcome, and Magellan's enterprise was, what it had been at the outset, his own idea and his exclusive deed. To him alone would accrue the burden and the trouble, the planning and the danger, but likewise the greatest happiness of a creative spirit—which craves always, responsible to itself alone, the unassisted fulfilment of its mission.

Chapter Six

DEPARTURE

September 20, 1519

Departure

ON August 10, 1519, a year
and five months after Charles I, the ruler of two worlds, had
signed the capitulación, the five ships at length left the port
of Seville and dropped downstream to San Lucar de Barrameda, where the Guadalquivir debouches into the Atlantic.
Here the last overhaul and the victualling of the fleet were to
take place. Substantially, farewell to Spain was already said
at Seville. In the church of Santa María de la Victoria, Magellan, having with bended knee taken the oath of fealty, was,
before his assembled crew and a reverent crowd of spectators,
given the royal standard by Corregidor Sancho Martínez de
Leyva. At this solemn moment he may well have recalled
that he had taken an oath of loyalty in a cathedral before setting forth on his first voyage to the Indies. It was to another
flag, the Portuguese, that he had then devoted himself; to
another king, Emanuel of Portugal and not Charles of Spain,
that he had given a pledge. Still, just as respectfully as the
youthful sobresaliente had then contemplated Admiral Almeida when the latter unrolled the silken banner and waved
it above the kneeling crowd, so now did his two hundred and
sixty-five followers look upon him as the lord and leader of
their destiny.

Magellan held the final muster in the port of San Lucar

opposite the castle of Duke Medina Sidonia. Before the start, he examined and re-examined the fleet with the tender affection of a conductor surveying his orchestra before a concert. He already knew these five ships as well as he knew the palm of his own hand. He must have been horrified when he looked at them for the first time at Seville, worn, old, and battered. Since then, however, a lot of work had been done on them. The galleons had been thoroughly renovated; rotten timbers had been replaced; from stem to stern they had been caulked and scoured. Magellan had personally tested every one of the planks, lest it should be perished or worm-eaten; had examined every rope in the rigging. The sails were of new and strong linen, stamped with the cross of St. James, patron saint of Spain. The shrouds were new; everything was in its proper place; no envious tongues would now dare to make mock of the ships which had been so thoroughly renovated. Of course they were not speedy, and little fitted to take part in a regatta, the craft that were so cumbrous and so broad in the beam; but, for that very reason, they had abundant room for freight, and would be safe in a heavy sea. As far as anyone could foretell, they would endure the hardest tests of storm and battle. The largest of the five was the "San Antonio," whose displacement was one hundred and twenty tons. For some unknown reason, Magellan put Juan de Cartagena in command of this ship, choosing for his flag-ship (which he himself captained) the "Trinidad," although her displacement was ten tons less. Next in size came the "Concepción," of ninety tons, commanded by Gaspar Quesada; the "Victoria" —destined to do honour to her name—under Luis de Mendoza, having eighty-five tons' displacement; and finally the

"Santiago," of seventy-five tons, under the command of João Serrão. The smaller ships, having a smaller draught and being more mobile, were to be used mainly for reconnaissances and for plumbing the depths of unknown waters. There were many advantages in these differences of tonnage and type, which had been arranged by Magellan of set purpose; but it would need remarkably skilful seamanship to keep five heterogeneous craft together upon the open sea for a year or more amid storm and fog.

Magellan went sedulously from one to another, being determined, before all, to inspect the freight. Again and again did he check the inventories, and even today the archives disclose to us with what extreme care one of the wildest adventures in history was prepared and calculated. Down to half a maravedi the voluminous accounts show what every hammer, every rope, every ream of paper on board the armada cost, and these cold, correct columns of figures, transcribed by some dispassionate copyist, show, with their specifications and fractions, perhaps more than does anything else, more than could any string of gushing words, Magellan's wonderful patience. As a tried seaman, the commander was fully aware what immense responsibility is incurred by one who is preparing for a voyage into the unknown. He knew that even the most trifling object which was forgotten before the start would be irreplaceable throughout the voyage, that there would be no subsequent possibility of atoning for initial mistakes. Every nail, every hank of oakum, every piece of lead, every sheet of paper would have, in the unexplored regions to which he was going, a value greater than its weight in gold, for the sacrifice of blood would never provide what was lacking. One item of forgetfulness might make a ship useless, and the enterprise might be wrecked by a false calculation. Magellan's responsibility as admiral would not begin upon the open sea, but must be discharged to the full before the ships left port.

It need hardly be said that, during this final inspection, the victualling of the fleet demanded supreme care. What would five ships need, what would two hundred and sixty-five men consume, upon a voyage whose goal and duration were indeterminable? This is a difficult calculation. None but Magellan knew (what caution made him keep to himself) that the journey would last many months, and perhaps years, before fresh stores could be provided. It would be better, therefore, to take too much rather than too little; and, in view of the scanty space available, the figures are imposing. The alpha and the omega of nautical diet in those days was ship's biscuit, the only breadstuff that keeps sound at sea. At a cost of 372,510 maravedis, Magellan had provided 2138 quintals of biscuit. According to his estimate, this huge amount would last for two years. In other respects, too, when we read the list of provisions, we think rather of a modern transatlantic liner of 20,000 tons than of five vessels not much bigger than fishing-smacks comprising in all from 500 to 600 tons, the displacement ton of those times being about one-tenth more than the present one.

What else, besides biscuit, was stored in the dark holds? In addition to sacks of flour, beans, lentils, rice, and other legumens and cereals, there were fifty-seven quintals (5700 pounds) of pickled pork, 200 barrels of anchovies, 984 cheeses, 250 strings of garlic and 100 of onions. Also there were various dainties, such as 5402 pounds of honey, 1800 pounds of Malaga raisins, almonds in their shells, an abundance of sugar, vinegar, and mustard. At the last moment there were driven on board seven cows, but these useful quadrupeds were not destined to live long. Anyhow, for a while the crew would get fresh milk, and subsequently fresh meat. But the vigorous fellows had more interest in wine than in milk. To keep his men in good humour, Magellan had bought of the best wine that Jerez could produce no less than 417 pipes and 253 butts; this was calculated to supply each man with a daily glass of wine at dinner and supper.

Lists in hand, Magellan went from ship to ship, verifying the presence of one article after another. What a labour it had been to bring all the supplies together, to examine them for quality, to work out the cost, and to pay! What arguments and bargainings day after day with officials and traders; and how much anxiety night after night lest anything should have been forgotten or wrongly assigned. Still, it seemed now as if he had really provided everything that two hundred and sixty-five stomachs would need upon the voyage. Yes, the men would have all they required. But ships, likewise, as he had frequently had occasion to notice, lived lives of their own; each one of them was mortal, consuming on a voyage a part of its own substance.

Storms tore the sails and broke the ropes, sea water gnawed away the wood and rusted the iron, the sun scorched the paint, and in the dark hours oil and candles were gradually used up. There must, consequently, be a twofold or manifold supply of all necessary things: anchors and hawsers; articles of wood, iron, and lead; spare masts and sails. The fleet had on board no less than forty loads of timber, so that damages could be promptly repaired, that planks and ribs could be replaced in case of need; there were also tons of pitch and tar, of beeswax and oakum, to keep the seams watertight. It need hardly be said that there was an ample supply of pincers and saws, of awls and other tools, of spades and hammers and nails and pickaxes. Thousands of fish-hooks, harpoons by the dozen, with an ample provision of nets for catching the fish which would be as important a constituent of the crew's diet as would ship's biscuit.

For light during the dark hours there were eighty-nine lanterns and many hundredweight of candles and grease for making them, in addition to the large and heavy wax candles for the consecration of the ships. There were also the various articles needed for navigation: mariner's compasses, hourglasses, astrolabes, quadrants, and planispheres; and fifteen blank account-books. The certainty of undesirable incidents was taken into consideration: there were medicine chests for the apothecaries, lancets and cutting utensils; handcuffs and irons for the undisciplined. Amusement would be furnished by five big drums and twenty tambourines; while it is probable that a few fiddles, flutes, and bagpipes were also taken along.

The foregoing are no more than a few trifling extracts from Magellan's Homeric ship's inventory; only some of the thousand kinds of articles which crew and ships would need upon a journey of such incalculable duration. A well-equipped fleet which had cost eight million maravedis was not sent forth haphazard into the unknown. The five ships

of which it was composed were not dispatched merely to
gather cosmographical information, but to make as much
money as possible for those who had financed the venture.
Consequently, articles to be used in barter must be carefully
selected and kept in store. Magellan's experience in the Indies had made him well acquainted with the simple tastes of
the indigenes. He knew that two things were especially
coveted by such folk: mirrors in which the black, brown, or
yellow-skinned natives could clearly see their own faces; and
bells large and small, which are a perpetual delight to children. There were no less than twenty thousand of these
noise-producers on board, with nine hundred small and one
hundred large mirrors, most of which, unfortunately, were
smashed during the voyage. There were four hundred dozen
knives of the commonest kind "made in Germany" (as the
list expressly specifies, "400 docenas de cuchillos de Alemania
de los peores"); fifty dozen pairs of scissors; the inevitable
coloured kerchiefs and red caps; brass bracelets, paste jewels,
and brightly tinted glassware. Some Turkish robes were taken
as fine raiment for the big chiefs, together with the customary
stock of coloured satins and wool. In a word, "junk," worth
as little in Spain as were spices in the Moluccas, but ideal
"trade goods," which would be appraised at ten times or a
hundred times their original value by the purchaser.

These combs and caps, these mirrors and other toys, would
be of use only if the indigenes should prove ready for peaceful barter. But for the other event, for bellicose possibilities,
there were also ample supplies. Fifty-eight culverins, seven
long falconets, and three large bombards grinned fiercely
from the gun-ports; deep in the hold were stored abundant

quantities of iron and stone shot, with many tons of lead for
the casting of more. A thousand lances, two hundred pikes,
and two hundred shields showed the resolute character of
the promoters of the enterprise, and more than half the crew
were provided with helmets and breastplates. For the admiral
two suits of armour had been obtained from Bilbao so that
he would be armed cap-à-pie and, to savages unacquainted
with the use of iron, would seem an unnatural, invulnerable
creature. Thus, although Magellan hoped to avoid fighting,
from the military point of view his expedition was as well
equipped as that of Hernando Cortez who, in the same summer of 1519, was marching with a handful of men to conquer an empire peopled by millions. This was to be a heroic
season in the history of Spanish conquest.

Having, for the last time, with the invincible patience
which was one of the man's signal characteristics, examined
each of the five ships as to seaworthiness and perfection of
equipment, Magellan proceeded to inspect the crew. It had
not been easy to enlist them. Weeks and weeks had passed
before they had been gathered from the alleys and the taverns. They arrived in rags, dirty and undisciplined, talking
to one another in a babel of tongues: Spanish, Italian, French,
Portuguese, Greek, Catalan, and German. Yes, it would take
a good while to convert this olla podrida into a sound, trustworthy, well-behaved crew. Still, by the time he had had
them at sea for a few weeks, he would hold them in his grip.
The man who for seven years had been a sobresaliente, quartered among the common sailors and soldiers, knew the needs
of ordinary seamen, how much could be asked of them, and

how they had to be treated. The admiral had little anxiety about his crew.

He was less easy in his mind when he looked at the four Spanish captains who had been placed in command of the other ships. His muscles grew tense, like those of a wrestler at the beginning of the struggle. Here was Juan de Cartagena, the king's veedor or chief inspector, who had replaced Faleiro in command of the "San Antonio," looking at him coldly, arrogantly, and with ill-concealed (perhaps purposely ill-concealed) disdain. No doubt Juan de Cartagena was an experienced seaman, and a man no less honourable than he was ambitious; but would this Castilian nobleman be able to hold his ambitions in leash? King Charles had appointed him veedor-general, supreme inspector of material concerns; Faleiro's retirement had made him captain of the largest ship in the fleet, and had given him the title of "conjuncta persona" —a plethora of offices and honours. Would this cousin of the Bishop of Burgos (who, having invested some of his own money in the venture, was a member of Christopher de Haro's combine) be content with purely mercantile control? As Magellan studied him, he remembered the words which Alvarez had whispered when the spy declared that Cartagena had received secret instructions and plenipotentiary powers of which Magellan would learn only when it was too late to save his honour. No less hostile was the aspect of Luis de Mendoza, who was in command of the "Victoria." Before leaving Seville he had, on one occasion, refused to obey orders; but Magellan could not discard this secret foe whom the Emperor had appointed tesorero of the expedition. It counted for little that in the church of Santa María de la

Victoria, beneath the unfurled banner, the officers had sworn him loyalty and obedience, for in the depths of their hearts they remained his envious foes. He would have to keep close watch on these Spanish noblemen.

Lucky, therefore, that he had succeeded in over-riding the royal rescript and the angry protests of the Casa de Contratación, and had been able to smuggle a few trustworthy Portuguese friends and relatives into the fleet. Above all he had brought with him Duarte Barbosa, his brother-in-law, and, though very young, an experienced navigator; then there were Alvaro de Mesquita, a near relative, and Estevão Gomez, the best pilot in Portugal. There was also João Serrão, enrolled as a Spaniard (for he had been in Castilia del Oro with Pizarro and Pedro d'Avilas), but presumably Portuguese, being a relative of Francisco Serrão, Magellan's old chum. He had gained much too by bringing along João Carvalho, who had visited Brazil years before, and had with him the son born to him in the New World by a brown-skinned wife. Both these men might do much service in Brazil by their knowledge of Indian dialects and of topography. If, having found the strait of which they were in search, the explorers reached the Malay-speaking areas in the Spice Islands and Malacca, Magellan's slave Enrique would be a valuable interpreter. But taking it all in all there were not more than from half a dozen to a dozen men among the two-hundred and sixty-five upon whom he could unconditionally rely. A scanty number, indeed, but he who has no choice must venture, even though time and number should be against him.

Grave of mien, as he made his lengthy review, Magellan walked along the front, secretly reckoning whom he could count on at a decisive moment, and who would be against him. Without his becoming aware of it, the strain had furrowed his brow. Then the tension relaxed, and involuntarily he smiled. Here was a man he had almost forgotten, a supernumerary, a superfluous hand, whom Fate had brought at the last moment. Or was it really by chance that the quiet, modest, youthful Italian, Antonio Pigafetta, sprig of a noble family in Vicenza, had joined this motley company of adventurers, gold-hunters, and desperadoes? He came to Barcelona to attach himself to the court of Charles V in the train of the papal protonotary. A beardless lad, though a Knight of Rhodes, he heard tell of a mysterious expedition which was to set out for unknown regions. It is probable that, in his native town of Vicenza, Pigafetta had read Vespucci's book (printed there in 1507) *Paesi novamente ritrovati*, in which the chronicler announced his longing "di andare e vedere parte del mondo e le sue meraviglie." It is, further, likely enough that the widely read *Itinerario* of his fellow-countryman Ludovico Vartema had fired the young Italian's enthusiasm. Beyond question he was greatly moved at the thought of seeing with his own eyes some of the "magnificent and dread things of the ocean." When he applied to Charles V with the request to be allowed to participate in this mysterious expedition, the Emperor recommended him to Magellan, and consequently, with these professional navigators, gold-hunters, and adventurers, there now became associated a remarkable idealist who rushed into danger, not for glory and not for pelf, but from a simple longing to see the world. Pigafetta was a dilettante in the best sense of the term, from pure delight in seeing, experiencing, admiring, wondering, staking his life for adventure's sake.

The upshot was to be that this supernumerary would become for Magellan the most important participator in his voyage. For what is an action worth when there is no one to describe it? A historical deed is not perfected when it has merely been achieved, but only when an account of it has been handed down to posterity. What we term history does not represent the sum-total of all conceivable things that have been done in space and time; history comprises those small illuminated sections of world happenings which have had thrown upon them the light of poetical or scientific description. Achilles would be nothing save for Homer. The figures of the world's heroes would be shadows, and the deeds they did would have slipped unnoticed into the infinite azure of the past, had it not been for the chronicler who preserves them in his story or for the artist who creatively reconstructs them. Thus we should know little of Magellan and his exploits had we nothing but the *Decades* of Don Peter Martyr, the bald letter of Maximilian Transylvanus, and a few dry sketches and log-books penned by the various pilots. Only Pigafetta, inconspicuous supernumerary and Knight of Rhodes, has preserved an adequate narrative of Magellan's voyage.

This worthy fellow was, indeed, neither a Tacitus nor a Livy. In authorship as in adventure, he was nothing more than a likeable amateur. We cannot say that knowledge of human nature was his forte; and the most important episodes of the mental tension between Magellan and the captains seem to have escaped his notice. But though Pigafetta pays little heed to psychological connexions, he observes details with remarkable accuracy, depicting them with the cheerful sobriety of a pen-portraitist who, as an exercise in school composition, is writing a description of a Sunday jaunt. Nor is he always trustworthy, for, in his naïve way, he often allowed himself to be hoaxed by the old pilots, who quickly perceived him to be a greenhorn. But Pigafetta compensates for such minor flaws by the zeal and care with which he describes whatever swims into his ken. Owing to the sedulous way in which he questioned the Patagonians in accordance with the Berlitz method, this Knight of Rhodes has unexpectedly acquired a niche in the Temple of Fame as the first to have written a vocabulary of an American dialect. An even more signal honour has accrued to him. No less distinguished an author than Shakespeare transcribes in *The Tempest* a scene from Pigafetta's *Book of Travels*. What can there be more splendid for a mediocre writer than that a genius shall take from his perishable work something to include in the imperishable, and thus, on an eagle's wings, lift the name of the nonentity into his own eternal sphere?

Magellan has finished his inspection and his review. With an easy conscience he can say to himself that he has done everything which can be expected of fallible man, making every conceivable calculation. But a voyage of adventure, a voyage of discovery, demands higher powers than attach to anything that can be weighed and measured on earth. In so bold an undertaking as this, a man who tries to reckon with all the possibilities of success must likewise take into account the most probable eventuality, must resolutely face the idea of death and of failure to return. In Seville, therefore, on August 24, 1519, immediately before departure, Magellan drew up and signed his will.

Not without emotion can we read this will of Magellan. Speaking generally, one who prepares his last will and testament has some sort of idea as to the amount of which he can dispose. But how could Magellan estimate what he had to bequeath? It still lay upon the knees of the gods whether in a year's time he would be a beggar or one of the wealthiest men in the world. At present his earthly goods consisted of a contract with the Crown of Spain. If the voyage were a success, if Magellan should find the legendary "paso," if he reached the Spice Islands and got back again with a rich freight, then he who had set out from Seville an impoverished adventurer would return thither a Crœsus. If, on the way, he were to discover new islands, his son and his grandson would acquire, in addition to this wealth, the hereditary title of governor and adelántado. But should the enterprise miscarry, should he not find the strait, or should his ships be wrecked, his wife and children, to avoid starvation, would have to hold out their hands for alms in front of church doors, invoking the aid of the pious. The decision must be left to the supreme powers, those who control the winds and the waves. Magellan, being an ardent Catholic, bowed himself humbly before God's unsearchable decrees.

But even in pious dispositions such a man as Magellan will never be vague and confused, so to the life after death he devotes the same amazing art of foresight that he displayed in his life on earth. All possibilities are foreseen and carefully graded. "When my present life shall end for the life eternal, I desire that if I die in the city of Seville my body may be buried in the monastery of Santa María de la Victoria . . . in the grave set apart for me. And if I die in this said voyage, I desire that my body may be buried in a church dedicated to Our Lady, in the nearest spot to that at which death seizes me and I die." Piously and precisely he now enumerates the religious legacies. A tenth part of the fifth share allotted to him in the profits of the venture is to be divided as follows: one-third of the said tenth part is to be given to the monastery of Santa María de la Victoria in Seville, and the remaining two-thirds of the said tenth part shall be divided into three equal parts, of which one part shall be given to the monastery of Santa María de Montserrat in the city of Barcelona, another to the monastery of San Francisco in the town of Aranda de Duero, and the third to the monastery of San Domingo in Oporto. One thousand maravedis are bequeathed to the chapel in Seville where he received the Holy Sacrament before departure, and where, with God's will, he hopes to receive it after his safe return. To the Holy Crusade he bequeaths a real of silver; another real in aid of the redemption of such faithful Christians as may be captives in the country of the Moors; a third real to the Infirmary of San Lázaro; a fourth and a fifth to the Hospital de las Bubas and to the Casa de San Sebastián, "that they may pray to God Our Lord for my soul." He desires that in the monastery of Santa María de la Victoria a thirty-day mass may be said for his soul. Further, "I desire that upon the day of my burial three poor men may be clothed, and that to each may be given a cloak of grey stuff, a cap, a shirt, and a pair of shoes, that they may pray to God for my soul; and I also desire that upon the said day of my burial food may be given to the said three paupers, and to twelve others, that they may pray to God for my soul; and I desire that upon the said day of my burial a gold ducat may be given as alms for the souls in purgatory."

When the Church has been assigned her share in the inheritance, we expect the last will and testament to specify bequests to wife and child. We are touched, however, to find that this deeply religious man is even more occupied about the fate of his slave Enrique. Perhaps before writing his will he had been troubled by scruples as to whether a true Christian was entitled to have a slave (especially one who had been baptized and was therefore a brother in the faith), and to treat as his own property a being with an immortal soul, as he might treat a plot of land or the coat that he wears. However that may be, Magellan does not wish to face his Maker with such disquiet on his mind, and he therefore specifies: "I declare and ordain that from the day of my death thenceforward for ever, my captured slave Enrique, mulatto, native of the city of Malacca, of the age of twenty-six years more or less, shall be free and manumitted, and quit, exempt, and relieved of every obligation of slavery and subjection, that he may act as he desires and thinks fit; and I desire that of my estate there may be given to the said Enrique the sum of ten thousand maravedis in money for his support; and this manumission I grant because he is a Christian and that he may pray to God for my soul."

Only now, when he has devoted careful attention to a future life and has thought of the "good works which, at the Last Judgment, can speak on behalf of the most sinful," does Magellan turn to the needs of his family. Even here he thinks first of something immaterial before troubling about the disposal of his property. Amid all the legacies we see that there is nothing which troubles him so much as what will happen to the arms and to the noble name of the Magellans, for he makes the most precise stipulations about what is to be done should (gloomy foreboding) his son die without leaving sons or daughters born in wedlock, stating who shall adopt the name and bear the arms of Magellan. Even as does the Christian, so does the nobleman, in this last will and testament, ardently crave for immortality.

At length all has been arranged, every clause is finished, and, with steady hand, the admiral signs the will as "Hernando de Magallanes," that thereby and by the attestation clause the document shall be guaranteed in perpetuity. But not by strokes of the pen does Destiny allow itself to be bound, nor to be coerced by vows, the eternal will of Fate being stronger than the will of any mortal. Not a single one of the wishes expressed by Magellan in his testament was fulfilled, not one of these carefully thought-out dispositions was respected. Magellan's testament was to remain null and void. Those whom he had appointed his heirs were never to become heirs; the poor whom he had thought to console were not to be consoled; his body was not to be interred at the appointed place; and his coat of arms would cease to exist. Nothing but his great deed would survive the circumnavigator of the world, and all mankind, but no individual, would be his grateful inheritor.

His last duty in the homeland had been discharged. The time had come to take farewell. His wife stood tremulous before him, the wife with whom he had been happy for a year. She held their son in her arms, while her body was shaken with sobs. He embraced her for the last time and pressed the hand of his father-in-law Barbosa, whose only son was to accompany him on his adventurous journey. Then quickly, that he might not be unmanned by the tears of the wife he was leaving, he took ship for San Lucar, where the fleet awaited him. Having confessed his sins in the little church of San Lucar, Magellan, with the assembled crew, received the Holy Sacrament. In the grey of morning, on Tuesday, September 20, 1519 (a day to be momentous in history), the anchors were heaved, the sails filled, salutes were fired at the departing land. The longest voyage of discovery, the boldest adventure in the records of our race, had begun.

Chapter Seven

FRUITLESS SEARCH

September 20, 1519–April 2, 1520

Fruitless Search

MAGELLAN'S fleet sailed from San Lucar on September 20, 1519. In those days the grip of Spain already extended far beyond Europe. When a week later the five ships touched at Tenerife, to take on further supplies and fresh water, they were still in the dominions of Emperor Charles V. Once more the would-be circumnavigators could set their feet on Spanish ground, and talk their familiar tongue before steering away into the unknown.

This rest was brief. Magellan was about to hoist sail once more, when there appeared in the offing a caravel from Spain, bringing the admiral secret tidings from his father-in-law Diego Barbosa. Secret tidings meant, as so often, evil tidings. Barbosa warned his son-in-law that he had learned of the existence of a privy pact among the Spanish captains, who intended to mutiny during the voyage; the head of the conspiracy was Juan de Cartagena, cousin of the Bishop of Burgos. Magellan had no reason to doubt the honesty and accuracy of the warning. It merely came as confirmation of the obscure threat uttered by the spy Alvarez, "others have been sent with contrary orders, of which you will learn only when it is too late for you to save your honour." However, the die was cast, and the manifest danger served only to intensify Magellan's natural stoutness of heart. Proudly he wrote in answer to Seville that, whatever happened, he would persist in his service to the Emperor, and that his life would be the pledge. Without letting anyone on board suspect what a gloomy and truthful warning had been brought by the caravel—the last letter he was ever to receive—he gave orders to weigh anchor, and within a few hours the peak of Tenerife was growing hazy in the distance. Most of the two hundred and sixty-five men were bidding eternal farewell to the homeland.

The hardest task for the commander of this motley squadron was to keep as a unified group five sailing-ships of such varying tonnage and speed. If one should stray from the flock it would be lost in the pathless ocean. Before the start, in understanding with the Casa de Contratación, Magellan had elaborated a special system to enable the members of his flock to keep in contact. True, the "derrota," the general course, had been communicated to the "contramaestres" (ships' captains) and the pilots. But on the open sea, standing orders were: Follow in the wake of the "Trinidad." By day this was easy enough, for even during a big storm the members of the fleet could keep in sight of one another. More difficult was it when darkness fell, so light-signals had been arranged. When the sun set, on the stern of the "Trinidad" a wooden torch was kindled in a lantern (farol), which the other ships were to keep in sight. If, in addition to this wooden torch, two other lights were shown on the flag-ship, that indicated to the consorts that they were to sail slower, or were to tack if the wind became unfavourable. Three lights signified that a storm was imminent and that the other ships were to shorten sail; four lights meant that all sails were to be lowered. A flickering light upon the flag-ship or gun-

shots were warnings to navigate cautiously, since shoals or
sand-banks were near at hand. This ingenious system of night-
signalling was worked out to meet every possible eventuality.

Each sign made by the light-telegraph on the flag-ship had
to be answered in like manner by the other ships, so that the
captain-general could be sure that his orders had been understood and would be obeyed. Furthermore, every evening,
just before it grew dark, the four ships had to steer close to
the flag-ship, and hail the admiral with the words, "Dios vos
salve, señor capitán-general y maestre y buena compañía,"
and thereafter receive orders for the three night watches. By
the organization of these daily contacts of the four captains
with the admiral, discipline during the early days seems to
have been secured. The flag-ship led and the others followed;
Magellan set the course, and the captains had to adopt it without question.

But precisely because the leadership was kept thus rigidly
and unyieldingly in the hands of one man, and because this
inaccessible, taciturn, self-contained Portuguese commander
made them come to him day after day to receive their orders
as if they had been mere hodmen, the captains of the other
boats grew more and more restive. No doubt they had felt
that, whereas in Spain Magellan was justified in keeping the
mystery of the "paso" close, lest it fall into the hands of gos-
sips and spies, once on the open sea this precaution would no
longer be needed, since the silence and loneliness of the ocean
made leakage impossible. Surely they would be invited on
board the flag-ship, would be shown the maps, and would be
told the details of his jealously guarded plan. Instead, they

found Magellan increasingly reserved, cold, and inaccessible. He did not summon them to a council, he did not ask their opinions, not even that of the most experienced among them. They had to follow the flag by day, the farol by night, with the dumb obedience of a well-trained dog. For some days the Spanish officers made no remonstrance at the way in which Magellan, without a word to them, kept his own course. But when the admiral, instead of sailing, as they had expected, south-west for Brazil, steered southward along the coast of Africa as far as Sierra Leone, Juan de Cartagena, on the occasion of one of the evening reports, bluntly asked why the course had been changed contrary to the original instructions.

An open inquiry was not in any way presumptuous on the part of Juan de Cartagena. (It is needful to insist upon this, for, in most of the accounts of the matter, in order to exonerate Magellan, Juan de Cartagena is described as having been a traitor from the outset.) We cannot but regard it as reasonable and right that the captain of the largest ship in the squadron, who was also the veedor of the Spanish Crown, should civilly ask the admiral why the prearranged course had been departed from. Besides, from a navigator's point of view, there were good grounds for Juan de Cartagena's question, since the alteration in the course seemed preposterous, and likely to cost the fleet a round fortnight. We do not know why Magellan changed the route. Perhaps he sailed along the coast of Africa as far south as Guinea in order there (following a technical rule of Portuguese navigators, a rule unknown to the Spaniards) "tomar barlavento"—to catch a favourable wind. Or it may be that he departed from the usual course in order to avoid the ships which King Eman-

uel of Portugal sent to Brazil by a more northerly route. In
any case, it would have been easy for Magellan to tell his
colleagues plainly, trusting in their loyalty, the why and the
wherefore of what was certainly unusual.

Magellan, however, was not concerned with this particular
instance, not with sailing a few miles more or less to the
south-west, but with the principle that led him from the
start to maintain strict discipline in the fleet. If, as his father-
in-law had warned him, there were conspirators among his
followers, he would rather force them into the open. Should
secret instructions have been issued to some of them, he
wanted to know what these instructions were and to enforce
his supreme authority. It suited his purposes, therefore, that
Juan de Cartagena was the captain who questioned him, for
now he would find out whether this Spanish hidalgo had
come as his equal or as his subordinate. In actual fact this
question of precedence had become somewhat dubious. Orig-
inally Juan de Cartagena had been sent by the Emperor as
veedor-general; both in this capacity and as captain of the
"San Antonio," he was subordinate to the admiral, without
any right to question or advise. But the situation changed
when Magellan shook off his partner Faleiro, since Juan took
Faleiro's place as "conjuncta persona," the term "conjuncta"
signifying "associate and equal." Each of them, therefore,
could produce a document in support: Magellan the one
which gave him supreme command of the fleet, and Juan de
Cartagena the cedula by which he was appointed "conjuncta
persona." Magellan was determined that this question should
no longer remain debatable. He therefore answered the query
of Juan de Cartagena, which was apparently justified by the

latter's coequal position, by bluntly stating that "no one was entitled to demand explanations from him, and all they had to do was to follow him as directed" ("que le siguisen y no le pidiesen más cuenta").

This was certainly rude, but Magellan thought it better to wave the bludgeon than merely to bluster or to negotiate. Metaphorically speaking, he hit the Spanish captain a sound crack upon the head, this implying that Cartagena was to be under no illusions, for the captain-general held the commandership in an iron grip. But though he had an iron grip, he lacked many excellent qualities, and especially the tact which would have enabled him to smooth over a rough answer. Never did he acquire the art of saying harsh things in a friendly way, of dealing with either his superiors or his subordinates in a cordial and courteous manner. Thus there necessarily became diffused around the commander who was bubbling over with energy a tense, hostile, and irritant atmosphere, which was likely to increase latent dissensions all the more, since Juan de Cartagena honestly regarded Magellan's change of course as a blunder.

There were reasons for this view. The favourable wind did not come, and the fleet was becalmed for twenty days. Then there ensued such violent storms that, according to Pigafetta's romantic imaginings, the expedition was saved only by the appearance of a luminous vision of the Corpo Santo, the Holy Bodies of the Patron Saints, Anselm, Nicholas, and Clara (St. Elmo's fire).

Much time had been lost by Magellan's arbitrary change in the course, so that in the end Juan de Cartagena could no longer disguise his spleen. Since the admiral regarded himself as above criticism, the whole fleet should see how little respect he, Juan de Cartagena, had for so bad a navigator. True, every day at nightfall his ship, the "San Antonio," steered close to the "Trinidad" to report and to receive Magellan's orders. One evening, however, Juan did not appear personally on deck, sending instead the quartermaster, who gave only the abbreviated greeting, "Dios vos salve, señor capitán y maestre."

Not for a moment did Magellan believe that this defective salute had come about by chance. If Juan de Cartagena addressed him merely as "capitán," and not as "capitán-general," this was to acquaint the fleet that Juan de Cartagena, as "conjuncta persona," did not recognize Magellan as a superior officer. At once the admiral let Juan know that he expected, henceforward, to be greeted in the proper terms. Juan, however, putting his cards on the table, sent back a curt answer that he must beg to be excused. This time he had made his greeting through the instrumentality of the best man on board the "San Antonio," but next time he might convey the greeting through the mouth of the cabin boy. For three days the "San Antonio," within sight of the whole fleet, gave no further greeting, in order to make it plain to everyone that Juan de Cartagena did not acknowledge the unrestricted supremacy of the Portuguese commander. Frankly (and this is to the credit of Juan, who was not—as he is often represented— a secret conspirator) the Spanish hidalgo flung down the gauntlet before his Portuguese rival.

A man's character is best disclosed by his behaviour at decisive moments. It is danger which brings to light hidden powers and capacities. Those overshadowed qualities which, when the temperature is moderate, lurk beyond the range of measurement, are, of a sudden, unmistakably disclosed. Magellan's reaction to danger was always the same; whenever great matters were at stake, his silence and coldness grew sinister. He froze, as it were. Even in face of the grossest insults, the eyes beneath the bushy brows did not flash, nor did the corners of his inscrutable mouth twitch. He always kept his temper, but in his icy brain at such times his senses were as clear as crystal, while he remained frostily silent, thinking out his plans. Not once in his life did Magellan deliver a blow hotly or hastily, but always struck after a long and obscure meditation, even as a cloud draws itself together before the lightning flashes.

This time, as on other occasions, Magellan kept his own counsel. One who did not know him (and his Spanish subordinates did not yet know him) might have supposed that he had not noticed Juan de Cartagena's challenge. Really he was preparing a counterstroke. He knew that, on the high seas, he could not forcibly dismiss the captain of his largest and best-armed ship. Patience then, patience. It would be better to seem indifferent. Magellan, therefore, made no answer to the insult, having the supreme gift of taciturnity, conjoined with the ardour of a fanatic, the tenacity of a peasant, and the passion of a gamester. Apparently unmoved, he walked to and fro on the deck of the "Trinidad," completely absorbed, it might have been supposed, in the petty details of shipboard life. He did not seem disturbed because the evening salute from the "San Antonio" remained unuttered; and the Spanish captains were somewhat surprised when this enigmatic man revealed what they looked upon as an inclination to compromise. For the first time, on the pretext of a breach of discipline by one of the soldiers, the admiral summoned the four captains to a council on the flagship. He found it inconvenient, they thought, to be on bad terms with his comrades. Having realized that the southward course had been a mistake, he felt it would be wiser to take the advice of old, experienced captains, instead of treating them as nonentities. Juan de Cartagena came to the council with the others, and, being now able to address the admiral in person, he repeated his inquiry why the course had been changed. In accordance with his preconceived plan, Magellan remained cool, well aware that his non-committal attitude would irritate Cartagena more and more. Cartagena's position in the fleet gave him the right of free speech; but his anger led to a violent outbreak, to a public refusal of obedience. Magellan, as a skilled psychologist, expected, and even hoped for, open insubordination. Now he could strike. At once, seizing Juan de Cartagena by the breast, he said: "Sed preso"—you are my prisoner—and commanded the alguacil to arrest the mutineer.

The other Spanish captains looked on, dumbfounded. A few minutes before, they had been wholly on the side of Juan de Cartagena; even now, at bottom, they espoused the cause of their countryman and were opposed to the tyrannical foreigner. But the speed of the blow, the formidable energy with which Magellan had had his adversary laid by the heels, paralysed them. In vain did Juan de Cartagena appeal to them for help. Not one of them dared do anything, or to make front against the stocky little man who had for the first time shown his claws and emerged from the tough envelope of silence. Only as Juan was about to be led away did one of them turn humbly to Magellan and beg that the prisoner, being a Spanish nobleman, should not be put in irons. It would be enough that he should give his word of honour not to break his arrest. Magellan agreed, on condition that Luis de Mendoza, to whose care Cartagena was entrusted, should swear to hold the prisoner at the admiral's disposal. This was arranged. An hour later another Spanish officer, Antonio de Coca, was in charge of the "San Antonio," and at nightfall, from the deck of his ship, greeted the admiral in due form as "capitán-general." Nothing seemed to be changed, and the fleet sailed onward without incident. On November 29, the look-out man at the masthead hailed those below to announce that he had sighted the Brazilian coast, which they reached, without landing, in the neighbourhood of Pernambuco; and at length, on December 13, the five ships, after an eleven weeks' voyage, entered the bay of Rio de Janeiro.

To the weary crew, this bay, which in those remote days was no less beautiful than now when a splendid city lines its shores, must have seemed a paradise. Rio de Janeiro, thus named because discovered on January 1, and erroneously called "Rio" because the mouth of a great river was mooted behind the medley of islands, was within the Portuguese sphere. Magellan, therefore, had been instructed to avoid landing there. But the Portuguese had not yet established any settlement; there was no threatening fortress with ominous guns; the place was substantially No-Man's-Land, so the

Spanish fleet could anchor unconcernedly. As soon as this was done, the natives emerged from their huts on the edge of the forest to welcome the soldiers in armour, showing much curiosity but no suspicion. They were gentle and trusting, although Pigafetta, in his journal, deplored that they were doughty cannibals who were wont to roast the corpses of conquered enemies upon great spits and to cut dainty morsels of the meat as from an ox. Anyhow, as regards these divine-looking white foreigners they showed no such inclination, so the soldiers had no need to use their arquebuses or their pikes.

After a few hours a brisk barter was in progress. Now the worthy Pigafetta was in his element. During the eleven weeks' voyage he had found nothing to describe, nothing to enter in his record, beyond a few anecdotes about man-eating sharks and strange birds. He must have been asleep when Juan de Cartagena was arrested, for he tells us nothing about the matter. Now his pen could hardly move swiftly enough to describe all the wonders that were happening. Of the magnificent scenery, indeed, he breathes no word, which must not be taken amiss, for descriptions of nature were first introduced more than two hundred years later by Jean-Jacques Rousseau. But he makes up for this by talking about a new fruit, pineapples, "which are like huge, rounded cones, but very sweet, and more tasteful than any other fruit." He speaks also of "battate," which he describes as having a flavour resembling that of chestnuts; and likewise of sugar-cane. His enthusiasm carries him away when he tells how cheaply these poor fools sell provisions. For a small fish-hook they give five or six fowls; for a comb, a couple of geese; for a mirror, ten gorgeous parrots; for a pair of scissors, as many fish as would provide an ample meal for a dozen men. For one bell (and we must not forget that the ships had brought twenty thousand of them), they exchanged a great basket of potatoes; and Pigafetta himself swapped the king from a pack of cards for six fowls, the Guaranis believing themselves to have bested the inexperienced Knight of Rhodes in the deal. Extraordinarily cheap, too, were the girls, who, as Pigafetta delicately puts it, "were clad only in their hair." For a knife or a hatchet, you could procure two or three of them for life.

While Pigafetta was busy with his notebook, and the sailors whiled away the time bartering fish-hooks for an abundance of fresh food or amused themselves with the easy-going brown girls, Magellan was preparing for the continuance of the voyage. He had no objection to the reasonable amusements of the crew, but he kept his men under strict discipline none the less. In accordance with a pledge he had given to the King of Spain, along the whole length of the Brazilian coast he forbade the purchase of slaves or any act of violence, so that the Portuguese owners of the territory might have no grounds for complaint.

This decent behaviour proved extremely advantageous to Magellan. Since no wrong was done to the natives, such fears as they might have entertained speedily vanished. Crowds of them, good-humoured and childlike, assembled on the shore when mass was being said. Inquisitively they looked on at the strange ceremonies and, seeing that the white strangers (whose arrival, they believed, had put an end to a long drought) bent the knee before a cross, they kneeled likewise, uplifting their hands as if at prayer—this to the pious Spaniards seeming to betoken that unwittingly they had accepted the mysteries of the Christian faith. When, after thirteen days, at the end of December, the fleet sailed southward out of the splendid bay, Magellan could resume his journey with a better conscience than any other conquistador of the time. For, even though he might not conquer the country for his emperor, he had, as a pious Christian, won new souls for his heavenly Lord. Not the slightest harm had been done to any of the indigenes during the Spaniards' stay; no one had been forcibly carried away from home and country. Magellan came in peace and departed in peace.

Reluctantly the sailors left the paradise of Rio de Janeiro, and reluctantly they steered without landing along the alluring coast of Brazil. But Magellan had no more time to spare. Imperturbable though he seemed, burning impatience drove him perpetually onward towards that "paso" which was inscribed on Schöner's globe, and which report had led him to expect in a particular region. The way through the Americas must, if the tale of the Portuguese pilots and the latitude given by Schöner were correct, be situated immediately behind the Cabo Santa Maria, so it was towards this cape that Magellan directed his course. Finally he reached it on January 10, 1520. Beyond it they saw a small hill rising out of an immense plain, and they called this hill Montevidi, today Montevideo. The weather being stormy, they took refuge in the huge inlet, which appeared to stretch indefinitely towards the west.

The enormous bay is, in reality, nothing more than the estuary of the Rio de la Plata, but of this Magellan had no inkling. He found himself at the precise spot described in the secret report, the inlet stretching westward, in the direction of the Moluccas. He fancied he had reached his goal. Everything tallied with the description. Assuredly this must be the place from which, twenty years before, the Portuguese had hoped to continue their voyage to the west. Pigafetta expressly declares that the ships' companies, without exception, were convinced that the desired strait had been discovered. "Si era creduto una volta esser questo un canal che mettesse nel Mar del Sur"—an error which may suggest that those who made it were simpletons, though we ourselves would be simpletons to laugh at them for having made it. How could the uninformed Spaniards suppose this gigantic estuary, whose western shores were out of sight, to be a mere indentation of the sea, when we ourselves, steering from Montevideo to Buenos Aires, find it hard to believe that we are merely entering the mouth of a river and not sailing into an open sea? If we, who are taught at school the accurate geography of America, are astonished, and doubt despite our better knowledge, how should mariners, most of whom had seen only the mouth of the Tagus, the Po, or the Rhine, fail to let their hopes cheat them into the belief that they were entering a strait like that of Gibraltar, the Hellespont, the English Channel? Assuredly, though it might narrow for a few hours, it would then widen again, to lead into the South Seas.

The persistency with which Magellan explored the estuary of the Rio de la Plata proves that, at his first glimpse of this vast sheet of water, he was convinced that he had discovered the "paso" of which he was in search. He spent a fortnight upon the fruitless quest. Directly the storm which broke out

THE HARBOUR OF SAN LUCAR
Copper engraving from de Bry's Travel Book (1594)

Le Breſilien;

L'homme du lieu auquel le Breſil croiſt.
Eſt tel qu'icy, à l'oeil il apparoiſt,
Leur naturel exercice s'applique
Coupper Breſil, pour en faire trafique,

BRAZILIAN INDIAN
Woodcut from a French Costume Book (1567)

at the time of his arrival had abated, the admiral divided his fleet. The smaller ships were sent westward to discover the presumed channel, in reality upstream. The two larger ships simultaneously sailed southward across the mouth of La Plata, "para ver si había pasage." Bitter was to be his disillusionment. After he had waited a fortnight in "Montevidi," the returning members of the squadron hove in sight. No pennant was waving joyfully at the masthead, and the captains brought the crushing intelligence that this huge indentation in the coast of Brazil, which they themselves had likewise supposed to be the channel of which they were in search, was nothing but the mouth of an unusually large river, for they had come to a place where the waters ran fresh. In honour of Juan de Solís, who had hoped to reach Malacca by the same route early in the year 1516, and had instead met his death, the river was provisionally christened Rio de Solis, for the name of Rio de la Plata was not applied to it until a later date.

Now, Magellan's only resource was to keep a stiff upper lip. None of the captains and none of the crew must discover how fearful was the blow he had sustained, how deadly the disappointment. For one thing, at least, had become plain to him, that Schöner's globe (or whatever map he was depending on) was untrustworthy, and that the news of the Portuguese concerning their discovery of a passage through the Americas in the fortieth parallel was erroneous. False had been his information, false were Faleiro's calculations, false his own contention, false were the promises he had made to King Charles and the Privy Council. If a strait really existed —and for the first time the man who had been so confident had to admit that there was an "if"—it must lie much farther to the south. But to steer southward meant to steer away from the warm seas. Since they were many degrees south of the Equator, it meant an approach to the Antarctic. February, here in the far south, was not the end of winter but its beginning. Unless they could soon find a passage into the South Seas, unless the strait could be quickly discovered, the favourable season would be over, and there would remain only two possibilities: either to get back to a warmer clime, or to winter in these bleak southern latitudes.

From the moment when the scouting ships returned with the evil tidings, gloomy thoughts must have predominated in Magellan's mind; and just as there was gloom within, so was there gloom without. The coast became increasingly hostile, barren, and desolate; the skies darkened. The white light of the south was extinguished, the blue zenith was overcast with grey, the steaming forests with their sweet aroma had vanished, balsamic odours were no longer wafted to the ships from the distant shore. Disappeared for ever had the friendly landscape of Brazil, with its luxuriant fruit trees, its waving palms, its multicoloured animals, its hospitable brown-skinned natives. On the strand there was nothing to be seen but penguins, which waddled away when approached; while sea-lions moved oafishly and lazily upon the reefs. As far as eye could reach, there were no other living creatures, for both man and beast seemed extinct in this disheartening waste. Once, indeed, on land huge savages—men clad like Eskimos in skins—fled wildly at sight of the strangers. They would not heed the lure of the little bells, or of the brightly tinted caps that were held out to them. With threatening and renunciatory gestures they vanished, and the explorers vainly attempted to discover a trace of their dwellings.

Slower and more laborious became the voyage, but Magellan held stubbornly southward, hugging the coast. Every bay was examined, with leadsmen at work in the chains. It was true that Magellan had long ceased to believe in that accursed globe which had enticed him into so fruitless a journey. But a miracle was still possible; there was still a chance that at some unexpected spot the "paso" would be found, and that before the beginning of winter the fleet would sail into the Mar del Sur. It was plain that the admiral, though no longer confident, clung to the last hope 'that perhaps Schöner and the Portuguese navigators had been mistaken only in the latitude, and that the strait of which he was in search lay somewhat farther to the south than they had declared. When, on February 24, the fleet reached the entrance of another bay whose western shores were out of sight, the Gulf of San Matias, hope flickered up once more. Again Magellan sent the smaller ships to explore, "viendo si había alguna salida para el Maluco." No, there was nothing. Another closed bay. The pilots came back crestfallen; and no less vainly were two other bays explored, the Bahia de los Patos, so called because of the numerous penguins seen there, and the Bahia de los Trabajos (Bay of Toil), thus named because of the terrible hardships suffered by members of the crew who landed there. The half-frozen men brought back only the bodies of sea-wolves they had slaughtered, instead of the longed-for tidings of the strait.

Farther and farther south sailed the fleet along the gloomy coast beneath gloomy skies. More and more horrible grew the prospect, shorter the days, longer the nights. The gentle breezes of latitudes nearer the Equator had long been left behind, to be replaced by cold and vicious storms. Snow and hail whitened the sails, while the grey waves towered dangerously high. Two months were spent by the fleet, constantly fighting bad weather, in traversing the thousand miles of coast between the estuary of La Plata and Port San Julian. There were hurricanes almost daily, shattering the masts and carrying away the sails, but the "paso" continued to elude them. They had to pay heavily, now, for the wasted weeks, for, while the ships had been exploring bay after bay, winter had overtaken them. The time had come when they would have to face this southern winter, wild and dangerous, blocking the southward course with its storms. Half a year had passed, and Magellan seemed no nearer his goal than on the day when he left Seville.

The crew began to show uneasiness, instinctively aware that something was wrong. When they signed on in Seville, had they not been told that the voyage was to the Spice Islands, to the sunny south, to a paradisaical world? Had not the admiral's slave Enrique assured them that his country was the land of the lotus-eaters, a place where the most precious spices grew ready for the picking, without labour? Had they not been promised wealth and a speedy return? Instead, this silent and sinister man was leading them into a cold and poverty-stricken world. On some days they could see the sun, pale yellow, as it described a low arc in the sky; but as a rule the heavens were overcast, and the smell of snow was in the air. The biting wind whistled through their worn clothing, the ice-encrusted ropes took the skin off their chilled hands, and their breath steamed. As for the land, how god-forsaken it looked. Even the cannibals had fled from the cold. When the men went ashore, there was no fresh fruit to be found, nothing but fish and sea-wolves; the cold waters were almost as barren of life as the storm-lashed strand. Whither had this crazy Portuguese brought them? Whither was he bound? Was it his aim to winter amid the ice, or to conduct them to the South Pole?

In vain did Magellan try to allay their discontent, telling them not to lose courage, and not to be alarmed at a little cold weather. The coasts of Norway and Iceland were in much higher latitudes, but in spring were as favourable for naviga-tion as the coast of Spain. Let them content themselves for a few days more. In case of need, they would lie up for the winter, and continue their journey when the skies grew kinder. But the men would not be consoled with empty words. The comparison with Northern Europe did not hold water. Norway and Iceland were another story, and the King of Spain had never foreseen a voyage in these icy soli-tudes. The mariners of Norway and Iceland were accustomed to the cold from childhood onward, and never sailed farther than a week or a fortnight from home, whereas the admiral had brought them into an icy waste which no Christian had ever visited before, and one which even the heathen and the cannibals, even the bears and the wolves, avoided. Why had he steered this devious course, when there was another route, the one by the East Indies, which led conveniently to the Spice Islands without touching upon such murderous zones? Such were the answers openly made by the crew to Magel-

lan's assurances. No doubt when they were among themselves
in their own dark quarters, they used stronger language. Once
more there stirred the suspicions which had been no more
than whispers in Seville, whether this infernal Portuguese
was not playing a "trato doble," a double game. Was it not
likely enough that, in order to reinstate himself in King
Emanuel's favour, he purposed to destroy five good Spanish
ships with all on board?

The Spanish captains watched the growth of this mutinous
spirit with tacit gratification. They took no part in fomenting
the disturbance; they avoided speaking to the admiral; they
were conspicuously silent; but their silence was perhaps more
dangerous than the frank discontent of the sailors. Being
themselves experienced navigators, it did not escape them
that Magellan was inwardly suffering from disappointment,
and that he no longer felt sure of his "secret." If he really
knew the precise latitude and longitude of the alleged "paso,"
why had he wasted a fortnight exploring the estuary of the
Rio de la Plata? Why did he continue to squander precious
time by investigating every inlet that they sighted? He must
have deceived either the King or himself when he declared
that he knew the route, for plainly he did not know it but
was looking for it. With malicious delight they watched him,
at each new indentation of the coast, scrutinizing the inhospitable shore. Well, let him go farther and farther south, en-
tangling himself in the rime; they need not protest, or try
to persuade him. Soon would come the moment when he
would be compelled to admit that he did not know his course,
and that it was impossible to go any farther. Then they would
be able to bend his arrogant neck beneath the yoke.

It is hardly possible to conceive a more terrible position than that of Magellan during these weeks. Having been twice cruelly disappointed, first in the estuary of the Rio de la Plata, and a second time in the Gulf of San Matias, he could no longer conceal from himself that his faith in Schöner's globe and in the reports of the Portuguese navigators had been misplaced. He was faced by a terrible alternative: either this strait, this "paso," this "estrecho," did not exist, in which case he had himself been deceived and had deceived his new master; or else, although the strait did really exist, it was farther south, nearer the Antarctic, so that, in the best event, he could not hope to get through until the cold season was over. Winter had him in its grip. Even should he discover the passage, he could not, till spring came, avail himself of it, with his worn ships and his discontented crew. He had spent nine months on the voyage without reaching the Moluccas as he had prematurely pledged himself to do. Threatened by storm, frost, and winter, the fleet was wandering no man knew whither, fighting for dear life against the hurricanes.

The most reasonable course would be to disclose the truth. Let him call the captains together, inform them that the globe and the reports of the Portuguese pilots had led him astray, and that a search for the "estrecho" would have to be renewed next spring. Better, now, about ship, evade the storms, sail northward along the coast to Brazil, where they would find a warm and friendly climate in which to spend the winter months, patch their battered craft, and rehabilitate the crew —to return south next spring.

That would have been the most obvious thing to do, as it would have been the most humane. But Magellan had ven-

tured so far that he was unwilling to turn back. Self-deceived,
too long he had deceived others by declaring he knew an
unexplored and shorter route to the Moluccas. Too roundly
had he dealt with those who had expressed even the faintest
doubt as to his omniscience: he had insulted the Spanish captains; he had deposed the King's highest officer in the fleet,
and treated the man like a criminal. Nothing but a great, a
decisive triumph could excuse his actions. Not for an hour,
not for a minute, would the captains and the crews fail to
rise against his command if he uttered the slightest hint (to
say nothing of a frank admission) that he was no longer so
sure as he had told King Charles. The youngest of the cabin
boys would refuse to salute him. For Magellan there was no
turning back. The instant he decided to about ship and sail
for Brazil, he would no longer be his officers' commander,
but their prisoner. He therefore made a desperate resolve.
Even as Cortez, in that same year, burned his ships in order
to deprive his men of the possibility of return, so did Magellan determine to keep ships and crews in a place so out-of-
the-way that they would not be able to return, even should
they wish to do so. If, when spring came, he found the passage, he would have won the game. If he failed to find it, all
was lost. Now that his original plan had miscarried, there was
no middle course for Magellan. Nothing but stubbornness
could give him strength, nothing but boldness could save him.
Once more, while keeping his own counsel, the incalculable
calculator prepared for a decisive blow.

From day to day the weather grew wilder and more wintry. The ships could advance only with great difficulty. Two
whole months had been spent in travelling no more than

fourteen parallels of latitude southward. At length, on March 31, 1520, another indentation appeared. With a transient gleam of hope, the admiral looked into it. Was it open? Could it be the long-desired "paso"? No, it was a closed bay. Still, Magellan entered. It was a sheltered place, and the water seemed well stocked with fish, so he gave orders to anchor. Then, to their astonishment and perhaps to their dismay, the captains and the crews learned that their admiral (without consulting any of them) had decided to winter in this Port San Julian, this unknown and uninhabited bay on the forty-ninth parallel, the gloomiest and remotest place they had yet struck, where no European had ever been before them, and from which Europe seemed to be at an inaccessible distance. This was to be their winter quarters.

Chapter Eight

MUTINY

April 2, 1520 - April 7, 1520

Mutiny

COOPED up as they were in Port San Julian, which, though well sheltered, was a gloomy place in which to spend the winter, it was inevitable that dissensions between commander and crew should become intensified. Matters grew worse than they had been on the open sea. Nothing can show more clearly Magellan's strength of character than that, in spite of the tension he knew to exist, he did not shrink from a measure which could not fail to foster dissatisfaction. He alone knew that the fleet, in the best event, could not reach the fruitful islands of which he was in search until many months had elapsed, and he therefore put his men on short commons. It was amazingly courageous—at the end of the earth, with hostile subordinates—to anger everyone on the first day by declaring that henceforward the allowance of bread and of wine must be considerably reduced.

In actual fact this energetic step was what subsequently saved the fleet. Never would the circumnavigators have been able to make their hundred days' voyage across the Pacific had not an iron ration been kept in store. But the crew, which had grown indifferent to an adventure they failed to understand, were by no means inclined to accept such restrictions. A sound instinct told the sorely tried sailors that even if their admiral should acquire eternal fame through this voyage, at least three-fourths of themselves were destined to perish miserably from cold and hunger, from toil and hardship, and from the evil fortune of the sea. If there was a shortage of provisions, they grumbled, that was a reason for the return voyage. They had pushed farther south than any ship had been known to travel in the memory of man. When they got home, no one would be able to charge them with having shirked their duty. Some had already died of cold. They had signed on, not to navigate the polar seas, but to reach the Moluccas. According to contemporary Spanish historians, Magellan answered these rebellious words with a speech that ill accords with the man's blunt and uncongenial nature, and smacks too much of Plutarch and Thucydides to be credible. He marvelled, we are told, that Castilians should be guilty of such weakness, forgetting that the voyage had been undertaken at the King's orders and for the sake of their country. When he had taken command, he had expected to find among his comrades in the expedition that spirit of valour which had always animated the Spanish nation. For his own part, he was determined rather to die than return to a life of shame. Let them have patience until the winter had gone by. The greater their labour and privation, the greater would be their reward.

Fine speeches have never allayed the pangs of an empty stomach. It was not rhetoric that saved Magellan in this critical hour, but his determination not to yield a jot. He provoked resistance, that he might the better be able to crush it. He would rather have matters settled here and now than procrastinate like a coward. Better face the foe than allow himself to be forced to the wall.

Magellan entertained no doubts that settlement must ensue, and speedily. The tension of reciprocal silence and mutual supervision between himself and the captains had been growing for weeks, during which, within the narrow limits of their ships, they had daily encountered one another with cold aloofness. Sooner or later the silence must end in tumult and in violent deeds.

The blame for this dangerous state of affairs attaches rather to Magellan than to the Spanish captains, and there is no warrant for the customary descriptions of the subordinates as a clique of black traitors, or as some of those little men who are typically hostile to genius. In so critical a situation, the captains had not only the right, but one may even say the duty, of asking the commander to inform them of his intentions, since besides their own lives those of two hundred and sixty subordinates were at stake. When Charles V appointed Cartagena, Mendoza, and Gaspar Quesada respectively veedor, tesorero, and contador of his fleet, he assigned them, not only their titles and their salaries, but also a share of responsibility. They had to keep watch over these five ships that represented an important amount of the royal property, and to defend that property in case of need. No doubt at Valladolid, by decree, supreme power had been vested in Magellan, but only upon his promising to reach the Spice Islands by a shorter route. Nine months had passed without his discovering the shorter route and without his reaching the Mo-

luccas. There was nothing to complain of, therefore, in view
of Magellan's being obviously at a loss, because the sworn
and salaried inspectors of the King insisted upon their commander's at least partly lifting the veil which occluded his
"great secret"; no occasion for him to resent their demanding that he should lay his cards on the table in token that he
was straightforward. It was both natural and reasonable for
the Spanish officers to request their chief to have done with
secrecy, to hold council with them round a table and discuss
the subsequent course of the fleet—or, as Juan Sebastian del
Cano subsequently put the matter in his report, "que tomase
consejo con sus oficiales y que diese la derrota a donde que-
ría ir."

But Magellan—this being both his torment and his fault—
dared not show his cards so long as he did not know whether
he held a strong suit of trumps. He could not appeal to
Schöner's globe, since there the "paso" was erroneously depicted as being in the fortieth parallel of latitude. Now that
he had deposed Juan de Cartagena, he could not say: "I was
led astray by false reports, and have led you astray likewise."
He could not face questions about the exact situation of the
promised "paso," because he himself did not know where it
was. He must feign blindness and deafness, must keep his
mouth shut, prepared for a counterstroke should these inconvenient inquiries press him too closely. Substantially the
situation was as follows: The King's controllers, weary of
his evasions, wanted to pluck him by the sleeve and to insist
on holding him to account for his future dealings with the
five ships and two hundred and sixty men entrusted to him.
Magellan, on his side, could not allow himself to be held to

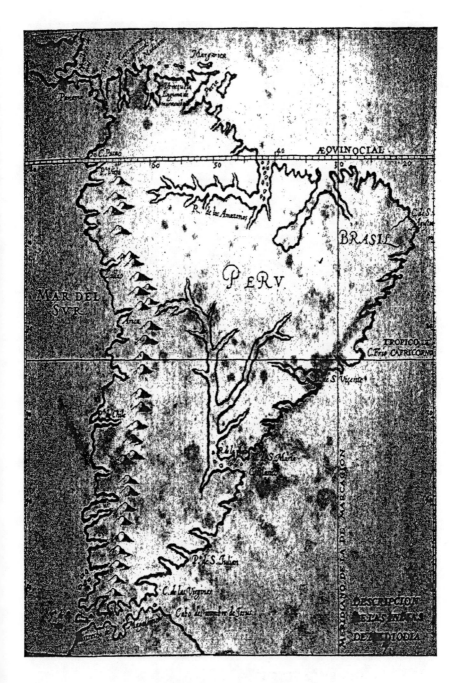

MAP OF SOUTH AMERICA
Copper engraving from de Bry's Travel Book (1624)

SOUTH AMERICA

Detail from the map of the world in Sebastian Münster's Cosmography
(Basle, 1544)

account until he had discovered the "paso," could not call such a council as the Spanish captains wanted without forfeiting his credit and losing his authority.

Right, therefore, was clearly on the side of the officers; and it was not idle curiosity but a plain discharge of their duty when they showed mistrust of Magellan and anxiety about the fate of the fleet. Urgency was justified by the admiral's previous shifts. To their honour it must be said that the Spanish captains did not make a dastardly attack upon the admiral. They gave plain warning before having recourse to violence. They had waited week after week for a council; and not until they found that Magellan, without consulting them, took a decisive step and issued orders to winter in Port San Julian, did they make up their minds to use strong measures in order to force an answer from one who maintained so stubborn a silence. They gave him a last hint that their patience was exhausted, a hint which Magellan could have understood had he wished to do so. Hoping by a courteous gesture to assuage the captains' anger at his arbitrary orders, he formally invited them to attend mass with him on Easter Sunday, and then to join him at dinner on the flag-ship. The Spaniards, however, would not allow themselves to be fobbed off in this way. The hidalgo Fernão de Magalhães had, they considered, obtained his proud title of Knight of the Order of Santiago by fraud; they themselves were experienced navigators and high officials of the King of Spain who had sailed with him for nine months without having once been invited to give their opinions as to the course of the fleet; so they declined his invitation to dinner. Indeed, they did not even decline, omitting this courtesy. Without troubling to explain that they were not coming to dinner, Juan de Cartagena, Gaspar Quesada, Luis de Mendoza, and Antonio de Coca, the captains appointed by King Charles, contemptuously ignored the invitation. Their places at his table remained vacant, their plates untouched. Magellan sat at board with, as only companion, his cousin Alvaro de Mesquita, whom Magellan had, on his own authority, made captain of the "San Antonio" after dismissing de Coca as "untrustworthy." The dinner party was a frost. By their deliberate and collective insult, Magellan's captains had warned him once more that they stood together, and that he was alone against them all. They had thrown down the gauntlet.

Magellan could not fail to understand the challenge, but nothing could shake this man's iron nerve. Without showing anger or disappointment, he ate his dinner quietly with his kinsman, issued the customary orders on the flag-ship, and, when night fell, lay down to sleep. Soon the lights were extinguished; in the shadows of the bay the five ships lay motionless like slumbering leviathans; so profound was the darkness of this long wintry night, when the heavy clouds hung low, that from the deck of one the outline of the others could scarcely be discerned. A sullen darkness veiled all. There was nothing to be heard above the plashing of the waves; no one on watch was aware that at midnight a boat with muffled oars had set out from one of the ships to approach the "San Antonio"; no one could suspect that the three royal captains, Juan de Cartagena, Gaspar Quesada, and Antonio de Coca, were in this boat, advancing to the attack. The plan of the mutineers had been well thought out. They knew that nothing but overwhelming force would enable them to press to

the wall so bold and resolute an adversary as Magellan. Very
sagaciously had Charles V appointed the Spanish captains in
large majority. When the fleet sailed, only one of the ships,
the flag-ship, was under Portuguese command, the four
others being under the control of Spaniards.

The Emperor's arrangement had, however, been arbitrar-
ily changed by Magellan, who had first degraded Juan de
Cartagena, replacing him by Antonio de Coca on the "San
Antonio," and had then dismissed the latter and appointed
Cousin Mesquita as captain in his place. With these two
large ships at his disposal, he was master of the fleet, all
the more since Serrão, captain of the fifth ship, the "Santiago," was one of his supporters. To the mutineers it seemed
that there was only one way of depriving the admiral of his
advantage, only one way of re-establishing the Emperor's
will. They must regain control of the "San Antonio" by
deposing the improperly appointed Alvaro de Mesquita—if
possible without shedding blood. Then the Spaniards would
be in control of three ships against Magellan's two, and could
hold the admiral at bay until he agreed to give them the desired information.

This scheme was carried into effect with as much care as
it had been planned. With a crew of thirty armed men, the
boat drew alongside the sleeping "San Antonio." All climbed
on board by rope ladders, led by Juan de Cartagena and Antonio de Coca. Both of them having captained this ship, they
knew where to find the commander's cabin. Before Mesquita
could get out of bed, he was surrounded by men with drawn
swords, who put him in irons and thrust him into the purser's
cabin. By now some of the crew of the "San Antonio" were

awake. One of them, Maestre Juan de Lorriaga, realizing that treachery was afoot, bluntly asked Quesada what business he was about. Quesada answered with six dagger-thrusts, and Lorriaga fell bleeding to the deck. All the Portuguese on board were clapped in irons. Thus Magellan's supporters were put out of action. Now, in order to win over the rest of the crew, Quesada had the storeroom opened, and allowed the men to supply themselves with ample rations of wine and bread. Except for the stabbing of Lorriaga, which made what had been intended to be a kidnapping into a bloody rebellion, everything went off according to plan. Juan de Cartagena, Gaspar Quesada, and Antonio de Coca returned tranquilly to their ships and got them ready for any eventuality, leaving the "San Antonio" in command of a man whose name now turns up for the first time, Juan Sebastian del Cano. At this hour he was summoned to hinder the realization of Magellan's idea; but, on a day to come, Destiny would choose him to complete Magellan's work.

The ships lay undisturbed once more in the shadow of the bay, like slumbering leviathans. No noise had been made and no light had been shown to betray what had taken place.

The gloomy dawn of these inhospitable regions at wintertide broke. The five ships were anchored in the icy prison of the bay. By no outward sign could Magellan be led to suspect that his faithful cousin and friend, with all the other Portuguese of the "San Antonio," were in irons, and that a mutineer was in command. The usual flag waved at the masthead, there was nothing outwardly changed, and on the admiral's ship the routine of the day began as usual. As on every other morning, Magellan sent a boat ashore from the "Trinidad" to fetch the daily supplies of wood and water for the various members of the fleet. As on every other morning, this boat called first on the "San Antonio," which always sent a couple of its crew ashore for the same purpose. It was strange, however, that when the boat drew near the "San Antonio" no rope ladder was lowered, nor did any of the seamen appear; and when the oarsmen angrily hailed the decks, telling the lazy lubbers to look alive, there came the amazing reply that on the "San Antonio" they no longer took orders from Magellan, but only from Captain Gaspar Quesada. So astounding was this answer, that the boat promptly returned to the flag-ship to report to the admiral.

Magellan immediately reviewed the situation. The "San Antonio" was in the hands of mutineers. He had been overreached. But even so murderous a surprise could not quicken the pulse, make tremulous the hand, or cloud the thoughts of this unbending man. His first business was to survey the gravity of the peril. How many of the ships were on his side, and how many had gone over to the mutineers? He sent back the rowboat to inspect. The "San Antonio," the "Concepción," and the "Victoria" all declared themselves for the rebels; only the inconsiderable "Santiago" was true to him. That meant three against two, or even three against one, since the "Santiago" would not count if there were a fight. The game was lost, then, or any other man would have regarded it as lost; the enterprise to which Magellan had devoted years of his life had been ruined betwixt night and morning. He could not make a voyage into the unknown with nothing but his flag-ship; he could not get on without the other craft, nor could he enforce their obedience. No help could be expected in waters which they were the first Europeans to visit. There were but two possibilities open in this disastrous position. One, the more reasonable course, which seemed the obvious one in view of the superior strength of Magellan's opponents, was to bow before the storm and come to terms with the Spanish captains. The other alternative, heroic though absurd, was to stake everything upon the turn of a card; to attempt a decisive counterthrust, try to defeat the mutineers, futile though the prospect seemed.

Everything spoke in favour of yielding. As yet the Spanish captains had made no hostile move against the admiral, nor voiced any demands. No sign had come from their ships, no act of war. Although they had so much stronger a force at their disposal, his adversaries did not seem, thousands of miles away from home, to desire foolish and fratricidal strife. Too clearly did they recall the oath they had sworn in the church at Seville, too well were they aware how shameful was the punishment for mutiny and desertion. Such distinguished noblemen as Juan de Cartagena, Luis de Mendoza, Gaspar Quesada, and Antonio de Coca, whom the King had, in his own handwriting, appointed to positions of trust, did not wish to return to Spain with their fair names tarnished by treachery. They therefore did not build upon their superior strength, but at the outset declared themselves ready for peaceful negotiation. In seizing the "San Antonio," they had done so not with intent to begin a bloody rebellion, but only in order to exert pressure upon their chief, to compel him to break his stubborn silence, and at length to make a clear statement regarding the destination of the royal fleet.

The letter now sent to Magellan by Gaspar Quesada, as spokesman of the Spanish captains, was therefore in no sense a challenge. On the contrary, it was humbly entitled a "suplicación," a petition, and was couched in the politest terms It opened with a justification of the mutineers' actions. Solely because they were so badly treated by Magellan, had they found it necessary to seize the "San Antonio," which had been entrusted to him as admiral by His Majesty King Charles. Magellan was not for a moment to suppose that they wished to repudiate the supreme authority which the monarch had granted him. All they asked for was better treatment. If he would comply with this reasonable request, they would not only obey his orders, as their duty was, but would serve him with the utmost respect. The Spanish text of the letter is so grotesquely high-flown that literal translation is almost impossible. "Y si hasta allí le habían llamado de merced, dende en adelante le llamarían de señoría y le besarían pies y manos."

Since the Spanish captains obviously held the key position as far as armed force was concerned, this might have seemed an extremely favourable offer. But Magellan had already decided upon strong, heroic measures. With rapid insight he saw his adversaries' weak point, their sense of insecurity. Something in the tone of the letter must have disclosed that the four or five leaders of the mutiny were not firmly resolved upon proceeding to extremities, and that their hesitation made them weaker than himself despite their numerical superiority. If he seized his opportunity, if he struck like lightning, before they had ceased to hesitate and had steeled their hearts against him, he might, by supreme audacity, win the game after all.

It is necessary here to insist once more that in Magellan audacity, boldness, invariably assumed a peculiar complexion. To act boldly did not, in his case, mean to act on the heat of impulse, but to lay his plans craftily, to do the dangerous thing with the utmost caution and after most careful calculation. His most venturesome schemes were, like good steel, forged in fire and then hardened in ice. It was by this mixture of imagination and caution that, again and again, he triumphed in moments of danger. His plan was instantly formed, and the brief time before it was to be put into execution served merely to perfect the details. Magellan realized that he must do what his captains had done, he must seize one of their ships to get the upper hand once more. But their task had been comparatively easy. At dead of night, they had attacked an unsuspecting craft, a ship whose captain and crew were sleeping soundly. No one was armed for defence, not one of the seamen had a weapon to hand. Now it was daytime. Suspiciously, from the three ships of the mutineers, the captains kept watch on the flag-ship; cannon and arquebus were ready for use; the mutineers were too well acquainted with Magellan's courage not to know how likely he was to attempt a bold stroke.

They knew his courage, but they did not know his cunning. They never suspected that this swift calculator would venture a most improbable hazard, would in broad daylight with a mere handful of men try to recapture one of three heavily armed ships. It was by a brilliant ruse that he did not make this attempt upon the "San Antonio," where his cousin Mesquita lay in irons. He knew full well that that was what his enemies would expect. For that very reason, he chose the "Victoria."

Every detail of the coup was brilliantly thought out. His first step was to seize the "San Antonio's" boat which had brought Quesada's message. Thus he gained two things: should it come to blows, he had deprived the mutineers of a number of their fighters; secondly, he now had two rowboats in hand, and this apparently trifling advantage would soon prove decisive. Keeping his own boat in reserve, he sent the captured boat in command of the thoroughly trustworthy master-at-arms, the alguacil of the fleet, Gonzalo Gómez de Espinosa, with five men, to the "Victoria," carrying a letter to its commander, Luis de Mendoza.

The mutineers on board this well-armed ship had no suspicions when they saw the tiny boat approaching. What cause was there for uneasiness? How could six men attack a ship manned by sixty and commanded by so able a captain as Mendoza? They did not know that the men in the boat carried concealed weapons, nor the momentous instructions given to Gómez de Espinosa. In a leisurely way (feigned leisure, for he knew that every second was of the utmost importance), Espinosa climbed on board, and handed Captain Luis de Mendoza Magellan's letter summoning him to the flag-ship.

Mendoza read the message. He could not fail to recall how, on board the "Trinidad," Juan de Cartagena had unexpectedly been arrested. No bait should lure Luis de Mendoza into a trap. "You won't catch me going there"—"no me pillarás allá"—he said with a laugh. But this laugh ended with a hideous gurgle, for the alguacil stabbed him in the throat.

At this critical instant, Magellan having calculated time and distance to perfection, fifteen heavily armed men climbed on board. They had arrived in the "Trinidad's" own boat, under command of Duarte Barbosa. The crew of the mutineers' ship stared at the corpse of their captain, who had been cut down by another of Magellan's men even as the alguacil stabbed him. The attack was too sudden for them to concert resistance. Duarte Barbosa was already issuing orders, which the intimidated mutineers hastened to obey. In a trice the anchor was weighed, the sails were hoisted, and before the mutineers' two other ships had grasped what had befallen with this thunder from a clear sky, the "Victoria," as the admiral's lawful prize, was steering to take up her position beside the flag-ship. Now the "Trinidad," the "Victoria," and the "Santiago" faced the "San Antonio" and the "Concepción," guarding the mouth of the harbour to prevent any attempt at desertion.

By this brilliant counterstroke the balance had been readjusted, the seemingly lost game had been won. The captains had been outmanœuvred, and for them there remained only three possibilities: to fly, to fight, or to surrender.

As already explained, the admiral had taken precautions against flight. Nor had the remaining mutineers any stomach for battle. Magellan's coup had undermined the courage of his opponents. In vain did Gaspar Quesada, armed with lance and shield, call upon his men. They were thoroughly cowed, and refused to obey. Magellan had merely to send a boat, for resistance to collapse both on the "Concepción" and on the "San Antonio." Within a few hours Alvaro de Mesquita was freed from his irons, and the surviving mutinous captains were given a dose of the same medicine.

The tension had been dispelled with the first flash, like that of a thunderstorm in summer. Perhaps this phase of open struggle had been the easier part, for now, in accordance with martial and maritime law, atonement must follow. There must have been a terrible conflict in Magellan's mind. The King had expressly endowed him with right of life and death, but the chief among the guilty enjoyed the special confidence of the Crown. To maintain his own authority he must inflict severe punishment, and yet he could not punish all the mutineers. How would it be possible for him to continue the voyage if, as he was entitled to do, he made an example of one-fifth of his men? Thousands of miles from home, in these inhospitable regions, the admiral could not venture to cut off his own right arm; he would have to take the guilty along with him; he must win them over by kindness, and yet he must, at the same time, terrify them by severity.

Magellan resolved to have only one victim, and he chose Gaspar Quesada, the man who had used arms and stabbed Juan de Lorriaga, maestre on board the "San Antonio." The proceedings against the offender were formally opened. The writers, the escriberos, took their places; the witnesses were summoned; and with the same prolixity as if the trial had been held in Seville or in Saragossa, the clerks made notes. Mesquita, as chairman of the court, opened the case against

Gaspar Quesada, former captain in the armada, for mutiny and attempted murder. Magellan passed sentence. Gaspar Quesada was condemned to death, and the only grace the admiral would accord the Spanish nobleman was that of being executed by the sword instead of by the garrotte.

But who was to act as executioner? It would be hard to induce any member of the crew. At length a man was found to consent, at a horrible price. Quesada's servant, Luis de Molino, had participated in the homicidal attack on Lorriaga (who did not die of his wounds until more than two months later). Now a pardon was offered to Molino if he would cut off Quesada's head. The choice between being himself executed and slaying his master may have been a cruel one, but in the end he declared himself willing. With one blow he struck off Quesada's head, and thus saved his own life. In accordance with the barbarous practice of the day, Quesada's body was quartered, as Mendoza's had already been, the quarters being spitted on poles. Thus for the first time were these dreadful customs of the Tower of London and those of other places of public execution in Europe introduced into the Antarctic.

There remained another sentence for Magellan to pass, and it is hard to say whether this was more clement or more cruel than death by the sword. Juan de Cartagena, the real leader of the mutiny, and a priest who tried to foment a second mutiny were no less guilty than Quesada had been, but even Magellan's courage was not equal to having these two offenders put to death. He was unwilling to hand over to the executioner the man whom King Charles had appointed as "conjuncta persona," or (being a pious Catholic) to shed the blood of an anointed priest. Nor did it seem to him feasible to carry the pair of them half round the world in chains. He decided, therefore, to maroon them. When the fleet set sail once more, they were left behind on the shore at Port San Julian, furnished with a supply of food and wine, it being left to God Almighty to decide whether they should die there.

Was Magellan right or wrong to pass these sentences at Port San Julian? Was it fair, the trial of which his cousin Mesquita kept the minutes, and which allowed no scope for defence? What view are we to take of the subsequent utterances of the Spanish officers who got back to Seville, and who declared that Magellan paid the alguacil and certain members of his crew twelve ducats for their murderous onslaught on Mendoza, also promising to divide among them the possessions of the slaughtered nobleman? When these assertions were made, Magellan, being dead, could not contradict them. Immediately a contentious deed has been done, conflicting accounts of it are apt to be circulated; and when we find that historians incline to justify Magellan, we must not forget that the victor is almost invariably held to have been right.

Had Magellan failed to find the strait of which he was in search, had he failed to complete his exploits, he would have been bluntly accused of murder for sweeping out of the way a Spanish captain who raised objections to his dangerous adventure. Magellan, however, was endorsed by a success which conferred on him immortal fame, whereas those who died ingloriously have been forgotten, and the chroniclers.

judging by accepted standards, approve his harshness and un-yieldingness.

Magellan's bloody sentence was to become a precedent for Francis Drake, the most brilliant of his successors. When, fifty-seven years later, this British hero, making the same dangerous voyage, was menaced in like manner by mutiny, he landed in this unlucky Port San Julian, and paid a sinister tribute to Magellan's martial activities by imitating them. Drake was perfectly well informed as to what had happened during his predecessor's voyage, was familiar with the min-utes of the former trial and with Magellan's pitiless dealings with the leading mutineers. It is probable that he found in Port San Julian the very block on which, two generations before, Quesada had been decapitated. Drake's rebellious captain was named Thomas Doughty, and, like Cartagena, he had been insubordinate during the voyage. Sentence was passed on him in this very same "puerto negro" of San Julian, the same sentence—death. Drake gave his former friend the choice between dying honourably under the sword as Gas-par Quesada had done or being marooned like Juan de Car-tagena. Doughty, having also read the story of Magellan's voyage, knew that no trace had ever been discovered of Cartagena or of the priest who was marooned with him, and that presumably they had died a slow, painful death. He chose, therefore, like a brave man, to die by the sword, and once more a head rolled in the sand. Is it not the eternal doom of man that his most memorable achievements should so often be stained with blood, and that those who are harshest are those who usually accomplish the greatest deeds?

Chapter Nine

THE GREAT MOMENT COMES

April 7, 1520–November 28, 1520

The Great Moment Comes

FOR four or five months Magellan's fleet was secluded by winter in the harbour of misfortune. Time moved on leaden feet in this solitude, and the admiral, doubtless aware that nothing tends to make men dissatisfied and unruly so much as boredom, kept his crew hard at work. The ships, which had now been almost a year on the way, were thoroughly overhauled; fresh timber was cut, beams were made; perhaps he invented superfluous tasks if only to make his subordinates feel sure that the voyage would soon be resumed, and that, from these wintry wastes, they would find their way to the Fortunate Isles.

At length there came the first sign of spring. Throughout these frosty and fog-ridden weeks, the men had come to the conclusion that they had reached a No-Man's-Land, a place utterly deserted by man and beast; and their dread at a sojourn in a primeval den remote from human kind may have increased their gloom. One morning, however, there appeared on a neighbouring hill a strange figure, that of a man whom at first they hardly recognized as one of their own kind, for in their alarm and surprise he appeared to them at least twice the ordinary human stature—"duobus humanum superantes staturam," as Peter Martyr writes. The statement is confirmed by Pigafetta in the following words: "So tall was he, that we reached only to his waist-belt. He was well enough made, and had a broad face, which was painted red, with yellow rings round his eyes, and two heart-shaped spots on the cheeks. His hair was short and was coloured white; and he was dressed in the skins of an animal cleverly stitched together."

Especially astonished were the Spaniards by the gigantic feet of the huge creature, and because of this "big-foot" (patagão) the natives were called Patagonians and the country Patagonia. But the first alarm at the son of Anak was soon dispelled. The enormous man clad in skins stretched out his arms with a grin, danced and sang, and busily sprinkled sand upon his white hair. Magellan, being well acquainted with the ways of savages, recognized the signs of a desire to be friendly, and told one of the sailors to dance in like manner and to scatter sand upon his head. To the delight of the worn and weary mariners, the wild man accepted this pantomime as a token of welcome, and drew near. After the "Tempest," the Trinculos had at length found their Caliban, someone who could provide them with diversion in the wilderness. For when they unexpectedly held a metallic mirror before the nose of the good-natured giant, he jumped with the surprise of seeing his own countenance for the first time; jumped violently backward, and tumbled down, dragging four of the sailors with him. His huge appetite made them forget the smallness of their own rations. They stared at this Gargantua as he swallowed a bucket of water at a draught, and stuffed half a hamper of ship's biscuit into his mouth as he might have stuffed one or two gingerbread nuts. What a shout did they give when, to the horror of the bystanders, on being presented with a couple of rats, he devoured them alive, skin and hair included! But the savage and the crew were inspired with mutual sympathy, and when Magellan bestowed a few little bells on the visitor, he hastened off to fetch some other "giants," as well as one or two "giantesses."

His nonchalance was to prove disastrous to the children of nature. Like Columbus and the other conquistadors, Magellan had received strict orders from the Casa de Contratación to collect specimens, not only of plants and ores, but also of all new varieties of man that he might encounter on the journey, and bring back some of them to Spain. To the sailors it seemed that the attempt to catch one of these "giants" alive would be as dangerous as tackling a whale with their bare hands. Anxiously they crept close to the Patagãos, but again and again, at the last moment, their courage failed them. At length a mean trick occurred to them. Magellan loaded the natives with presents, so that their hands were full; then he offered them a pair of irons, and, as they were unable to hold these, showed how they could be fitted upon the legs. A couple of strokes of the hammer riveted the bolts, and the two unlucky savages were prisoners before they realized their position. They were pleased, at first, with the beautiful rings round their ankles, which made merry music. But now it was easy to sandbag them, since, fettered, they were no longer dangerous. In vain did they howl, thrash with their arms, and call Setebos, their Great Spirit, to their aid. (Shakespeare borrowed this name from the Patagonians.) The Emperor wanted them as curios, so like pole-axed oxen they were borne on board the ships, where they perished miserably from lack of proper food.

By this perfidious behaviour on the part of the representatives of Christian civilization, good understanding with the savages was destroyed. The Patagonians kept aloof from the deceivers, and when a troop of Spaniards pursued them on one occasion (Pigafetta's report lacks clearness about this matter) to catch or to visit some of the Patagonian women, the white men were forcibly repulsed, and one of the sailors paid for the attempt with his life.

Neither to the indigenes nor to the Spaniards did this unhappy Port San Julian bring anything but disaster. Magellan had no luck here. The blood-stained strand was fraught with doom. "Let us get away," was the cry of the crew. On with the voyage, on with the voyage, was Magellan's supreme desire. The impatience of both parties increased as the days grew longer. As soon as the worst storms of winter were over, the captain-general made a move. He sent the handiest of his ships, the little "Santiago," under the command of Serrão, to sail southward along the coast on an exploring voyage, even as Noah sent the dove from the Ark. Serrão was to come back and report after a specified number of days. He overstayed his time, and Magellan impatiently watched the sea. The first tidings, however, came from the land. Two strange, tottering figures were seen on one of the hills. Believing them to be Patagonians, the sailors made ready their crossbows. But the naked men, half frozen, almost starved, exhausted and spectral, shouted words in Spanish. They were two of the crew of the "Santiago" and brought evil tidings. Serrão had got as far as a river which he named the Rio de Santa Cruz. It was conveniently situated, and there were abundant supplies of fish; but when he was about to continue his reconnaissance a squall from the east drove the ship ashore. Only one life was lost, that of the captain's Negro slave. The rest, thirty-seven in all, got safely to land. They were waiting at the mouth of the Rio de Santa Cruz in the extremest need while the two speakers had made their way along the coast to Port San Julian. Chosen for the task as the strongest of the party, they had just managed to keep themselves alive by devouring roots and grass.

Magellan promptly sent a boat to the rescue. The ship-wrecked men were brought back. They were saved, but their ship, the most mobile in the fleet, had been utterly destroyed. She was a total loss, and like every loss in this uttermost part of the world she was irreplaceable. When, on August 24, 1520, Magellan gave orders to weigh anchor and leave the unlucky Port San Julian, giving a last glance to the two poor wretches he had marooned, in his secret soul he perhaps cursed the day and the hour when he had landed here. One of his ships was sunk, two of his captains had been killed, a whole year had passed since the beginning of a voyage in which nothing had been gained, nothing discovered, nothing done.

These must have been the gloomiest days in Magellan's life, perhaps the only ones in which he, whose faith was usually not to be shaken, secretly despaired. His uncertainty was betrayed by the pretended firmness with which he declared himself resolved to sail down the Patagonian coast as far as the seventy-fifth parallel, and only then, if he had not yet discovered the way through, to turn eastward and take the customary route to the Indies round the Cape of Good Hope. This was the first time on which he admitted to his officers that there was a possibility of retreat, that the strait of which they were in search perhaps did not exist, or existed only in Antarctic waters. Obviously his innermost conviction had been undermined; his intuitive certainty that he would find the "paso" had at length been dispelled.

Seldom in history has anyone been in a more deplorable situation than was Magellan, when, after holding on his southward course for two days, he halted once more at the mouth of the Rio de Santa Cruz, to spend there another two months inactive until the winter was fully over. Only from the vantage point of our better knowledge can we perceive how paradoxical was this determination. Here was a man inspired with a great idea, who, misled by an erroneous report, had staked his life upon finding a navigable way from the Atlantic Ocean into the Pacific, and thus becoming the first to circumnavigate the globe. Thanks to his strength of will he had overcome material opposition, had found helpers for his almost unrealizable scheme, had (through the suggestive power of his plan) extorted a fleet from the monarch of an alien land, and had sailed this fleet farther south along the American coast than any navigator before him. He had mastered the winds and the waves, suppressed a mutiny; no obstacles, no disappointments, had, so far, been able to shake his belief that he must be close to the "paso," the goal of his dreams. Now, when on the threshold of victory, this man, who was usually so clear-sighted, lost his "hunch." It was as if the gods, regarding him with disfavour, had spitefully hoodwinked him. On August 26, 1520, when Magellan again called a halt which was to last a couple of months, he was already close to his destination, was approaching the entrance to the strait. Only two more degrees of latitude, only two days' voyage after eleven months, no more than one hundred and fifty miles or so added to the thousands he had already travelled, would have brought him to that of which he was in search, and have filled him with rejoicing. But, through the spite of Destiny, the unhappy man had no inkling of this.

For two tedious months he waited off the barren, godforsaken coast at the mouth of the Santa Cruz, like one who, caught in a blizzard and not knowing where he is, waits and freezes within a stone's throw of his own house, unaware that a few steps would bring him safe to shelter. Two months, two endless, senseless months, did Magellan brood in this desolate spot, wondering whether he would or would not ever reach the "paso." Yet only two days south was the Strait of Magellan, which would bear his name for all eternity. Until the last moment he who, with Promethean gaze, was to unveil the last great mystery on the surface of our planet, had, like Prometheus, to endure the rending of the eagle's claws of doubt.

All the more splendid would be the reaction when it came, for bliss is more glorious when we rise from the depths of despair. On October 18, 1520, Magellan gave orders to get the fleet under way once more. Before the start, mass was said, the men having first been confessed. After the ceremony, the anchors were weighed and the ships steered south under full press of sail. Even now they were baffled for two days by head-winds, and every inch had to be conquered. At length the wind shifted to the north, and they made good progress. But the land off which they coasted did not cheer their hearts with a brave show of green, for sand and rocks, such as had depressed them all the winter, stretched inhospitably before their eyes. Sand and rocks, rocks and sand. Then, on October 21, 1520, they sighted a cape with white cliffs rising above a strangely indented shore. In honour of the day, St. Ursula's, Magellan christened it Cabo de las Virgenes. On the farther side of it they entered a deep bay with black waters. The fleet sailed into this bay. Strange, harsh, and tremendous was the prospect. There were steep hills, uneasy-looking and fissured. Far in the distance were snow-clad peaks, such as they had not seen since their last winter in Europe. How dead was the landscape! No sign of human life, no vegetation; naught but the howling and roaring of the wind disturbed the silence of this ghostly spot. The men looked dubiously at the dark inlet. To all of them it seemed absurd to suppose that this land-locked bay, encircled by mountains, its waters black as Hades, could lead to the Mar del Sur, the bright, the sunny southern seas. Unanimously the pilots declared that the deep indentation in the land could be nothing but a fiord, like those found on the coast of Norway. Why waste time and energy upon exploring it, or upon soundings? Too many days and weeks had already been spent in reconnaissances along the Patagonian coast, to find that none of the bays led into the expected strait. Let there be no more hesitation. Let the chief give orders to sail on along the coast, and then, if the "estrecho" did not soon disclose itself, return home while the weather was still warm; or, if he did not do that, let him make for the Cape of Good Hope and round it into the Indian Ocean.

But Magellan, obsessed by his idea of a hidden strait, insisted upon thoroughly exploring this remarkable bay. Reluctantly his companions heard the order, "for we all believed that it was a blind alley" (Pigafetta's words). The flag-ship and the "Victoria" stayed behind, anchoring on the southern side of the inlet. The "San Antonio" and the "Concepción" were instructed to sail as far westward as they could, but to return and report in five days at the utmost. Time was precious, for supplies were running short. Magellan could no longer allow a fortnight for exploration, as he had in the estuary of the Rio de la Plata. Five days was all he could spare for the adventure.

The dramatic moment had come. Magellan intended the "Trinidad" and the "Victoria" to cruise round the outer part of the bay until the "San Antonio" and the "Concepción" returned from their exploratory voyage. Once more, however, nature showed herself adverse to the revealing of her last secret. The wind freshened to a gale, and then to one of the hurricanes common in this part of the world, of which the Spanish maps of the times warningly assure us "no hay buenas estaciones"—there are no good seasons here. In a trice the waters of the bay were lashed by the storm, the ships dragged their anchors, had to weigh them, and to make sail for the open, lucky not to be dashed on the rocks. For a day, and then for another, they were in great peril. But it was not the risk to these two ships which disturbed Magellan, who continued to weather the storm as best he could in the mouth of the bay. It was the "San Antonio" and the "Concepción" about which he felt grave anxiety. The hurricane must have overtaken them in the narrows, where they would have no room to tack, no possibility of anchoring or of seeking shelter. Save for a miracle, they must be driven ashore and dashed to pieces.

Intense must have been the leader's disquietude, his impatience, during these days and hours when he was awaiting the decision of Fate. One day passed, and there was no sign. Another day, and the explorers had not returned. Then came a third and a fourth day of waiting. Magellan knew that if these two craft had been lost, all was lost. He could not venture to continue his voyage to the west with no more than two ships. His achievement, his dream, would have been wrecked as well as they.

At length the look-out man at the masthead hailed the deck. Alas, it was not the returning members of the fleet whom he had espied, but merely a pillar of smoke in the distance. What a terrible moment. A smoke-signal could only mean shipwrecked men calling for aid. The "San Antonio" and the "Concepción" must have foundered, and with them his whole enterprise, in this nameless bay.

Magellan gave orders to lower the boats, row towards the point from which the signal came, and save what lives could still be saved. But now came a turn in his fortunes. It was like the glorious passage in *Tristan and Isolde* when the plaintive, the despairing death-melody of the shepherd's flute is transformed as it swells into a pæan of happiness. A sail! A sail! A ship! A ship! God be praised, one ship is saved! No, both ships, both, the "San Antonio" and the "Concepción" are coming back, safe and sound. Hardly have Magellan and his companions caught sight of them, when, on the port bow, they see flashes, one, two, three, followed by the thunderous notes of large bombards, re-echoed from the hills. What has happened? Why are his subordinates, who have been strictly instructed to avoid wasting powder, firing one salvo after another? Why, thinks Magellan, who can hardly believe his eyes, are the returning craft dressed with flags? Why are the captains and the crews waving and shouting? What are they trying to say? Still too far away to hear the words or understand the signs, but those who have been so anxiously awaiting the return of the expedition are confident—Magellan most of all—that the language is that of triumph.

Yes, it was the yearned-for tidings which the "San Antonio" and the "Concepción" were bringing. With immense relief, Magellan listened to Serrão, now captain of the "Concepción." The ships had had a bad time to begin with. They had sailed deep into the bay when the storm broke. Though they promptly shortened canvas, they were driven farther and farther to the west, and it seemed inevitable that they would be wrecked upon the rocks which faced them. But, at the last moment, they became aware that the bay was not closed, for behind a headland a channel opened, the "First Narrows." Through this channel, where the sea was comparatively calm, they entered a second bay, followed by the "Second Narrows"; and the widening and narrowing of the waterway happened again and again. For three days they continued their voyage without reaching the end of this re-

markable strait. Though they had not found the western outlet, they had not seen anything to show that they were in
an estuary. The water was persistently salt, and the ebb and
flow of the tide continued regularly on the sides of the channel. It did not narrow steadily as the estuary of the Rio de la
Plata had done. On the contrary, after the narrows there
always recurred a new expansion. Practically certain, therefore, that this fiord, this canal, must lead into the Mar del Sur,
into the ocean which, a few years before, Núñez de Balboa
had been the first of all Europeans to behold.

Better news could not have reached the sorely tried Magellan after a year of tedious waiting and fruitless search.
We can only guess how immense must have been the relief.
He had almost surrendered to despair, had contemplated
leaving the South American coast for the Cape of Good
Hope, and must have made many fervent prayers to God and
the Saints. Now, when faith and hope had almost come to
an end, illusions were disclosing themselves as truth and
dreams as reality. Let there be no more hesitation. Heave
anchor and make all sail to the west. One more salvo in
honour of Emperor Charles, one more prayer to the Great
Admiral under whose command he was making his venturesome voyage. Then, with steady courage, forward into the
labyrinth. If, out of these Acherontine waters he could find
an exit into the new ocean, he would be the first man in
the world to discover the passage. Followed by the other
three ships, he steered into the strait, which, with a reference
to the calendar, he called Todos los Santos, but which posterity was to name the Strait of Magellan.

A strange, a ghostly sight it must have been to see these four ships gliding noiselessly into the dark and silent bay, which theirs was the first fleet to enter. Profound indeed was the silence. Like loadstone mountains the hills lined the channel; gloomy were the skies which here are almost perpetually clouded; overshadowed was the sea; like Charon's boat upon the Styx, shadows among shadows, steered the ships soundlessly through this Plutonic world. From afar gleamed the snowy peaks, white giants whose icy breath was blown to the voyagers by the wind. No living creature showed itself, yet surely there must be human beings somewhere in the region, since by night on the southward side of the channel could be seen flickering flames, for which reason the explorers called the country Tierra del Fuego, the Land of Fire. (These unceasing fires were seen for centuries to come. They flamed because the Fuegians did not know how to make fire, and therefore burned wood and dried grasses perpetually in their huts.) But no voice was heard, nor any moving form seen. When Magellan sent a boat for some purpose to the shore, the men found no signs of human habitation, but only an abiding-place of the dead, a few dozen forsaken tombs. The one animal they stumbled upon was dead, a mighty whale whose corpse had been washed ashore. He had come hither only to die in this domain of everlasting autumn. With astonishment the explorers stared into the spectral stillness, into vistas which looked as if they belonged to some dead and cold star. Sail on, sail on. Driven slowly before the breeze, the ships glided through the untravelled waters. Again and again they cast the lead, to reach no bottom; again and again they looked ahead to see if the bay would close in against them, with no free channel. But at each fresh turn, it remained open, the charmed passage meandering farther and farther.

Still, this part of the voyage, like the rest, was gloomy as well as dangerous. The strait did not in the least resemble the broad convenient passage which, in their comfortable studies, the home-keeping cosmographers of Nuremberg—Schöner and, doubtless before him, Behaim—had inscribed on their globes. Only for short, and by euphemism, is the Strait of Magellan called a strait. It really consists of a tangled, labyrinthine confusion of bays and other indentations, of fiords and complicated arms of the sea, and is navigable only with great skill and good fortune. The bays become pointed, or agglomerate into peculiar and incalculable shapes. Three or four times the passage forks, so that it is hardly possible to decide which can be the real way through, the channel that leads west, or north, or south. Shallows have to be avoided, rocks skirted, and again and again a wild squall comes to whip the waters, blowing down from the sinister hills. That is why, for so long, the Strait of Magellan has been a terror to mariners. In dozens of subsequent expeditions, ships were wrecked upon these inhospitable, still desolate strands; and nothing can testify better to Magellan's exceptional skill as navigator than that he, who was the first to traverse the strait which bears his name, remained for years the last to pass through it without mishap. When we recall the unhandiness of his ships, with their clumsy bellying sails and their wooden tillers, and remind ourselves how they had to seek out a way through the arteries and lateral passages,

and reassemble at appointed spots—doing all this at an in-
opportune season and harassed by storms—we cannot but
wonder at his success, and our wonder is shared by generations of seamen.

On this occasion, as throughout Magellan's career, he
showed his genius for patience, and his inviolable foresight
no less. He spent a month exploring the "paso." Unhurry-
ingly he studied the various channels, although inward impulses were urging him on to make an end of it and reach
the southern seas. Repeatedly, when the channel forked, he
divided the fleet, sending two ships to the north while the
others investigated the south. As if this lonely man, born under a dark star, knew that he could never trust his luck, he
did not leave to chance his choice among the many ways
that offered, or decide matters by spinning a coin. He explored all the seaways to find the right one, and, while hitherto he had prevailed through the strength of his imagination, he now triumphed thanks to the soberest of the virtues—
stubbornness.

The First Narrows had been successfully passed, and the
Second Narrows as well. Once more Magellan reached a
parting of the ways, where the widening passage divided
to right and to left. Once more he split his fleet in twain. The
"San Antonio" and the "Concepción" were to try the south-
eastern route, while he himself in the flag-ship, accompanied
by the "Victoria," would follow the south-western channel.
They were to reassemble, after five days at most, at the
mouth of a little river which, because of the multitude of
sardines it contained, they proposed to name the River of

Sardines. Detailed instructions were given to the captains. The ships were ready to make sail, when something unexpected occurred. Magellan summoned the captains to report upon the amount of stores that were available, and to ask their opinion.

Ask their opinion? What could have happened? Why, of a sudden, this democratic gesture? Why did the dictator, who hitherto had been unwilling to admit that his captains had any right to ask a question or to dispute a command, now treat his officers as comrades on so trifling an occasion? In truth, nothing could have been more logical than this change of front. After an overwhelming triumph, dictators often find it advisable to let humane considerations hold sway for a while, since now the granting of the right of free speech will serve only to safeguard their position.

Having found the "paso," the "estrecho," the admiral no longer had any reason to dread questions. Since, at long last, he held the trumps, he could meet the others more than half-way and show his cards. It is always easier to be just in days of good fortune than in days of bad. The taciturn, self-contained man therefore broke the long silence. His mystery having been made public, he could afford to be frank and communicative.

The captains appeared according to orders, and delivered their report. It was not encouraging. Supplies were running short, and at best could not last for more than three months longer. Magellan replied. The first aim of the voyage had been achieved, he said; the passage into the South Seas had been found. Of that there could be no doubt. What did his

PASSAGE THROUGH STRAIT OF MAGELLAN
After a woodcut now lost (1801)

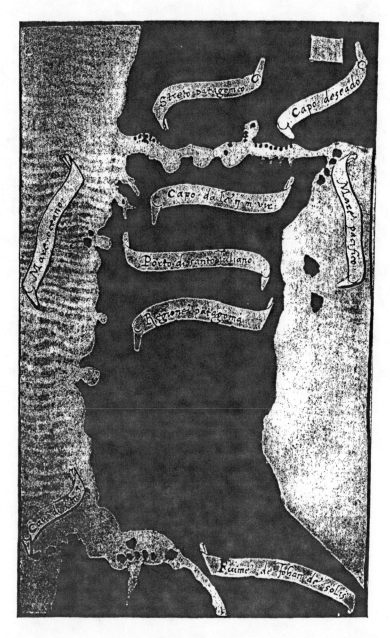

Streto patigonico C.

Capo deseado C.

Capo da 11 m. uir.

Mar del paçifico

Porto di santo Juliano

Mare oceano

Regione patagonia

Capo de 11 m.

Fiume de Johan de solis

STRAIT OF MAGELLAN, IN PIGAFETTA'S HANDWRITING
THE UPPER PART IS SOUTH; THE LOWER, NORTH
From the Ambrosian MS. *in Milan*

captains think? Would it be better for the fleet to be content with having done so much, or should they go on, in order to finish what he had promised to the Emperor, find the Spice Islands, and take possession of them for Spain? He could not deny that the shortage of provisions entailed serious danger. Still, great would be the renown and enormous the wealth that would await them on the successful completion of their task. He himself was undismayed. He wished, however, to come to a final decision as to whether they should return home with the honours they had gained, or, for the sake of still more honours, they should push forward to the goal. What did the officers think?

There is no record of the answers of the various captains and pilots, but we are not likely to go far wrong in supposing that few of them had much to say. Their memories of the beach at Port San Julian and of the sight of the quartered corpses of their Spanish comrades must still have been vivid, and they cannot have felt much inclined to run counter to the will of this Portuguese who had shown himself to be a man of iron. One voice, however, was raised in opposition, that of Estevão Gomez, pilot of the "San Antonio," Portuguese by nationality, and, it is supposed, a kinsman of the admiral. Gomez unhesitatingly declared that, since to all seeming the "paso" had now been discovered, it would be better to return to Spain, and come back with a freshly equipped fleet to take advantage of the newly disclosed strait leading to the Spice Islands. Their present craft, he considered, were no longer seaworthy, were inadequately supplied, and no one could tell how far it might be to their destination across this new and unknown ocean, the Mar del Sur. They should not fail to remember that unless they speedily got to port across the waters of the trackless sea, all on board the fleet would perish miserably from starvation.

The advice of Estevão Gomez was eminently reasonable, and it seems probable that Pigafetta (who was always inclined to regard as suspect anyone who dissented from his idol Magellan) did the experienced navigator an injustice by accusing him of cowardice. From the logical, the objective outlook, Gomez's proposal to return forthwith to enjoy the honours they had won was eminently sound. Had it been accepted, the commander and nearly two hundred other members of the expedition who were foredoomed to perish would have got home safely. Magellan, however, was more interested in his imperishable deed than in his mortal life. One who wishes to act heroically, must act unreasonably. The leader again took up his parable. No doubt they were faced with difficulties; they would probably suffer hunger and other hardships; but (and here he was strangely prophetic) "even if they had to eat the leather on the ships' yards, he would still go on, to discover what he had promised to the Emperor, and he trusted that God would aid them and give them good fortune" ("de pasar adelante y descubrir lo que había prometido"). With this bold utterance the council came to an end, and loud calls passed from ship to ship announcing that the voyage was to be continued. Privily, however, Magellan ordered the captains to conceal from their crews the grave shortage of supplies. Anyone who allowed even a hint of it to transpire would be punishable with death.

Silently the captains obeyed orders. The ships that were
to take the south-eastern channel—the "San Antonio" under
Mesquita and the "Concepción" under Serrão—could hoist
sail and depart, and soon they disappeared in the devious passage. The other two craft, Magellan's flag-ship and the "Victoria," were to have an easier time of it. They anchored at
the mouth of Sardine River, for Magellan, instead of immediately taking the south-western route, provided a well-
manned boat with stores. For a preliminary reconnaissance
in these peaceful, narrow waters, a minor craft would do
very well. Magellan ordered the commander to be back in
three days with his report; then he would have two days for
recuperation, since the two other big ships were not expected back until five days had elapsed. Magellan and his
companions had a pleasant rest in their quiet anchorage.
During the last few days, as they made their way westward,
the scenery had greatly improved. Instead of bald reefs, the
shore disclosed meadowland and forest. The outline of the
near-by hills was lofty, the ice-capped mountains were more
remote. The air was milder, and springs of fresh water re-
animated the crew, who for weeks had had nothing to drink
but the foul, brackish water in the tanks. They lay at ease
on the soft grass, watching the wonderful exploits of the
flying fish and the other denizens of the sea. There were so
many edible plants that at length they could eat their fill.
The aspect of nature was so beautiful, so pleasing, that
Pigafetta enthusiastically exclaimed: "Credo che non sia al
mondo un più bello e miglior stretto, come è questo!"

But what was this trifling interlude of comfort and relaxation, what were these days of idleness, in comparison

with the great, the exciting news which was about to reach Magellan? It was not long delayed, for on the third day the boat obediently returned, and from afar its men were seen to be hailing the flag-ship with excited gestures like those which had been made by the sailors on All Saints' Day, when they came back after discovering the entrance to the strait. This time—and it was a thousandfold more important—they had found the outlet. With their own eyes they had seen the Mar del Sur, the great unknown sea into which this channel opened. "Thalassa! Thalassa!"—such was the cry, two thousand years before, uttered by the Greeks when, returning from manifold perils, they at length caught sight of the sea. Now it was re-echoed in another tongue, and at sight of an ocean which only on Balboa's expedition had heard the jubilant tones of European voices.

This was Magellan's supreme minute, the minute of the utmost rapture that any man can ever have enjoyed. All his expectations had been fulfilled. He had kept his word to the Emperor. He first in the world, he alone, had done what thousands before him had dreamed of doing; he had found his way into a new ocean. His life was justified by its fruit, and by this moment in it he was destined for immortality.

Then there happened what no one would have dared to expect from a man so harsh and reserved as was Magellan. The stern soldier was suddenly overcome; he who had never before betrayed his inner feelings, surrendered to a surge from within. His eyes filled with tears, which, scalding hot, ran down his weather-beaten face and dropped into his black beard.

For the first time since he had grown up, the iron man wept for joy ("il capitano-generale lacrimò per allegrezza").

For a brief moment in his dark and toilsome life Magellan was able to taste the highest rapture vouchsafed to men of creative type. He had realized the idea which had so long dominated him. But it was also his fate that he should know no happiness without having to pay for it with extortionate interest. Every one of his successes was associated with some heartrending disappointment. He could catch only a glimpse of delight, but could not grasp it; and even this brief hour of rapture, the most rapturous of his life, was sped before he had fully savoured it. For what had become of the two other ships? Why did they tarry? Now that the scouting boat had returned to announce the discovery of the exit into the South Seas, further search, further reconnaissance, had become a waste of time. Why did they not come, the "San Antonio" and the "Concepción," to learn the good tidings? What had delayed them? More and more impatiently did Magellan scan the depths of the bay. The appointed time had long been exceeded, the fifth day had passed.

Had there been an accident? Had they gone off their course? Magellan could no longer wait. He ordered the sails to be set, and he steered into the channel in search of his missing consorts. But the horizon remained blank. There was no trace of them on the cold, dead waters. Not a sign was to be seen.

At length, on the second day of the search, a sail was sighted. It was the "Concepción," under the command of the trusty Serrão. Where was the other ship, the "San Antonio," the most important of the fleet because it was the largest? Serrão could not say. On the first day she had outstripped him, and had vanished. For a little while, Magellan did not guess that there was anything wrong. Perhaps the "San Antonio" had merely gone astray, or the captain had misunderstood his orders. He therefore, with all three craft, explored the remotest corners of the main channel, now known as Admiralty Sound. He lighted beacons as signals; made cairns, marked with flags,. and containing letters of instruction, in case the "San Antonio" should return after having lost her way. But she did not return. Some disaster must have taken place. She must have struck a rock and foundered with all hands—but this was improbable, for the weather had been calm. More likely did it seem that Estevão Gomez, pilot of the missing "San Antonio," who in the council a few days back had insisted upon the desirability of a prompt return to Spain, had now rebelliously followed his own rede. He and the Spanish officers must have overpowered their captain, who was faithful to Magellan, and have deserted with all the stores they had on board.

Magellan did not know what had happened. All he knew was that it must be something terrible. The ship had disappeared, the best, the largest, and the most amply provisioned in his fleet. But what had become of it? There was no one to inform him, in this forsaken region, whether it was at the bottom of the sea, or had deserted and was making for Spain with the utmost speed. Nothing but the unfamiliar constellation, the Southern Cross, surrounded by the other stars of the Antarctic heavens, had witnessed the affair. They alone knew what had become of the "San Antonio," they alone might have answered Magellan's questioning. It was natural, therefore, that the admiral should summon Andrés de San Martín, astrologer and astronomer, who was with the fleet in place of Faleiro, and was the only man competent to read the stars. Let the star-gazer cast a horoscope. He did so, and (influenced, no doubt, by what he remembered of Estevão Gomez's behaviour at the recent council) announced the message of the stars, which happened, on this occasion, to speak the truth. The "San Antonio," he said, had deserted, and her captain was a prisoner.

Once more Magellan was faced by the need for an important decision. He had been too ready to rejoice. What had happened to him was what would, by a remarkable parallelism of the second circumnavigation of the globe with the first, happen in like circumstances to Francis Drake, his successor. His best ship had deserted, secretly, during the night. When victory was in his hands, a fellow-countryman, a man of his own blood, had treacherously stabbed him in the back. If, before this, the fleet had been poorly supplied, now the need had become pressing. On board the "San Antonio" was the major share of the provisions, which had been further depleted, as far as the remaining three craft were concerned, by the needless delay of six days. To launch forth into the unknown South Seas, which a week ago, when the prospects were far more favourable, had seemed unduly venturesome, would now, after the flight of the "San Antonio," be practically suicidal.

From the topmost peak of pride and confidence, Magellan had been plunged into the lowest abyss of perplexity and confusion. Almost superfluous seems Barros's report: "He was so much confused that he did not venture upon any decision" ("Quedó tan confuso que no sabía lo que había de determinar"). The disturbed state of his mind is shown all too plainly by the statement that in these circumstances his disquiet spread to the other officers of the fleet. For the second time within a few days he summoned a council and asked them their opinion as to whether the voyage should be continued, or whether they should return to Spain; and he now demanded written answers to his questions, wishing, with remarkable foresight, to provide a written record, an incontrovertible proof, of his having consulted his captains. "Litera scripta manet."

It was plain to him, and the facts were to justify his prescience, that the mutineers and deserters on the "San Antonio," directly they got back to Seville, would lodge an accusation against him, to avoid being themselves accused of insubordination. They would describe him (being absent and unable to justify himself) as a man who ruled only by terror. They would give an exaggerated account of how he, a Portuguese alien, had cruelly kept in irons officers duly appointed by King Charles, had had Castilian noblemen decapitated and quartered, and had marooned others, that he might, contrary to the King's orders, maintain the control of the fleet exclusively in Portuguese hands. To deprive these (not wholly unjustified) accusations of their force, to counteract the charge that, throughout the voyage, he had terrorized his officers and refused them any chance of expressing their opinions, Magellan now issued a remarkable order which partook more of the nature of self-defence than of comradely inquiry. "Given in the Channel of Todos los Santos off the mouth of the Rio del Isleo on November 21, fifty-three degrees south of the Equator," this command begins. It goes on as follows:

"I, Ferdinand Magellan, Knight of the Order of Santiago and captain-general of this armada, have fully realized that to all of you it appears a grave decision to continue the voyage, since you regard the season as already far advanced. Now I am a man who never despises the opinion or the advice of another, but who wishes to discuss and to carry out his affairs after general consultation."

It seems likely that the officers must have chuckled when they read this remarkable self-characterization, for if there was anything typical of Magellan it was his unbending autocracy as leader and commander. They could not fail to remember clearly how the very man who now sought their opinions had for nine months crushed with the mailed fist every attempt to offer advice.

Magellan himself knew that they could not have forgotten his ruthless dictatorship, for he continued: "Let no one, therefore, be timid because of what happened in Port San Julian, for it is the duty of each of you to tell me without fear what his opinion is regarding the safety of this armada. It would conflict with your oath and your duty were you to hide your views from me."

He asked each one of them severally (cada uno de por si) to communicate plainly and in writing (por escrito) his opinion as to whether it would be better to continue the voyage or to return immediately to Spain. The reasons for the opinion were to be adduced.

Not in one hour, however, is confidence which has been lost for many months to be restored. His officers had been too seriously alarmed to risk candour. The only answer that has come down to us, that of Andrés de San Martín, shows how little inclined he and the others were, now when the responsibility had grown so heavy, to take any part of the load off Magellan's shoulders. The astrologer replied, appropriately for one of his craft, in ambiguous and nebulous terms, adroitly shifting from one foot to the other. It seemed doubtful, he said, whether this Canal de Todos los Santos was really the right way to the Moluccas ("aunque yo dudo que hay camino para poder navigar a Maluco por este canal"), but he advised the continuance of the voyage (so long as they had the full bloom of the summer with them). On the other hand it would be a mistake to voyage too far, and would be better to put about in the middle of January, seeing that the crew were toil-worn and weak. Perhaps it might be wiser to sail east rather than west, but let Magellan do whatever seemed to him right and take the way that God would disclose to him. We can hardly doubt that the other officers must have replied with like vagueness.

Magellan, of course, had not consulted his officers in order to get their opinions, but only to provide evidence, for subsequent use, that he had consulted them. He knew that he had ventured too far to draw back. He could only return to Spain as a conqueror, for otherwise he would be lost. Even if the verbose astronomer had prophesied his death, he would have continued on his course. On November 22, 1520, upon his orders, the three ships left their anchorage, and a few days later they emerged from the strait which would henceforward bear his name. From a cape which he gratefully named Cabo Deseado (Cape Desire) he set sail into the pathless Pacific. Somewhere beyond the horizon must lie the Spice Islands, the islands of wealth; farther on still must be China and Japan and Hindustan; and beyond them, in the vast distance, must be the homeland Spain, and Europe. Let them rest for a little while—the last rest before thrusting forth into an ocean which had never been traversed since the creation of the world. Then (on November 28, 1520) it was up anchor and away, flags flying. With a salvo of artillery, three lonely little ships respectfully greeted the unfamiliar seas, as a man chivalrously greets a great adversary who has challenged him to a life-or-death struggle.

Chapter Ten

DISCOVERY OF THE PHILIPPINES

November 28, 1520 - April 7, 1521

Discovery of the Philippines

THE story of the first crossing of this hitherto nameless ocean—"a sea so vast that the human mind can scarcely grasp it," as we read in the letter of Maximilian Transylvanus—is one of the deathless deeds of mankind. The voyage of Columbus into the unlimited expanse of waters has, by those of his own time and of all times, been regarded as marvellously courageous; but even that journey is not to be deemed comparable with the one made by Magellan amid unspeakable hardships and privations. Columbus sailed with three ships fresh from the yards, newly rigged, and thoroughly well supplied. His outward voyage lasted no more than thirty-three days. A week before he sighted San Salvador, the appearance of tufts of grass and of fresh driftwood upon the sea and of land-birds in the air, encouraged him to believe that he must be approaching a continent. His crew were hale, his ships so provisioned that, in the worst event, he could sail home again even if he failed to reach the land of which he was in search. Though steering into the unknown, at his back he had his homeland as last refuge.

Magellan was journeying into the void, while the land astern of him was not familiar Europe with its safe and comfortable harbours but the strange and inhospitable Patagonia. His men were exhausted by long months of hardship. Hunger and privation lay behind them, hunger and privation accompanied them, hunger and privation lay threateningly before. Their clothing was threadbare, the sails were rotten, the rigging was frayed. For weeks they had seen no new faces, nor felt the touch of a woman's hand. Although they may have kept their thoughts to themselves, they must in the depths of their hearts have envied the bold comrades who had deserted and made for home before it was too late, instead of being adrift or little better in an endless desert of water. Such was their mood as they sailed on for twenty days, thirty days, forty days, fifty, and sixty, and still there came no land, nor any sign to give hope that they were drawing near the land. Week followed week and week followed week until a hundred days had passed since leaving the Patagonian coast—thrice as long as the westward voyage of Columbus. For thousands upon thousands of hours did Magellan's fleet move onward into vacancy. Since November 28, when Cabo Deseado had faded out of sight on the horizon, they had had neither maps nor means of measurement. False had proved Faleiro's estimate of distances. Long since, thought Magellan, he must have got beyond Cipangu (as Marco Polo had called it), beyond Japan, Dai Nippon, the Land of the Rising Sun. Yet at the time when he believed this, he had not yet traversed as much as a third of the width of the vast ocean which, because it was so peaceful, he called the Pacific.

Peaceful though it was, its peace was cruel, for the monotony of its stillness was a martyrdom. Continually the same blue mirror was the ocean, perpetually cloudless and burning

MAP OF STRAIT OF MAGELLAN

Copper engraving from Hulsius's Travel Book (1626)

NATIVES OF STRAIT OF MAGELLAN
Copper engraving of the eighteenth century

was the sky, silent and toneless the atmosphere, interminably distant and equably rounded the horizon, a metallic line separating the water from the air, heartlessly unvaried. Always the same gigantic but empty blueness round the tiny ships, which were the only things that moved amid a changeless world; always the same cruelly glaring daylight, offering the same unchanging prospect; always at night the same cold and silent stars, which were fruitlessly questioned for their message. The same objects in the circle of vision; the same sails, the same masts, the same decks, the same anchors at the bows, the same bombards and falconets showing at the gun-ports, the same tables. Always the same sweetish stink of corruption that rose from the sweltering bowels of the ships. Morning, noon, and night the same inevitable companions, the same faces growing rigid with despair, modified only by emaciation from hunger and sickness. The eyes grew increasingly sunken, losing their sheen more and more as day followed day; the faces became more haggard, and the gait less resilient. They were like ghosts walking, hollow-cheeked and pale, those who a few months before had been fresh and lively fellows as they climbed the shrouds to shorten sail during a storm. Like sick men they tottered, or lay inert on the decks. Each of the three ships which had set forth on one of the boldest adventures in the history of man was now peopled by spectres who could hardly be regarded as human; each of them was a floating hospital, a moving lazar-house.

Upon this unexpectedly long voyage, supplies were running out until there was a disastrous shortage. Muck rather than food it was that the purser was now able to serve. The wine, which, while it lasted, had moistened the lips and refreshed the mind a little, had been drunk to the last drop. The fresh water, heated by the pitiless sun, had grown brackish in the filthy containers, had (as sailors say) "gone sick," and gave off such a pestilential odour that the unhappy men had to hold the nose while swallowing the scant daily ration with which they tried to assuage the dryness of their throats. The biscuit, too, which as food was supplemented only by such fish as the men could catch, had crumbled into a grey, dirty powder, alive with worms or maggots, and further contaminated by the droppings of rats which, themselves driven crazy by want, were ravaging the last pitiful remnants of food. These repulsive creatures had become coveted delicacies, and when the robbers of the last provisions were now hunted in all corners of the ships, this was done, not merely to slay them, but to preserve the bodies as valuable dainties. "Rats were so much in request," writes Pigafetta, "that we paid half a ducat apiece for them." The lucky purchaser roasted and greedily swallowed the repulsive prey. To ease the gnawing of their stomachs, to create the semblance of a meal, the men chewed sawdust which they had mixed with the trifling allowance of decayed biscuit. At length the need became so pressing that Magellan's prophecy was fulfilled, and "the famine-stricken fellows were forced to gnaw the hides with which the mainyard was covered to prevent the chafing" (Pigafetta, once more). "These hides," he writes, "exposed to the sun and rain and wind, had become so hard that we were obliged to soften them by putting them overboard for four or five days, after which we cooked them on the embers and ate them thus."

We need not be surprised that even the most vigorous

among these men of iron, though inured to suffering, could not long tolerate such a diet. Scurvy broke out for lack of fresh elements (vitamins, we call them today) in the victuals. The gums swelled, bled, and festered; the teeth became loose and fell out; sores formed in the mouth, while the palates of the sufferers grew so painful that they could not take nutriment when they wanted, and some perished miserably of malnutrition. Those who survived were weakened by famine. Their limbs paralysed or covered with ulcers, they hobbled about with the aid of sticks, or lay exhausted in out-of-the-way corners. No less than nineteen, being about one-tenth of those still left with the expedition, died thus in torment on this dreadful journey across the Pacific. One of the first to succumb was the poor kidnapped Patagonian, whom they had christened Juan Gigante, and who, a few months before, had been so greatly admired because of his power of eating half a bushel of ship's biscuit and swallowing a pailful of water at one meal. As day followed day, the number of men fit for duty continually diminished; and Pigafetta was right when he declared that, with a crew so enfeebled, the three ships could not have weathered a storm. "But for the grace of God and the Blessed Virgin in sending us such magnificent weather, we should all have perished in this gigantic ocean."

For ages, as it seemed, the lonely fleet crept across the deserted waters, those on board suffering all manner of torment, being not spared even the worst of these, the agony of disappointed hope. Just as men who, crossing the desert, catch sight of an oasis, and see the palms fluttering in the

breeze, fondly picture the coolness of the shade they will enjoy as protection from the glaring sun which has dazzled
them for days, and fancy themselves already listening to the
gurgle of refreshing springs, so that they press forward with
the last remnant of their strength—to find they have been
fooled by a mirage, for the phantom vanishes and the endless
hostile sands stretch around them as before—so did Magellan
and his followers fall victims to a cruel illusion. One morning there came from the look-out man at the masthead a
hoarse hail: "Land-ho!" Land for the first time after so many
days and weeks. The parched and famished mariners rushed
on deck; even the sick, who had not been able to rise for a
long time, struggled to their feet. Yes, it was really an island
that they were approaching. The boats were quickly manned.
All dreamed of fresh water and of lying in the shadow of
the trees. What a delight it would be to feel firm ground
beneath their feet once more instead of these restless planks.
Pitiful was to be the disappointment. As they drew near,
this, and later another, was found to be a desert island, uninhabited and uninhabitable, a barren rock in the midst of the
sea, providing neither fresh water nor fresh fruit. Waste of
time to land. "Since we found there neither people, nor con-
solation, nor sustenance of any kind, the name of Desaven-
turadas—the Unfortunate Islands—was given to this and to
St. Paul's Island." The voyage across the blue desolation was
resumed. On and on and on for days and days, for weeks
and weeks, in what was perhaps the most dreadful voyage,
the one most full of hardships and hopelessness, in the chronicles of human suffering.

At length on March 6, 1521, for the hundredth time since leaving Cabo Deseado, the sun rose to show what they had expected to be nothing more than the usual vacancy. This morning, however, there was again a cry from the masthead: "Land-ho!" It was time. Two or three days more in the void, and probably no record of this heroic exploit would have come down to us. With crews dying of hunger, the ships (wandering cemeteries) would have continued an aimless journey until sunk by a storm or dashed to pieces on the rocks. But this island, praise God, was inhabited, and could supply water for the thirsty. Hardly had the fleet entered the bay, dropping anchors and lowering sails, when agile prahus put off from shore, little painted boats, with sails made of palm-leaves stitched together. Nimble as monkeys, the nude children of nature scrambled on board, and so foreign to their thoughts were any of the conventions of civilized life that these light-fingered visitors were quick to appropriate anything that was not nailed down. In a trice objects disappeared as if by magic or a conjuring trick. The painter which attached the "Trinidad's" skiff having been cut, the tiny craft was paddled off in triumph to the shore. The savages seized this fine piece of plunder without dreaming that they did anything wrong. To the simple-minded pagans their behaviour seemed perfectly natural, it seemed reasonable and right for them (since naked men have no pockets) to stick whatever they fancied into their hair, as it seemed natural and right to the Spaniards, the Pope, and the Emperor to declare all these undiscovered islands with their population of men and beasts the property of His Christian Majesty of Spain.

Magellan found that the natives were inclined to annex his goods, though they lacked an imperial and papal document. He must do something, for the skiff, entered in the inventory made at Seville as "purchased for the 'Trinidad' at a cost of 3937½ maravedis," was here, ten or twelve thousand miles away, of inestimable value. Their booty must be snatched from the skilful robbers. Next day, therefore, the commander landed forty armed seamen to bring it back and teach the dishonest islanders a lesson. Some of their huts were burned, but the indigenes offered no serious resistance, their weapons being most inadequate.

They were, says Pigafetta, "quite unacquainted with the use of bows and arrows, for when wounded by one of the latter they would draw it out of their bodies and look at it with great surprise, an incident that aroused the compassion of their antagonists. Their only arms were spears tipped with fish-bones." Panic-stricken, they fled out of range and took refuge in the bush from the missiles of these detestable white barbarians. The Spaniards could get a supply of fresh water, and make an effective raid in search of food. From the abandoned huts they took whatever they could see—fowls, fish, and fruit. Now that both sides had enjoyed a campaign of reciprocal thieving, the natives plundering the Spaniards and the Spaniards the natives, the civilized robbers punished the islanders by giving their habitat, for all time, the disgraceful name of "Thieves' Islands," the Ladrones.

Anyhow, this plunder-raid saved the Spaniards from destruction. Three days' rest, fresh fruit and fresh meat, and an abundant supply of fresh water quickly restored most of the crew to health. Some of the men had, indeed, gone too

far to recover, and died of their sickness during the later
stages of the voyage (one of them was the only Englishman
on board); while a few dozen were still too weak and exhausted to resume work. But the worst of the horrors were
over, and it was with renewed courage that the westward
voyage was resumed. When, a week later, another and yet
another island were sighted, Magellan knew that they were
saved. According to his calculations, these must be the Moluccas. He fancied he had reached his goal. But even his burning impatience, his urgent need to care for the sick and to
strengthen the hungry, did not make him incautious. Instead
of landing on Suluan, the larger of the two islands, he went
to a smaller one, called by Pigafetta "Humunu" but now
known as Malhou, since it appeared to be uninhabited; and,
owing to the weakened state of his crews, he wished to avoid
any clash with the aborigines. They should not have to trade
or to fight until their health had been re-established. The sick
were carried ashore, provided with fresh, sweet water, and
one of the pigs which had been stolen from the Ladrone
islanders was killed for them. Let them rest, and not be
too impatient. Next afternoon, however, a boat containing
friendly natives came over from Suluan. It brought fresh
fruit, by the sight of which Pigafetta was greatly astonished,
since never before had he seen bananas or coconuts, the milk
of the latter proving wonderfully good for the sick. Trade
now began: fish, fowls, palm wine, oranges, and all sorts of
vegetables and fruits were exchanged for a few bells, coloured glass beads, and other trifles; and at length, after weeks
and months of semi-starvation, both the sick and the hale
could satisfy their appetites.

Yes, Magellan believed that he had reached the Isles of Promise, the Spice Islands. Soon he realized that he must have miscalculated. Had these been the Moluccas, Enrique would have understood the speech of the natives. He did not. They were not his slave's fellow-countrymen, so the expedition must have reached some other archipelago. Once more mistake had led to discovery. Magellan had directed his course ten degrees too far northward, and had found his way to a completely unknown group of islands, to an archipelago whose existence had never been suspected by any European. In his search for the Moluccas, he had discovered the Philippines, thus securing for Emperor Charles a new province, which was destined to remain under the rule of the Spanish Crown longer than any of the regions discovered by Columbus, Cortez, or Pizarro. For himself, likewise, he had established a realm, since, in accordance with the terms of his contract, he and Faleiro were entitled to become owners of two of the new islands should they discover more than six. He who had yesterday been a poverty-stricken adventurer, a desperado on the edge of destruction, had become adelantado of his own territory, entitled to a perpetual share of all the profits which should accrue from these new colonies, and therewith one of the wealthiest men in the world.

How dramatic was this good fortune after so long, so gloomy, and apparently so fruitless a search. No less remarkable in its effect upon the sick than the abundance of fresh and wholesome food which the natives brought over daily from Suluan to the open-air hospital, was the marvellous spiritual elixir of certainty. After nine days' careful treatment on this tropical shore, nearly all were restored to health, and

Magellan made ready to visit the neighbouring island. At the last moment, indeed, an untoward incident came near to destroying the happiness of the sorely tried man. His friend and chronicler Pigafetta was fishing from the bulwarks when he put his foot upon a spar wet with rain, and, slipping, fell overboard without being perceived by anyone. This nearly put an end to the man who was to be the chief reporter of the first circumnavigation of the world, for the excellent Pigafetta could not swim, and was in imminent danger of drowning. Luckily he managed to grasp the mainsheet which was trailing in the water, and he clung to it while shouting for help. The indispensable chronicler was pulled safe on board.

Thereupon sail was joyfully made. All knew that the terrible expanse of ocean had been crossed, that they would no longer be depressed by vast expanses of water. Within a few days or hours, when the voyage had been resumed, there was an endless succession of islands on the horizon. At length, on the fourth day, March 28, the day before Good Friday, the fleet reached Mazzava, or Mazaba, where they rested awhile before pursuing their course in search of the goal which was no longer distant.

At Mazzava, a tiny islet of the Philippine group, so small that only with a lens can one find it on the map, Magellan had one of the most remarkable experiences of his life. Again and again had his dark and laborious existence been illuminated by such flashes of happiness, whose intensity compensated him for the stubborn patience with which he had endured so many lonely and care-fraught hours. The outward occasion of this one seemed of little significance. As soon as, under press of sail, the three large foreign ships drew near the shore of Mazzava, the inhabitants, inquisitive and friendly, flocked to the strand. Before Magellan landed, he sent his slave Enrique ashore as emissary, rightly supposing that the indigenes would have more confidence in a brown-skinned man of their own kidney than in the bearded whites, strangely clad and fully armed.

Now came the wonder. The islanders surrounded Enrique chattering and shouting, and the Malay slave was dumb-founded, for he understood much of what they were saying. He understood their questions. It was a good many years since he had been snatched from his home, a good many years since he had last heard a word of his native speech. What an amazing moment, one of the most remarkable in the history of mankind! For the first time since our planet had begun to spin upon its axis and to circle in its orbit, a living man, himself circling that planet, had got back to his homeland. No matter that he was an underling, a slave, for his significance lies in his fate and not in his personality. He is known to us only by his slave-name Enrique; but we know, likewise, that he was torn from his home upon the island of Sumatra, was bought by Magellan in Malacca, was taken by his master to India, to Africa, and to Lisbon; travelled thence to Brazil and to Patagonia; and, first of all the population of the world, traversing the oceans, circling the globe, he returned to the region where men spoke a familiar tongue. Having made acquaintance on the way with hundreds of peoples and tribes and races, each of which had a different way of communicating thought, he had got back to his own folk, whom he could understand and who could understand him.

Magellan knew, therefore, that he had reached his goal, had completed his task. He was back among the speakers of Malay, among those whom, twelve years before, he had quitted on his westward course when he sailed from Malacca, to which he would be able to bring back this slave of his. Whether that would happen tomorrow or considerably later, and whether not himself but another was destined to reach the Isles of Promise, seemed indifferent, for, substantially, the deed was done in the moment when it had been irrefutably established that he who persisted in his course around the globe, whether westward following the sun or eastward against the sun, must get back to the place from which he started. What sages had suspected for thousands of years, what learned men had dreamed, was now certain, thanks to the persistent courage of this one man. The earth was round, for a man had rounded it.

This time in Mazzava was the happiest and most restful part of the journey. Magellan's star had reached the zenith. In three days, on Easter Sunday, would come the anniversary of the evil day when, at Port San Julian, he had had, by violent means, to defend himself against conspiracy. Since then how much disaster, how much torment, how much distress! Behind him lay boundless horrors, the dreadful days of hunger, of privation, the nights of storm in unknown waters. Behind him lay the greatest of all his afflictions, the terrible uncertainty which had gnawed at his soul for month upon month, the burning doubt whether he might not have led his fleet astray. The unhappy dissensions in the ranks of his followers were over and done with. He who was so fervent a Christian could unhesitatingly celebrate this Eastertide as the Feast of the Resurrection, now that the cloud of danger had been dispelled, now that his work was accomplished. The imperishable deed he, a frail mortal, had for so many years ardently aspired to do, was done. Magellan had found the route to the west, the route which Columbus, Vespucci, Cabot, Pinzón, and other navigators had vainly sought. He had discovered lands and seas which none before him had seen; as the first European, the first man to do so, he had successfully crossed a new and mighty ocean. He had far outstripped all others in the exploration of our planet. After this splendid achievement, after this signal victory, how trifling was that which still remained to do. It would take but a few days, under the guidance of trusty pilots, to reach the Moluccas, the richest islands in the world. Then he would have fulfilled his pledge to the Emperor. How joyfully, when he got there, would he embrace his friend Serrão, who had steadied his courage and shown him the way; then swiftly, swiftly, he would fill the holds of his ships with spices, and sail home along the familiar route by way of India and the Cape, where every harbour and every bay were well known to him. Home across the western hemisphere to Spain, home in triumph, as a wealthy man, as adelantado and governor, his forehead crowned with imperishable laurels.

There was no hurry, no need for impatience. He could rest at length, could enjoy the happiness of fulfilment after the painful months of perpetual harassment. Let the Argo-

nauts have a spell of repose in this blessed port. Beautiful was
the landscape, paradisaical the climate; friendly were the natives who still lived in the Golden Age, pacific, carefree, and
untroubled by the curse of toil ("questi popoli vivano con
iusticia, peso e misura; amano la pace, l'otio e la quiete"). But
besides loving tranquillity, the children of nature loved eating and drinking; and the half-starved men of the Spanish
fleet, who had for so long been compelled to fill their stomachs with sawdust and rat's flesh, could have fancied themselves in Utopia.

The temptations of the excellent fresh food were overwhelming, so that even the pious Pigafetta, who never forgot
to thank the Madonna and the Saints, committed a great sin.
For it was not only Friday, an ordinary fast day, but Good
Friday, when Magellan sent him with one companion to the
king of the island. Calambu (this being His Majesty's name)
received him with much ceremony "under a canopy of canes
where there was a canoe like a galley, on the poop of which
we sat, conversing by signs, for we had no interpreter." Near
by was boiling a dish of fat pork, whence proceeded a pleasant odour. From civility to the monarch, and perhaps also
from greed, Pigafetta now committed his sin. Unable to resist the seductive aroma, on the holiest and strictest of all fast
days he ate the tasty flesh, washing it down with copious liba-
tions of palm wine. Hardly was this meal finished, hardly had
the mariners so unused to rich fare filled their bellies, when
Calambu invited them to a second banquet in his own hut.
Seated "upon a cane mat with our legs crossed like tailors
on a bench," the guests had to devour another meal, consist-
ing this time of roasted fish with freshly gathered ginger and

palm wine—so the sinner sinned once more. Worse still was to happen, for hardly had Pigafetta and his companion finished this second meal, when the king's eldest son entered to greet the visitors, and, for politeness' sake, the guests had to gorge themselves a third time. Two more dishes were brought, "one of fish with its sauce, and the other of rice." Pigafetta's companion, "having eaten and drunk too much, became intoxicated," and had, on a cane mat, to sleep off a European's first carouse in the Philippines. We can be sure that, thoroughly replete after months upon months of scanty fare, he must have dreamed of paradise.

The islanders were no less enthusiastic than were their hungry guests. What wonderful visitors had come to them across the sea, bringing such splendid gifts: polished mirrors in which a man could see his own nose with his own eyes; glittering knives; and heavy axes, which could cut down a thick bamboo with one blow. Calambu was pranking in a Turkish robe of red and yellow and a red cap, given to him by Magellan. The visitors had wonderful armour which made them invulnerable. On the admiral's command, one of the seamen put on a suit of steel, and the natives were allowed to shoot at him with their bone arrows, while the mail-clad soldier laughed them to scorn. What an amazing conjurer, too, was this Pigafetta! He held what appeared to be a feather in his hand and, when one of the indigenes spoke, he made scratching noises with it upon a piece of paper, producing black signs, which must be magical, for, having done so, two days later he could repeat what had been said to him. And how splendid a spectacle had these white gods prepared for Sunday, which they called Easter Sunday. They placed on the shore a strange object, a sort of box which they called an altar, and above it a cross glittered in the sun. Then they all came, two by two, the admiral and fifty men in their best clothes, and, while they kneeled before the Cross, lightnings flashed from the ships, and a noise like thunder (though the sky was cloudless) rolled across the sea.

Convinced that there must be something miraculous about these mighty white men, the natives timidly and reverently imitated their movements. They, too, kneeled and kissed the Cross. Joyfully those who had hitherto been pagans thanked the admiral when he told them he would order his carpenters to make them a Cross so large that, "set up on the summit of the highest mountain in the neighbourhood, all might see and adore it." Thus great things had been brought to pass within a few days. The king of these islands had not only become an ally of the King of Spain, but also a Christian brother. Not merely had new land been won for the Spanish Crown, but the simple souls of the children of nature had been gained over for the true Church and for the Saviour.

It was a glorious, idyllic time, this week spent in Mazzava. But Magellan had rested long enough. The mariners were refreshed and encouraged; it was time to continue the home-ward road. Why delay longer? What could it matter to him to discover another island more or less, since he had made the greatest discovery of the age? He need only visit the Spice Islands, fulfil his commission, discharge his vow; then let him make as quickly as possible for Europe, where his wife awaited him, and would show him the child born since his departure. Back to secure the punishment of the mutineers who had treacherously deserted him. Back to teach the world the courage of a Portuguese nobleman, the resolution and fortitude of a Spanish crew. He must not keep his friends waiting any longer, or leave in the lurch those who had trusted him.

Yet always a man's genius is at the same time his innermost danger; and Magellan's genius was patience, his power to wait, his capacity for silence. Stronger in him than his longing for a triumphal return that he might win thanks from the lord of the Old World and the New, was his sense of duty. Whatever he had hitherto undertaken, he had carefully performed and thoroughly completed. Nor, on this occasion, was Magellan willing to leave the Philippine Archipelago without having seen more of Emperor Charles's new province and without having made of it a permanent asset for Spain. It would not suffice him that he had visited and annexed one little island. Since his crew was too small for him to leave representatives and factors behind, he must enter into the same sort of treaty with the principal rulers of the archipelago as he had with this inconsiderable local chief Calambu, that the flag of Castile and Aragon might wave everywhere, and the Cross stand as a permanent sign of supremacy.

When he asked Calambu which was the largest of the islands, he was told that it was Zebu (Cebu), and when the admiral demanded a pilot, the Rajah said it would be an honour to be allowed to guide him thither. It is true that this high honour of royal pilotage delayed the departure a little, since Calambu overate and overdrank himself so grossly at the harvest festival that it was not until April 4 that the fleet could

SHIPS IN THE LADRONES
Copper engraving from de Bry's Travel Book (1620)

THE ISLAND OF MACTAN, WHERE MAGELLAN MET
HIS DEATH
In Pigafetta's *handwriting, from the* Ambrosian MS. *in Milan*

sail under the guidance of its Pantagruelian pilot. Then the ships set out from the blessed strand which had saved them in their utmost need. Through quiet waters they steered past gracious islands towards the destination chosen by Magellan —"for thus," writes the trusty Pigafetta, "his unlucky fate willed that it should be."

Chapter Eleven

MAGELLAN'S DEATH

April 7, 1521–April 27, 1521

Magellan's Death

On April 7, 1521, after a calm and pleasant three days' voyage, the fleet approached the island of Cebu. Numerous villages dotted along the coast showed that the place was thickly populated. The royal pilot Calambu steered straight for the capital, the first glance of which taught Magellan that he had here to do with a rajah or king of considerably more importance than his present companion, seeing that in the roads there lay a number of junks from foreign parts together with quantities of native prahus. It was desirable to make a big show and to disclose himself as the lord of thunder and lightning. Magellan signalled the fleet to fire an artillery salute, which, to begin with, aroused the horror of the unsophisticated islanders, who fled in all directions to hide. Thereupon Magellan hastened to send Enrique ashore as interpreter, with instructions to be diplomatic, and inform the ruler of the island that the thunder was not a sign of enmity, for the commander of the squadron intended by this magic to show his respect for the mighty Rajah of Cebu. The lord of the fleet was himself only a servant of the greatest monarch in the world, on whose command he had sailed across the mightiest ocean in the world to seek out the Spice Islands. On the way, having learned how wise and courteous a prince the Rajah of Cebu was, he had

determined to pay a friendly call. The admiral, declared
Enrique, commander of the thunder-ships, was prepared to
show His Majesty various costly goods never before seen in
that part of the world, and enter into trade with him. He
could not make a long stay, for, as soon as he had cemented
friendly relations with this renowned monarch, to whom he
wished to show his goodwill, he would leave the island.

Humabon, Rajah of Cebu, was no such unsophisticated
child of nature as were the naked savages of the Ladrones or
the "giants" of Patagonia. He had already eaten of the tree
of knowledge, knew about money and money's worth. This
yellowish-brown prince on the other side of the world was a
political economist who practised the highly civilized art of
exacting transit dues from every ship that cast anchor in his
port. A keen man of business, he was not impressed by the
thunder of the artillery or flattered by the honeyed words
of the interpreter. He coolly replied to Enrique that he had
no wish to forbid an entrance to his harbour. The white
strangers were welcome, and he would be glad to trade with
them. But every ship without exception must pay harbour
dues. It was therefore incumbent upon the great captain in
command of the three big ships to begin by paying the usual
tribute.

The slave Enrique knew that his master, being admiral of
a royal Spanish armada and Knight of Santiago, would never
consent to pay tribute to a duodecimo princelet. Any payment of that kind would implicitly acknowledge the supremacy or the independence of a country which Spain, in virtue
of a Papal Bull, regarded as one of her own provinces. Enrique therefore boldly advised Rajah Humabon to dispense

with tribute on this occasion, and not to risk entering into hostilities with the lord of thunder and lightning. The commercial-minded Rajah once more expressed his regret. Payment first, friendship afterwards. The foreigners could not be received unless the customary dues were forthcoming. There could be no exception. As witness he summoned a Mohammedan trader who had just arrived from Siam in a junk, and had paid without controversy.

This worthy appeared, and turned pale. At the first glance towards the big ships with the cross of St. James upon the taut sails, he grasped the situation. Alas, in this farthest corner of the East, where hitherto trade had been carried on without interference from the giaours, these children of Shaitan had appeared upon the scene. Here they were with their terrible cannons and arquebuses, these murderers, the enemies of Mohammed. Peaceful trade and big profits for such as himself were over and done with. He hastily whispered to the Rajah that caution was needed, and that a dispute with the unwelcome visitors must be avoided at all costs. They were the same, he explained (confusing the Spaniards with the Portuguese), who had pillaged and conquered Calicut, all Hindustan, and Malacca. No one could resist the white devils.

With this recognition another circle had been closed. At the other end of the world, under other stars, Europe had touched Europe once more. Hitherto Magellan, steering always to the west, had reached only lands untrodden by Europeans. Not one of the natives hitherto encountered had heard of white men; not one of them had ever before seen a European. Even Vasco da Gama, when he first landed in India, was addressed in Portuguese by an Arab; but Magel-

lan, since leaving Spain two years before, had not once been
recognized for what he was, a conquistador; the Spaniards
might have been wandering upon a remote, unpeopled star.
The Patagonians regarded them as heavenly beings; the inhabitants of the Ladrones fled from them as if they were
devils or evil spirits. Here at length, at the other end of the
world, Europeans were faced by ·persons who knew them
or had heard of them; a bridge had been built from Europe
across the oceanic distances to this new world. The circle
was closed. A few more days' sailing, over a few hundred
miles of sea, and he would encounter European faces after
two years, would meet Christians and comrades, brothers in
the faith. If Magellan still doubted whether he could really
be close to his goal, he was now confirmed in his expectations. Sphere had touched sphere, the miracle had been
worked, the world had been circumnavigated.

The Mohammedan trader's warning made a manifest impression upon the Rajah of Cebu. In his alarm, he instantly
abandoned his claim for harbour dues. As a first proof of his
hospitable intentions, he invited Magellan's envoys to a banquet. Now came a third unmistakable sign that the Argonauts were close to their destination. Food was no longer
served upon mats or upon wooden platters, but on porcelain,
which came direct from China, the semi-mythical Cathay of
Marco Polo. Cipangu and India, at the heart of Oriental
civilization, must likewise be close at hand. Magellan had
very nearly realized the dream of Columbus, who hoped to
reach the Indies by sailing west.

As soon as this diplomatic incident had been smoothed

over, the official interchange of courtesies and goods could begin. Pigafetta was sent ashore as plenipotentiary, and the Rajah of Cebu declared himself ready to enter into a perpetual treaty of peace with the mighty Emperor Charles, while Magellan, on his side, did his utmost to promote amicable relations. In marked contrast with such conquistadors as Cortez and Pizarro—who unleashed their wardogs the instant they landed, barbarously massacring and enslaving the population, thinking only of ruthless extortion—this more far-seeing and humane discoverer thought exclusively of peaceful penetration. From the first, he aimed at incorporating the new provinces rather by friendliness and treaty than by blood and violence. Nothing makes Magellan's figure stand out with such marked moral superiority, as compared with all the other conquistadors of his day, as does this inviolable will to humaneness. In himself he was a man of harsh and reserved temperament. As his behaviour in the case of the mutiny at Port San Julian showed, he maintained iron discipline in his fleet, showing no consideration. But, harsh though he was, it is to his honour that he was never cruel. His memory is not stained by any of the misdeeds which tarnished the scutcheons of Cortez and Pizarro—such as the burning of the caciques and the torture of Guatemozin. His voyage was not dishonoured by any of those breaches of faith which the conquistadors in general thought lightly of when their faith had been pledged to the "heathen." Down to the hour of his death, he loyally kept every pact he entered into with the native chieftains, this sterling honesty being his best weapon and contributing to his eternal renown.

Meanwhile trade had begun, and was carried on to mutual

satisfaction. Above all, the islanders were astonished at iron, this hard metal brought by the foreigners, which was so wonderful for making swords and spears, mattocks and ploughs. They had comparatively little interest in gold, and, like enthusiasts in the blessed war-year 1914, they were willing to give gold for iron. Fourteen pounds of the latter metal, so cheap in Europe, were worth more to them than fifteen gold ducats. The captain-general found it necessary to caution his men and issue strict orders that no great desire to obtain gold should be shown, "for otherwise," writes Pigafetta, "every sailor would have sold his all for gold, which would for ever have ruined our future trade." Too impetuous a demand for gold would have shown the natives that the Spaniards regarded it as precious, and this would have spoiled the market.

Magellan was ready to take advantage of their ignorance, but he insisted that the people of Cebu should not be cheated in weight and measure. He, who always looked ahead, was not concerned with winning temporary advantages that would cost him more in the long run, and would interfere with his gaining the goodwill of the inhabitants of the new province. Once more he proved right. The relations between the indigenes and the mighty strangers grew so cordial that the Rajah and most of his followers spontaneously expressed a desire to become Christians. What the other Spanish conquistadors achieved in the course of months and years with the rack and the Holy Inquisition, with cruel punishments, and with burnings at the stake, the profoundly religious but unfanatical Magellan secured in a few days without any violence whatever.

Let Pigafetta convince us how much humanity, how much

freedom of spirit, he displayed on the occasion of these whole-
sale conversions. "The captain warned them against adopting
Christianity either from fear or from the hope of pleasing
us. If they really wished to become Christians, they must do
so because of a genuine desire, and for the love of God. If
they did not become Christians, the Spaniards would do
nothing to harm them. Still, those who did become Christians would be loved the more and would be better treated.
Then they all exclaimed, as with one voice, that they wished
to become Christians, not from fear and not in order to please
us, but of their own free will. They put themselves in his
hands, and he could deal with them as with his own subjects.
Thereupon the captain embraced them with tears in his eyes,
took the hands of the princes and those of the Rajah of Mazzava, and told them that, by his faith in God and his loyalty
to the Emperor, he swore to them that thenceforward they
should live in perpetual peace with the King of Spain, and
they made him a like promise in return."

Next Sunday, April 14, 1521, the Spaniards celebrated
their greatest triumph. On the market-place in the centre of
the town a scaffolding was erected and decorated with hang-
ings and palm-branches. Carpets were brought from the ship,
and upon these, beneath the canopy, were two thrones
wreathed in satin, one for Magellan and the other for the
Rajah of Cebu. In front, visible from afar, stood the altar,
surrounded in a wide circle by hundreds and thousands of
brown-skinned natives, awaiting the promised spectacle. The
captain-general, who had wisely hitherto entered into the
bulk of the arrangements through Pigafetta, now approached,
making a dramatic entry. Forty men in armour preceded

him. Behind them, immediately in front of Magellan, marched the ensign, bearing the silken banner of King Charles, the banner bestowed upon the admiral in the church at Seville, and now for the first time unfurled in this new Crown colony. The banner was followed by Magellan and the train of his officers, in ceremonious march. At the moment when he set foot on shore, a salute was fired from the ship. In the first shock of terror, the spectators dispersed in all directions. But, seeing that their king (who had been warned what was about to happen) sat composedly on his throne, they returned, and looked on enthusiastically while a large Cross was set up, before which the Rajah kneeled, together with the prince his nephew, and others to the number of fifty or more, all of whom were baptized. Magellan, acting as the Rajah's godfather, gave Humabon, hitherto a pagan, the Christian name of Charles in honour of his European suzerain. The Queen, or Ranee, a pretty woman four centuries in advance of her European and American sisters, since her lips and her finger-nails were tinted bright red, was baptized Joanna, while the other princesses also received Spanish names, being christened Catarina and Isabella. It need hardly be said that the other notables of Mazzava and the neighbouring islands did not wish to lag behind their king and chieftain. The news spread far and wide. Next day there came from neighbouring islands many more of the indigenes to be initiated into these magical ceremonies. Within a few days almost all the chiefs had sworn alliance with Spain, and had been sprinkled with the waters of baptism.

Seldom has a deed been more splendidly accomplished. Magellan had gained his ends. He had discovered the strait leading to the other side of the world. New islands with abundant riches had been won for the Crown of Castile and Aragon; countless souls had accepted the true faith, and, triumph among triumphs, these things had been done without shedding a drop of blood. God had protected this man ardent in the faith. He had saved Magellan from privations and dangers worse than those any other mortal had ever endured. The admiral was permeated with a fervently religious sentiment of security. After the numerous difficulties he had overcome, what more difficult could remain to be accomplished; what, after this glorious victory, could still endanger his work? His mind was obsessed with the humble conviction that he could venture anything for God and the Emperor.

This faith was to bring him to his doom.

Magellan had succeeded in everything, as if angels had lighted his path. He had found the way, he had conquered new islands for his king, and another, a vainer man than he, would have hastened home to wear the laurel crown. But Magellan, the precise and incorruptible calculator, was chiefly concerned with the problem of how best to make the islands he had discovered permanent possessions of the Spanish Crown. He hoped and believed that the newly baptized Rajah Charles would keep troth. But Charles Humabon was no more than one of many kings in the Philippines, and to visit all these islands, to win over and to convert all their rajahs, would have taken too long. The admiral's duty was to reach the Spice Islands as quickly as he could. As far as consolidating Spanish power in the Philippines was concerned, there seemed to Magellan (always thinking far ahead) only one

way, namely, to make Charles Humabon, the only Catholic
Rajah, liege lord of the other chieftains in the region. Thenceforward Rajah Charles of Cebu was to rule as the Spanish
monarch's viceroy, and must gain higher prestige than that
of his fellow-rulers. A friend of the King of Spain could not
stand on a like footing with other princes, but, in virtue of
his alliance with the lord of thunder and lightning, must
hold unrivalled rank and authority throughout the archipelago. It was not in levity, but as the outcome of careful political reflection, that Magellan now offered the Rajah of Cebu
military aid, should any other rajah venture to rise against
him.

As luck would have it, during these very days there was
opportunity for such a demonstration. On a tiny isle called
Mactan, close to Cebu, there ruled a rajah named Silapulapu
who had always been inclined to rise in revolt against the
Rajah of Cebu. Since the arrival of the Spaniards, he had been
doing what he could to prevent the other chieftains from
supplying them with the necessary stores of food. Silapulapu's animus against the Spaniards would appear to have been
not altogether unjustified. Somewhere on his islet (probably
because the mariners of the fleet, sex-hungry after a long
voyage, were hunting the native women too eagerly) there
had been a broil, and a few of the huts on Mactan had been
burned down. The refusal of supplies seemed to Magellan
an excellent reason for a trial of strength. Not only the Rajah
of Cebu, but the other chieftains as well, should learn once
for all how much better it was to support the Spaniards, and
how grievous would be the fate of any who should resist the
lord of thunder and lightning. Such a spectacle (which need

not involve much bloodshed) would be more convincing than words. Magellan therefore informed Humabon of his wish to read this refractory princeling a lesson, that Silapulapu might behave better in future. Strangely enough the Rajah of Cebu does not seem to have been very enthusiastic in his acceptance of the proffered aid. Perhaps he dreaded lest the subjugated tribes rise against him, as soon as the Spaniards departed. Serrão and Barbosa likewise warned the admiral against so needless a military expedition.

Magellan, for his part, was not thinking of a serious campaign. All he sought to do was to ensure the authority of Spain's new ally, Rajah Charles, over all the other princes and chieftains. If the rebellious Silapulapu did but lower his crest, so much the better for him and for everyone. The sworn enemy of needless bloodshed, the very antithesis of other and more pugnacious conquistadors, Magellan began by sending his slave Enrique and the Siamese trader to Silapulapu, offering peace. Magellan asked nothing more of Silapulapu than that the latter should acknowledge the suzerainty of the Rajah of Cebu and place himself under the protectorate of Spain. If he would agree to this, the Spaniards would show him close friendship. If, on the other hand, he refused, and repudiated the suzerainty of Rajah Charles of Cebu, then he would be taught how sharp were the Spanish lances.

Silapulapu answered that his men had lances of their own. Though these were made only of bamboo, the points had been well hardened in the fire, and the Spaniards, should they venture to attack, would find them to be formidable weapons. Having received this arrogant message, Magellan had no choice but to maintain Spanish supremacy by an act of war.

He was compelled to have recourse to the arbitrament of arms.

For the first time in his career, we find Magellan lacking in what had hitherto been his most striking characteristics: caution and foresight. For the first time the good calculator apparently overlooked the best of his chances. The Rajah of Cebu had offered to send a thousand warriors against Mactan, and Magellan would have no difficulty in supplying one hundred and fifty of his own men for the assault on the island. Attacked by so preponderant a force, the rajah of this petty state would have sustained a crushing defeat. But Magellan did not want a butchery. He was concerned, in this expedition, with something much more important, the prestige of Spain. An admiral of the emperor of two worlds could not treat as equal adversary a brown-skinned rascal who had not a mat in his hut which was not worn into holes. It would never do to attack such a pack of islanders with a superior force. Magellan had other plans. What he designed to prove was that one vigorous, well-armed Spaniard could deal single-handed with a hundred such rapscallions. The myth of the invulnerability, of the invincibility of the Spaniards was to be established by this action, and tidings of the defeat of the bush-rajah who had dared to face the forces of the King of Spain would spread like wildfire through the islands. What Magellan had shown a few days before on his flag-ship as a farce to amuse the rajahs of Mazzava and Cebu was to be shown once more on a larger scale and in dead earnest—that twenty natives armed with lances and krises could attack a Spanish soldier in steel harness without being able even to

THE ISLAND OF MACTAN, SHOWING THE DEATH
OF MAGELLAN
Copper engraving from Hulsius's Travel Book (1626)

MAGELLAN'S DEATH
Woodcut from Thevet's Cosmographie Universelle *(1575)*

wound him. This would teach the refractory Silapulapu the same lesson. It was for these psychological reasons that a leader usually so circumspect took with him no more than sixty men, and requested the Rajah of Cebu, with his auxiliary force of a thousand warriors, not to land on Mactan, but to watch the contest from the prahus. They would not have to fight, but merely to enjoy the instructive spectacle of how a few dozen Spaniards could easily get the better of all the chieftains and rajahs and kings on the islands.

Had the experienced calculator miscalculated this time? Not a bit of it. The teachings of history show that to send a score or so of Europeans in coats of mail against a thousand naked savages, Indians, or what not, armed with fish-bone lances, was by no means absurd. With three or four hundred men Cortez and Pizarro, getting the better of hundreds of thousands of Mexicans and Peruvians, conquered huge realms. In comparison with the difficulties these faced, Magellan's expedition against a petty island must have seemed little more than a military parade. We know, indeed, that Magellan did not anticipate danger, for the pious Catholic, whose custom it was, before any decisive action, to hear mass, and, with his men, take Holy Communion, did not do this before attacking Mactan. A few gunshots, a few shrewd blows, and Silapulapu's poor fellows would be on the run like hares. Without any serious bloodshed, the inviolability of the Spanish warriors would be proved to these islands for all time.

On this Friday night, April 26, 1521, when Magellan embarked with his sixty men to cross the narrow strait between the two islands, the indigenes declared that they saw a strange,

black, unknown bird, looking something like a crow, perched
on a roof-tree. It seems to be true that, for some unknown
reason, all the dogs began to howl. The Spaniards, no less
superstitious than the savages, crossed themselves anxiously.
But was the man who had ventured upon the greatest voyage
in history likely to turn back because a raven croaked, or to
be afraid of a skirmish with a naked chieftain and his poor
rabble of followers?

Disastrously for Magellan, however, this puny prince had
a powerful ally in the structure of the shore. A little distance
out to sea there was a coral reef which the boats could not
cross, so the Spaniards were deprived from the start of the
effective use of their best weapon, the murderous fire of
arquebuses and crossbows, the mere thunder of the guns usually being enough to put the savages to flight.

Taking no trouble to cover their rear, forty of the heavily
armed men disembarked to wade, leaving the other twenty in
the boats. Magellan led the way, for, as Pigafetta writes, "being a good shepherd, he would not desert his flock." Girdle-
deep in the water, they waded a considerable distance to the
shore, where a great number of indigenes were stationed,
shouting and swinging their shields defiantly. Soon battle was
joined.

The most trustworthy of various accounts of this battle is
probably Pigafetta's, for the chronicler was one of the attacking party, and was himself wounded by an arrow. "We
jumped into the water," he writes, "which was waist-deep,
and then we had two long bow-shots to wade before we
reached land, while our boats could not follow us because of

the reef. On the shore we found fifteen hundred of the islanders divided into three bodies, of which one opposed our advance, while the others assailed us on the flanks. The captain,
accordingly, marshalled his men in two companies, as afford-
ing a better means of defence. Our musketeers and cross-
bow men fired for half an hour from the boats, without effect, for from so great a distance our bullets and bolts and
lances could not penetrate the wooden shields of the enemy,
and at best could merely wound them in the arm. The captain ordered the marksmen to cease fire (obviously wishing
to reserve the ammunition for a later stage of the encounter),
but his order was disregarded in the confusion. When the
islanders realized that our fire was doing them little or no
harm, they ceased to retire. Shouting more and more loudly,
and jumping from side to side to disconcert our aim, they
advanced simultaneously, under cover of their shields, assail-
ing us with arrows, javelins, lances with points hardened in
the fire, stones, and even filth, so that we were scarcely able
to defend ourselves. Some of them began to throw lances
with brazen points against our captain.

"To instil terror into the hearts of the enemy, the captain
now sent some of our men to set the islanders' huts on fire.
That only increased their ferocity. Some of them ran off to
cope with the flames, which were raging in twenty or thirty
of the houses, and there they slew two of our fellows. The
rest attacked us with redoubled fury. When they became
aware that, though our bodies were protected by armour,
our legs were exposed, they aimed chiefly at these. The captain's right foot was wounded by a poisoned arrow, where-

ipon he issued orders for a slow and steady retreat. But nearly all our men fled headlong, so that no more than six or eight of us stayed with him, who, having been lame for years, could not withdraw quickly. Now we were exposed to lances and stones hurled from all sides, and we were no longer in a position to resist. The bombard we had in the boat could not help us, for the range was too great. Retreating, therefore, step by step, and fighting all the time, we withdrew from the shore, till we were a full bow-shot away, and the water already rose to our knees. But the islanders followed us sturdily, continually picking up the spears they had already cast, so that one and the same spear could wound five or six men in succession. Recognizing the captain, they aimed chiefly at him, and twice the helmet was struck from his head. He, supported by the few of us who had stayed with him, fought like a valiant knight at his post, without attempting further retreat.

"Thus we fought for an hour or more, until at length an Indian succeeded in wounding the captain in the face with a bamboo spear. He, being desperate, plunged his lance into the Indian's breast, leaving it there. But, wishing to use his sword, he could draw it only half-way from the sheath, on account of a spear wound he had received in the right arm. Seeing this, the enemy made a combined rush at him, and one of them, with a long terzado, like a large scimitar, gave him a heavy blow upon the left leg which caused him to fall forward on his face. Then the Indians threw themselves upon him, with spears and scimitars and every weapon they had, and ran him through—our mirror, our light, our comforter, our true guide—until they killed him."

In this insensate way (like his successor James Cook, one of the greatest navigators in history), when hard upon the completion of his imperishable deed, Magellan was slain in a petty skirmish with a horde of naked islanders. The man of genius who, like Prospero, had mastered the elements, overcome storms, and constrained men, was felled by a ludicrous human insect named Silapulapu. Though death could deprive him of life, it could not rob him of victory, and his mortal lot seems of little importance after so immortal a deed. But the tragedy of his heroic doom was followed all too quickly by a satirical episode. The very Spaniards who, a few days earlier, had been revered as gods from heaven and had then looked down upon the princeling of Mactan, now debased themselves so low that, instead of instantly summoning the rest of their forces and snatching the corpse of their leader from those who had slain him, they, like cowards, sent a negotiator to Silapulapu, offering to buy the body. They wished to recover the mortal remains of their admiral in return for a few bells and scraps of coloured cloth. But the princeling who had triumphed over the Spaniards proved greater in spirit than the not very heroic companions of Magellan. Silapulapu would not surrender the corpse of his adversary in exchange for mirrors and glass beads and coloured satin. He valued the trophy he had won, for now the news was spreading through the islands that Silapulapu the Great had destroyed the white lord of thunder and lightning as easily as he would have destroyed a fish or a bird.

No one knows what became of Magellan's body, or to which element his mortal envelope was returned; whether to fire, to water, to earth, or to air. No witness was there to tell us; and his grave, if he was buried, remains secret. All traces of the man who wrested its last mystery from the unknown have vanished.

Chapter Twelve

A VOYAGE WITHOUT A LEADER

April 27, 1521 – September 6, 1522

A Voyage without a Leader

THE Spaniards lost no more than eight men in this trifling skirmish—a far from overwhelming proportion of their total forces. But the fall of their leader made the reverse catastrophic. With Magellan's death was dispelled the magical nimbus that had made the white strangers seem godlike to the simple islanders. Only upon this nimbus depended the power and success of the conquistadors. Despite their bravery, their staying-power, their strategy, and the strength of their weapons, neither Cortez nor Pizarro would ever have succeeded in overcoming foes by the myriad and by the hundred thousand, had not the myth of invincibility supported them like a guardian angel. These all-wise beings who could launch thunder and lightning from weapons which looked like bludgeons, seemed to the alarmed natives to be invulnerable; they could not be wounded, because arrows fell blunted from their armour; in the Americas, it was impossible to escape them by flight, for the huge quadrupeds with which they were, so to say, fused could gallop much faster than a man could run. Nothing shows better the paralysing influence of fear than does the story which has come down to us from the days of the conquistadors, telling how a Spaniard was drowned in a river. For three days the Indians watched the body in a hut, with-

out venturing to touch it, lest the strange god might come
to life once more. Only when putrefaction was well advanced did they pull themselves together and prepare for
further resistance. When one of the white gods was wounded,
when the invincibles sustained but one defeat, everywhere
the spell broke and the myth of invulnerability was no longer
believed.

Thus did it happen now. The Rajah of Cebu had surrendered unresistingly to the lords of thunder and lightning.
Humbly he had accepted their faith, believing that this new
god of the Cross must be stronger than the wooden idols he
had hitherto reverenced. He hoped, when he struck up a
friendship with these supernatural strangers, that he would
speedily become the mightiest monarch in the islands. Now
he himself and his thousand warriors had looked on from
their prahus while Silapulapu, one of the most insignificant
of the princes, had vanquished the white god. With his own
eyes he had seen that their thunder and lightning were pow-
erless; had watched the reputedly invulnerable men clad in
glittering cuirasses fleeing ignominiously from the naked
fighters of a petty chieftain. Finally, he had seen their leader
fall a victim to the spears of his jubilant and courageous
fellow-countrymen.

Perhaps an energetic counterstroke might still have saved
the prestige of the Spaniards. Had a resolute successor to
Magellan assembled the whole body of them, taken boat to
Mactan, and forcibly snatched away the corpse of the great
navigator, subsequently to inflict a terrible chastisement upon
the bandit chief and his tribe, then perhaps a wholesome terror would have been instilled even into the mind of the Rajah

of Cebu. Instead of this, Don Carlos Humabon (who would not long continue to use the imperial name bestowed on him in baptism) had seen how the vanquished Spaniards sent a negotiator to the triumphant princeling, hoping to buy back Magellan's corpse. But, lo, the petty chieftain of the petty island of Mactan snapped his fingers at the white gods, and contemptuously drove their representative forth from his palace.

It was inevitable that the cowardly behaviour of the whites should make the Rajah of Cebu think strange thoughts. Probably he felt the same disappointment that was experienced by Caliban as regards Trinculo when the poor fool found he had been over-ready to take a boaster for a god. Besides, in various ways the Spaniards did what they could to destroy their good understanding with the islanders. Peter Martyr, who immediately after the return of the expedition asked some of the seamen what was the cause of the islanders' change of mood after the death of Magellan, was told the undoubted truth by an eye-witness, Martin of Genoa: "Violation of the women was the main trouble." Despite his best endeavours, Magellan had been unable to prevent his men, sex-hungry after so long a voyage, from raping the wives of their hosts; vainly did he try to put an end to these acts of violence and lubricity, punishing his own brother-in-law, Barbosa, for staying ashore three nights in succession. In this respect, matters seem to have grown worse after the leader's death. Anyhow, as soon as Rajah Charles had ceased to value these fierce invaders for their military prowess, he ceased altogether to respect them.

The Spaniards must have realized the increasing hostility

of the islanders, for they speedily became impatient. Let them get together a stock of wares on which they could make a profit, and sail with all speed for the Spice Islands. Magellan's successors, more mercantile than their great leader had been, took little interest in his idea of winning the Philippines for Spain by a policy of peace and friendliness, and in his notion of spreading the Christian faith. To speed matters up, they had urgent need of the services of Enrique, Magellan's slave, since he was the only man able to facilitate barter with the natives by talking to them in their own language. Over this trifling matter it became apparent that the art of managing men, through which Magellan won his greatest successes, had died with him. The faithful Enrique had fought by his leader's side to the last moment. He was brought back wounded to the ship, and lay motionless, wrapped in his mat —perhaps because of his wounds, or perhaps because, with the faithfulness of a dog, he was mourning his beloved master. Thereupon Duarte Barbosa, who, jointly with João Serrão, had been elected to the leadership, was foolish enough, by deadly insults, to alienate the loyal servitor. He bluntly told the poor devil not to fancy that a dog could play the idler after his master's death, or that he had ceased to be a slave. When they got back to Lisbon, Enrique would be handed over to Magellan's widow, and meanwhile he would have to obey orders. If he did not get up promptly and go ashore to act as interpreter for the exchange of goods, he should have a sound drubbing. The Malays are a fierce and dangerous race, and will never endure contumely. Enrique made no sign at the moment, though doubtless aware that Magellan had manumitted him by the last will and testament, and had bequeathed him a handsome legacy. Privily he clenched his teeth while listening to Barbosa's insults. This man who wished to deprive him of his rights and who could not understand that he was wounded in mind as well as in body, should pay dearly for having called him a dog and for treating him like one.

The crafty Malay did not allow any sign of his secret intentions to escape. Obediently he betook himself to the market, and acted as interpreter. But he made another, a very dangerous use of his native tongue. He told the Rajah of Cebu that the Spaniards had already planned to carry off the rest of the unsold goods to their ships, and disappear with them next day. If Charles forestalled this attempt, he would turn the tables, seize the Spaniards' goods, and their three fine ships into the bargain.

It is likely enough that Enrique, when making this proposal, was merely suggesting a scheme which His Majesty of Cebu had already entertained on his own account. However that may be, the words fell upon willing ears. A plan was concocted between the pair, of which neither gave any outward sign. Barter went on briskly, in the most amicable way; the Rajah showed himself as cordial as ever towards his new brethren in the faith; and Enrique, having heard the crack of Barbosa's whip, seemed thoroughly cured of his alleged laziness. On May 1, 1521, four days after Magellan's death, with a radiant countenance Enrique brought peculiarly agreeable news to the captains. The Rajah of Cebu, he said, had got together the jewels which the monarch purposed to send to his suzerain and friend, the King of Spain. To hand over these gifts as ceremoniously as possible, he had

summoned his chieftains and other principal subordinates;
would Captains Barbosa and Serrão be good enough to come
ashore with the most distinguished of their followers and, on
the part of King Charles of Spain, receive the gifts of King
Charles of Cebu?

Had Magellan still been alive, he would certainly have
remembered his experiences in the East Indies, and how, having responded to a similar amiable invitation on the part of
the Rajah of Malacca, at the latter's signal the Portuguese
who had landed without suspicion were massacred, and nothing but his own dauntless courage had enabled him to save
Francisco Serrão. But Magellan was no longer there to warn
them, so João Serrão and Duarte Barbosa walked heedlessly
into their new Christian brother's trap. They accepted the
invitation. Once more it became plain how little power astrol-
ogers have of foretelling their own fate, for Andrés de San
Martín, having apparently omitted to cast his horoscope,
joined them in the visit. Pigafetta, usually so eager to gather
news, had better luck. He had been wounded by an arrow
in the battle of Mactan, kept his bed, and thereby saved his
life.

In all, twenty-nine Spaniards went ashore, and among
them were the best, the most experienced leaders and pilots.
Ceremoniously received, they were escorted to a palm-leaf
hut, where the feast had been prepared. Crowds of natives,
playing the part of curious onlookers, assembled, thronging
round the guests in the most cordial fashion. But the Rajah's
urgency to get the Spaniards inside the palm-leaf hut made
João Carvalho, the pilot, uneasy. He communicated his suspicions to Gómez de Espinosa, master-at-arms of the fleet,

and the pair of them decided to fetch the rest of their force from the ships as soon as possible, that they might, in case of treachery, rescue their comrades. A pretext was found. They withdrew from the gathering and rowed off to the ships. They had just got on board, when shouts and screams came from the shore. Precisely as had happened years before in Malacca, the indigenes attacked the Spanish guests before these had had time to prepare for defence. At one stroke the crafty Rajah of Cebu finished off his guests, and made himself master of their trade goods, together with the arms and the armour which were supposed to render the Spaniards invulnerable and invincible.

Their comrades on shipboard were, for a moment, paralysed with horror. Then Carvalho, whom the murder of all the other captains had raised to the command, issued orders to steer landward and train the guns on the town. One broadside thundered after another. Maybe Carvalho hoped, by this demonstration, to save some of the luckless men, but perhaps it was only a spontaneous outburst of wrath. When the first round of shots began to bombard the huts, there occurred one of those horrible scenes which those who have witnessed them are never able to forget. One of the men who were in the trap, the bravest of them, João Serrão, had, like his relative Francisco Serrão at Malacca, at the last moment torn himself out of the hands of the murderers and fled to the beach. The enemy pursued him, surrounded him, disarmed and bound him. There he stood defenceless, environed by assassins, shouting to those on board to cease fire, or the Malays would take vengeance on him. For God's sake, let Carvalho send a boat with sufficient goods to ransom him.

For a moment or two it seemed as if the bargain would be struck. The price of the valiant captain had been fixed at two bombards, some copper ingots, and some pieces of cloth. But the natives insisted that the ransom should be delivered on shore before Serrão was set free, and Carvalho was probably afraid that the rascals, who had already broken troth, would seize not only the goods but the boats. It is possible, however (as we learn from Pigafetta's account), that Carvalho was actuated by mean ambition, being afraid that he would not be confirmed in his captaincy should he rescue Serrão, and would merely serve as pilot under the latter. In any case, the horrible butchery occurred. On the shore there writhed, his limbs bound, a man bleeding from many wounds and with the sweat of death on his brow, surrounded by murderers armed with krises. Serrão's last hope was that three fully manned Spanish ships lay at little more than a stone's throw from the land, under the command of his fellow-countryman Carvalho, his compadre, his chum, with whom he had shared a thousand perils. Surely Carvalho would run any risk rather than abandon him to his fate! Again and again, in the name of their friendship, he shouted, imploring Carvalho to send the ransom. He stared eagerly at the boats that lay alongside. Why did Carvalho hesitate, why did he delay? All at once Serrão, with the quick eyes of a seaman who understands every move made on board a ship, saw that the boats were being hoisted. Treason! Treason! Instead of sending to his rescue, the ships put about, and made for the offing. A breeze filled the sails. For a moment the unhappy Serrão could not believe that his blood-brother was about to forsake him, the leader, the commander, to leave him bound and helpless in

PLAN OF MALACCA
From a manuscript in the British Museum, London

MARKET IN GOA

Copper engraving from de Bry's Travel Book (1599)

the hands of murderers. Once more he cried despairingly, in stifled tones, voicing the agony of his despair. When, at length, he realized that he was to be forsaken, that the ships were abandoning him, with such strength as was left him he yelled across the waters to João Carvalho a solemn curse, praying God that at the last great day He would require the false friend to render an account of his action.

The words of this curse were to be Serrão's last. With their own eyes his faithless comrades on board had to see their chosen commander butchered. Simultaneously, before the ships had cleared the harbour, amid cries of jubilation from the indigenes, another party of them was tearing down the great Cross which Magellan had erected. What the leader had achieved during weeks of careful and patient work came to naught in an hour. Covered with shame, the curse of their dying captain in their ears, the scorn of the triumphant savages pursuing them in their retreat, like hunted criminals the Spaniards sailed away from the island on which, under Magellan's leadership, they had landed as gods.

Painful was the review which the rescued men held as soon as they had escaped from the ill-starred harbour of Cebu. Of all the blows of Fate which the fleet had sustained since leaving Spain, those that resulted from the stay in Cebu were the most disastrous. Besides Magellan, the irreplaceable leader, they had lost the most experienced of their captains, Duarte Barbosa and João Serrão, who, being well acquainted with the East Indian coast, would have been most useful to them on the homeward voyage. The death of Andrés de San Martín had deprived them of their nautical expert, and the treason of Enrique had robbed them of their interpreter. After a careful enumeration, it appeared that, of the two hundred and sixty-five men who had signed on in Seville, there were left no more than one hundred and fifteen, so that the three ships were undermanned. Better, then, to sacrifice one of the three, in order that the remaining two might have approximately full complements. It was decided to abandon the "Concepción," which had long been leaky, and seemed in any case unlikely to keep afloat all the way back to Spain. Off the island of Bohol, therefore, the death-sentence was carried out. Everything worth saving, down to the last nail and the thinnest rope, was transferred to the other ships, and the wooden corpse was then fired. Gloomily the sailors looked on as the flames gathered strength, until they devoured the "Concepción," which for two years had been a home to many of them, and now, charred and hissing, sank in these distant waters. Five ships, gaily dressed with flags and fully manned, had dropped down the Guadalquivir from Seville. The first victim had been the "Santiago," wrecked on the Patagonian coast. In the Strait of Magellan, the "San Antonio" had basely deserted her consort. Now the "Concepción" had become her own pyre and her own coffin. Only two ships, the last two, set forth side by side, across waters still unknown: the "Trinidad," which had been Magellan's flag-ship, and the "Victoria," whose glory it would be to complete the admiral's task and immortalize his name.

How sorely this reduced fleet missed its real leader, the experienced Captain-General Magellan, was now to be shown by the uncertain course of the "Trinidad" and the "Victoria." As if blinded, they groped their way through the Malay Archipelago. Instead of steering south-east to the Moluccas, to which they were now quite close, for some unexplained reason they headed south-west, in uncertain zigzags. Six months were wasted in these wanderings, which led them to Borneo and to Mindanao. Even more plainly than by the lack of a steadfast course, was the loss of the great admiral disclosed by the failure of discipline. Under the firm guidance of Magellan there had been neither robbery by land nor piracy by sea. Strict order was kept and careful reckoning. Never had the captain-general forgotten that he was pledged to the King-Emperor to maintain the honour of the Spanish flag in the remotest parts of the earth. His puny successor Carvalho, who owed his promotion to the rank of captain-general only to the slaying of his superior officers by the rajahs of Mactan and Cebu, knew nothing of moral restraint. He was an unashamed pirate, and seized whatever he could lay hands on. When a junk was sighted, it was attacked and plundered; and the unconscionable Carvalho put in his own pocket whatever ransom he secured on these occasions. He kept no accounts, being his own contador and tesorero. Whereas for the sake of order Magellan had never allowed women on board, the new captain-general took three from a captured junk, on the pretext that he intended to present them to the Queen of Spain. By degrees the doings of this lawless pasha became distasteful even to his lawless crew. "Vedendo che faceva cosa che non fosse in servitio del Re"—seeing, Juan Sebastian del Cano reports, that Carvalho was pursuing his own advantage and not that of the King— they deprived him of his command, and authority was vested in a triumvirate: Gómez de Espinosa as captain of the "Trinidad," del Cano as captain of the "Victoria," and the pilot Poncero as "gobernador de la armada."

Still, this change of government did not put an end to the futile wanderings. The strayed ships had no difficulty, amid these richly populated islands, in replenishing their stores by barter and robbery; but they seemed to have forgotten their real task, that which Magellan had undertaken. At length a chance gave them the clue to an exit from the labyrinth of the Philippine Islands. While cruising up the Gulf of Mindanao they fell in with a large prahu, which, following their usual custom, they captured after desperate resistance. One of the survivors, its captain, proved to be a man from Ternate, who must, of course, know the way to his own home, the long-desired Spice Islands. Yes, he knew the way, and, what was more, he knew Francisco Serrão, Magellan's friend. At length they could set the right course. The last trial had been endured; they could make for the goal to which they had again and again been close during these senseless meanderings, and which had continually evaded them. A few days' easy sailing brought them to what they had been looking for throughout the last six months. On November 6 there rose above the horizon the mountains of Ternate and Tidore. They had reached the Fortunate Islands.

"The pilot," says Pigafetta, "told us that they were the Moluccas, for the which we thanked God, and to comfort us we discharged all our artillery. Nor ought it to cause astonishment that we were so rejoiced, since we had passed twenty-seven months, less two days, always in search of these

Moluccas, wandering hither and thither for that purpose among innumerable islands."

On November 8, 1521, they landed on Tidore, one of the happy islands of which Magellan had so long dreamed. Even as the deceased Cid, mounted by his men upon his trusty charger, gained another victory, so did Magellan's energy enforce his will long after life had fled. His ships, his crews, looked upon the Promised Land a sight of which was forbidden him, the pathfinder, even as Moses was forbidden to set foot upon the Land of Canaan. Nor was Francisco Serrão, who had called to him across the ocean, and inspired him with his great idea, still alive. In vain had the friend stretched forth his arms towards the friend whom he had sailed round the world to see. Serrão had died a few weeks before, presumably poisoned; thus both pioneers of this great circumnavigation paid for their ambition with their life.

But Serrão's enthusiastic description of the archipelago proved fully justified. Not only was the scenery splendid, not only was the earth here richly endowed by nature, but the inhabitants were friendly beyond compare. "What are we to say of these islands?" writes Maximilian Transylvanus in his famous letter. "Here everything is simple, and without high value, including peace, comfort, and spices. The best of these things, perhaps the best of earthly goods, to wit, peace, would seem, through the wickedness of man, to have been expelled from our world and to have taken refuge here." The King, whose friend and helper Serrão had been, came at once to call, being rowed in a prahu with a silken canopy. He received the guests in brotherly fashion on his boat.

"After such long tossing upon the seas, and so many dangers," he said, "come and enjoy the pleasures of the land, and refresh your bodies, and do not think but that you have arrived at the kingdom of your own sovereign." He willingly acknowledged the supremacy of the Spanish monarch; and, instead of, like the other chieftains whom they encountered, extorting from them as much as he could, this generous prince begged them to cease their gifts, for "he had nothing worthy to send to our King as a present."

Fortunate Isles. Everything the Spaniards could wish, was provided in abundance: the costliest spices, food, and gold-dust; and what the friendly Al Mansur could not himself furnish, he procured from neighbouring islands. The mariners were charmed by so much happiness after all their sorrows and privations. Frenziedly they bought spices and the precious birds of paradise, giving their shirts, their muskets, their crossbows, their cloaks, their belts in exchange; for now they were going home, and would soon become rich men by the sale of these easily secured treasures. Many of them would have liked to follow Serrão's example, and remain in this paradise. To a considerable proportion of them, therefore, the news was by no means unwelcome when it transpired, shortly before the time appointed for departure, that only one of the ships was sufficiently seaworthy to undertake the homeward voyage. Fifty of the mariners out of the hundred would have to stay on the Fortunate Islands, at any rate until the necessary repairs had been effected.

The ship thus condemned to wait was Magellan's former flag-ship, the "Trinidad." The "capitana," the flag-ship, had been the first to leave San Lucar, the first to enter the Strait of Magellan, the first to steer out into the unknown Pacific—always in the van, the embodied will of its leader and master. Now that the leader had passed away, it could sail no farther. Even as a faithful dog will not allow itself to be removed from its master's grave, so did the ship remain in the islands which had been Magellan's goal. The water-butts had been filled, the hold had been richly stored with provisions, many hundredweight of spices had been carried on board; the flag of St. James had been hoisted, bearing the inscription: "Let this be the sign of our happy return"; the sails were set—when the rotten old ship groaned and its seams opened. Water oozed in all over the place, and not from any definite leak. Hastily the freight had to be discharged, in order to beach the "Trinidad" before she sank. Many weeks would be required to make her water-tight once more, and her sister ship, the only other remaining craft of the armada of five, could not wait so long. Now that the third year had come, it was time to send a message to Emperor Charles V to relate that Magellan had fulfilled his pledge at the cost of life, and had performed the greatest deed in history beneath the Spanish flag. It was unanimously agreed that the "Trinidad," when she had been made seaworthy, should recross the Pacific in order to reach overseas Spain at Panama, while the "Victoria," taking advantage of favourable winds, should sail westward across the Indian Ocean and reach home by rounding the Cape of Good Hope.

The commanders of the two ships, now about to take leave of one another for ever after two and a half years of close companionship—Gómez de Espinosa and Sebastian del Cano —had once before stood together in a decisive moment. During that fateful hour of the mutiny in Port San Julian, Gómez de Espinosa, then master-at-arms, had been Magellan's most faithful helper. Thanks to his timely dagger-thrust, the "Victoria" had been reconquered, and saved to continue the voyage. Sebastian del Cano, on the other hand, then no more than a sobresaliente, a youthful Basque, had that night been on the side of the mutineers. With his active help, the other rebels had gained mastery of the "San Antonio." Magellan had thankfully rewarded the trusty Gómez de Espinosa, and had magnanimously pardoned the traitor del Cano. Had Fate been just, Espinosa, who had ensured the triumph of Magellan's idea, would also have been appointed to end the glorious voyage of circumnavigation. But, magnanimously rather than justly, the lot decided for the unworthy. Whereas Espinosa, with the doomed crew of the "Trinidad," was to perish ingloriously after many strayings and sufferings, forgotten by ungrateful history, the stars had decided to crown with imperishable glory the man who had tried to hinder Magellan's deed.

This was a pathetic scene on the other side of the world, when forty-seven officers and men who were going home in the "Victoria," bade farewell to the fifty-one selected to await on Tidore the repair of the "Trinidad." Down to the last hour, the latter group stayed on board the "Victoria" with their comrades, to embrace them once again, and to send home letters and greetings. Two and a half years of hardships shared had cemented unity among those who spoke different tongues and belonged to so many different races. No dissension could now disturb their harmony. When the "Victoria" heaved anchor, the crew of the "Trinidad" were still unwilling to depart. On rowboats, or paddling in Malay prahus, they kept alongside the "Victoria" as she gathered way, to see a little longer the faces of those who were homeward bound, and to shout a last message. Not until night fell and their arms were weary, did they put about and make for the shore, while a broadside was fired in last good-bye. Then the "Victoria" continued her ever-memorable voyage of circumnavigation alone.

This homeward journey of the battered galleon round the second half of the globe, after thirty months had been spent upon the first half of the journey, was one of the most heroic deeds in the history of navigation; and del Cano now compensated for his behaviour to Magellan by admirably fulfilling the will of the dead leader. At first glance the task assigned him did not seem particularly difficult. Since the turn of the century, Portuguese ships had frequently sailed with the monsoon from the Malay Archipelago to Portugal, and back again, with the regularity of a pendulum. The Indian voyage, which under Almeida and Albuquerque was an adventure into the unknown, now required nothing more than knowledge of a route which had been accurately surveyed, and where all the stopping-places had become familiar. At each port of call in the Indies and in Africa, at Malacca, Mozambique, and Cape Verde, there was a Portuguese factor with other officials; stores could be obtained at each one of them; everywhere a captain could find helpers and pilots. But the trouble which faced del Cano was, not merely that it would be impossible for him to touch at these Portuguese settlements, but that he must make long detours to avoid them,

and must travel by unfrequented ways. At Tidore he had
been informed by a Portuguese refugee how King Emanuel
had ordered that Magellan's ships were to be seized, and the
crews arrested as pirates; and, in actual fact, their unhappy
comrades on the "Trinidad" were not spared this cruel fate.
Thus, what del Cano had to undertake was to sail a worm-
eaten, leaky, and overladen ship (of which nearly three years
before, in the port of Seville, Consul Alvarez had declared he
would not dare to take a voyage in it to the Canaries) across
the wide Indian Ocean, round the Cape of Good Hope, and
up the west coast of Africa, without touching at any port.
We need merely glance at the map to see what a formidable
prospect this was, a voyage which, after the lapse of four centuries, would be difficult for a well-equipped modern steam-
ship.

This unexampled traverse from the Malay Archipelago to
Seville began at the island of Timor on February 13, 1522.
Once more del Cano had taken on board stores and fresh
water; once more, mindful of his dead master's foresight, he
had had his ship thoroughly overhauled and caulked before
surrendering for many months to the unceasing perils of
winds and waves. During the first days they sighted numerous islands with towering mountains, whose lower slopes
were wooded with tropical green to the water's edge. But the
season was too advanced for the voyagers to stop anywhere;
del Cano had to make the best use he could of the monsoon
while it lasted, so he did not land, and the navigators left
these enchanting spots unvisited, much to the distress of the
ever-curious Pigafetta, who had not yet seen enough "wonderful things." To save himself from boredom, he passed the

time in obtaining from the natives on board (there were nine-teen of them in addition to the forty-seven European mem-bers of the crew) information about the alluring isles, and the brown-skinned folk tickled his fancy with the most amazing fables, which might have come from *The Arabian Nights*. Upon one island, they told him, lived men who were not more than a span high, but their ears were as long as them-selves, so they used one of them to lie upon and the other as a coverlet. Then the travellers passed an island which was said to be inhabited only by women, and no man was allowed to visit it. Nevertheless, the women were impregnated by the wind. Any boys to which they gave birth were killed, only the girls being allowed to live and grow up. . . . Gradually the last of these islands faded away in the blue distance, and then, for what seemed an interminable time, the navigators sighted no more land as they sailed south-westward across the wide and monotonous stretches of the Indian Ocean. No hu-man beings, no ships, no sails, not a sound; nothing but the perpetual blue vacancy of vast and endless space.

Not a sound did they hear, nor did they see an unfamiliar face during all these weeks upon weeks. Then there emerged from the depths of the ship a well-known spectre, hollow-eyed and pale—famine. This spectre, who had been their in-separable companion on the Pacific Ocean, the murderer and torturer of their trusty comrades, must have come aboard as a stowaway, for he now stalked among them, staring greedily in their alarmed faces. An unforeseen catastrophe had frus-trated del Cano's careful calculations. The "Victoria" had been amply provisioned for five months, her stores including large quantities of meat. But in Timor no salt was obtainable,

and under the burning sun of the tropics the inadequately
pickled pork became putrid. To escape the pestilential odour
of this carrion they had to throw the whole stock overboard.
Now they were reduced to a diet of rice and water, water
and rice, continually less rice and water that grew fouler as
day followed day. Again scurvy broke out, and again death
exacted its toll. So fearful were their sufferings when May began, that some of the crew urged making for Mozambique,
and handing over their ship to the Portuguese instead of
starving.

But del Cano, when he assumed command, del Cano, the
sometime mutineer, had been inspired with Magellan's indomitable resolve. The very man who, at the time of the mutiny on the South American coast, had faint-heartedly wished
to compel his commander to abandon the voyage, being now
himself commander, insisted upon unflinching courage in his
men, and was able to bend them to his will. "Ma inanti de-
terminamo tutti morir che andar in mano dei Portoghesi"—
"We resolved to die rather than fall into the hands of the
Portuguese." Thus, in due course, he would proudly report
to the Emperor. A bold landing on an uninhabited part of the
South African coast, eastward of the Cape, proved fruitless,
for they found neither water nor fruit in the barren land, and
had to resume the voyage without any relief to their hardships.

When they came to round the Cape of Good Hope, which
their present experience led them to designate by its old name
of Cabo Tormentoso, they suffered from heavy weather
which, on May 16, carried away their foretopmast and sprung
their foreyard. Laboriously the sick and weary mariners re-

paired these damages; and slowly, painfully, like a wounded man, the ship crept northward along the western coast of Africa. Neither in storm nor in calm, neither by day nor by night, did their grim persecutor, the grey spectre of famine, depart from them, and his assaults were accompanied by new tortures and mockery, the tortures of Tantalus. For the holds were not empty to the last crumb, as they had been when crossing the Pacific Ocean. This time the ship was loaded to bursting. The "Victoria" was freighted with hundreds of quintals of spices—so the hungry men had with them enough of these flavouring agents to render palatable the meals of perhaps a million persons. But who, with parched lips and empty stomach, can chew pepper-corns, endure the nip of cinnamon, or swallow nutmeg instead of bread? Just as it is ghastly to be at sea with "water, water, everywhere, nor any drop to drink," so, on board the "Victoria," it was horrible to be dying of hunger amid mountains of spices. Day after day, one withered corpse after another was flung overboard. A score of the Spaniards out of the forty-seven had died, and all but four of the nineteen natives, when, on July 9, 1522, after five months' voyage, they anchored off Santiago in the Cape Verde Islands.

Here was a Portuguese harbour in a Portuguese colony. A landing meant to put themselves into the enemy's hands, to capitulate just before reaching home. But hunger left no choice, since the rationed food could last at most two or three days. Del Cano, before sending some of his men ashore, gave them strict injunctions not to inform the Portuguese that the "Victoria" was the last remnant of Magellan's fleet, on its way back from the East Indies. A fable was put into their mouths. They were to pretend that they came from America, that the other two ships had preceded them to Spain, but that they had been delayed by the loss of their foretopmast on the Line. The shattered condition of the vessel confirmed this story. Without making serious inquiries, without sending officials on board to examine, the Portuguese, inspired by the freemasonry of the sea, gave a cordial reception to the mariners whose famine-stricken condition was obvious. They sent the Spaniards an abundance of water and fresh food; once, twice, thrice the boat returned from the shore richly laden with provisions. The trick seemed to have succeeded; rest, good food, and fresh water had largely restored the men's strength. They had enough supplies on board to reach Seville. Once more del Cano sent the boat ashore to fetch a further stock of rice and fruit, then he would heave anchor and the "Victoria" would prove worthy of her name.

Strangely, however, the boat did not reappear, and the commander speedily guessed what had happened. One of the boat's crew had perhaps blabbed, or an attempt may have been made to barter a handful of spices for a bottle of brandy. The Portuguese authorities had doubtless recognized that this battered craft was one of the ships of their arch-enemy Magellan, for del Cano perceived that some caravels inshore were preparing to put off, doubtless in order to seize him. Nothing but boldness and resolution could save the situation. Better leave his comrades to their fate and run for it. Although the "Victoria" now had on board no more than eighteen Europeans and four natives—a scanty crew to work the leaky ship home to Spain—del Cano hastily heaved anchor and set sail. He saved himself by flight. But it was a flight to the great, the decisive victory.

Brief and risky as had been the stay in the Cape Verde Islands, it was here that Pigafetta, the industrious chronicler, at the last moment was able to observe one of the wonders that had led him to make the voyage of circumnavigation. This was a phenomenon which he was the first man in the world to notice, and its novelty and importance were to intrigue his contemporaries. The men who went ashore for supplies returned to bring the astounding news that it was Thursday on shore, although on board ship it was unquestionably Wednesday. Pigafetta was greatly astonished, having kept his diary with the utmost precision during a voyage which had now lasted hard upon three years. Without intermission he had written "Monday, Tuesday, Wednesday," and the other days of the week. Could he possibly have missed a day? He asked Alvo, the pilot, who had also kept a record of the days in the ship's log, and Alvo was equally sure that it was Wednesday. Steering persistently westward, in some unexplained way the circumnavigators must have dropped a day out of the calendar, and Pigafetta's report of this strange phenomenon mystified the European world. A secret had been disclosed which none of the sages of Greece, neither Ptolemy nor Aristotle, had suspected, and was first brought to notice through Magellan's enterprise. This discovery, that one who counters the earth on its rolling course will have gained a day when the full circle has been traversed, was as exciting to the humanists of the sixteenth century as has been the theory of relativity to those of our own generation. Peter Martyr hastened to demand from a "wise man" an explanation of what had occurred, and reported it to the Emperor and the Pope. Thus, while his shipmates brought home thousands of bushels of spices, the Knight of Rhodes, as fruit of his journey, brought the most precious thing on earth, a piece of new knowledge.

Not yet, however, had the "Victoria" reached home. With groaning timbers, slowly and wearily, exerting her last energies, she continued the final stage of the voyage. Of the sixty-six souls on board when she left the Spice Islands, only twenty-two were left; instead of one hundred and thirty-two hands there were no more than forty-four to do the work, just when powerful hands were most urgently needed. For, shortly before she reached port, there came another catastrophe. The old ship's seams were letting in water. "All hands to the pumps!" was the order. But the water seemed to gain on them. Would they not have to jettison some of the several hundred quintals of precious spices, to lighten ship? No, del Cano would not waste the Emperor's property. The tired men worked at the two pumps by day and by night, toiling like criminals at the treadmill, having all the time to make sail or shorten sail as the wind slackened or freshened, to handle the tiller, to keep watch at the masthead, and to discharge the hundred and one other tasks of their daily work. It was too much for them. Getting no sleep for night after night, they staggered and tottered at their posts. "They were feebler," writes del Cano in his report to the Emperor, "than men have ever been before." Yet each must continue to per-

PLAN OF GOA
From a manuscript in the British Museum, London

THE CAPE OF GOOD HOPE AT TABLE MOUNTAIN
Dutch engraving, c. 1670

form a double, a triple task. Even so, they were barely able
to hold their own against the leak. At length, with the very
last ounce of their failing strength, they reached the goal. On
July 13 the eighteen heroes left Cape Verde. On September
4, 1521 (when the third year of the voyage was drawing to
its close), there came a shout of jubilation, for the look-out
man had sighted Cape St. Vincent. To our way of thinking,
Europe ends at Cape St. Vincent; but to them, the circumnavigators, it was where Europe, home, began. Slowly the
crags rose above the horizon, and courage revived in their
hearts. Onward! Onward! Only two more days and two
more nights. Only two more nights and one more day. Only
one night and one day. But one night more, one night. Now
all crowded the deck, trembling with happiness. Yes, there
was a silver break in the shore, showing the place where, beside San Lucar de Barrameda, the Guadalquivir entered the
sea. From that anchorage, three years earlier, under Magellan's leadership, two hundred and sixty-five men had set sail.
Now one ship, manned by eighteen survivors, was returning
to the same port. They anchored, they went ashore. The
eighteen fell on their knees to kiss the good earth of the homeland. The greatest cruise in the history of the world, the first
circumnavigation of the globe, was over.

Instantly, as in duty bound, del Cano sent a message to the
Emperor. Then they were able to enjoy the taste of real
bread which was hospitably offered them. For years they
had not fingered the soft, aromatic crumb; for years they had
not known the flavours of the wine, the meat, and the fruit
of their homeland. People stared at them as if at ghosts from
the tomb. Then they flung themselves down on palliasses to

sleep, sleep the clock round, sleep an untroubled sleep after years of unceasing anxiety, their hearts pressed against the motherly bosom of Spain.

Next morning the "Victoria" sailed upriver to Seville. From the barks and boats she encountered came astonished glances and excited hails. People had almost forgotten the craft which had in 1519 departed on an almost interminable voyage. Seville and Spain had long since given up Magellan's fleet for lost, but here was the victorious ship proudly, triumphantly working her way upstream. At length, in the distance, shone the white bell-tower of La Giralda. It was Seville! It was Seville! "Fire the bombards!" shouted del Cano, and a salute resounded across the river. With the iron mouths of these guns, three years before, they had bidden farewell to Spain; with the same cannon they had solemnly greeted the Strait of Magellan, and again greeted the unknown Pacific. With the big guns they had saluted the newly discovered archipelago of the Philippines; as now, with the same thundering bombards, did they announce the completion of their duty on reaching Magellan's goal, the Spice Islands. Thus did they bid farewell to their comrades at Tidore, when the "Victoria" left the islands for Spain. But never did the iron voices sound so loud and so jubilant as now when they announced: "We have returned. We have done what no one ever did before us. We are the first circumnavigators of the world."

Chapter Thirteen

THE RETURN AND THE SEQUEL

FERDINAND MAGELLANUS

MAGELLAN

FIRST PAGE OF TEXT IN PIGAFETTA'S ACCOUNT
OF THE VOYAGE
In his own handwriting, from the Ambrosian MS. *in Milan*

The Return and the Sequel

HUGE crowds assembled on the river-front of Seville in order (as Oviedo writes) "to admire this famous ship whose voyage was the most wonderful and the greatest thing that had ever happened in the world since God created it and men to people it." With profound emotion they scrutinized the eighteen men as they left the "Victoria"; saw how they stumbled from weakness and fatigue; how worn, sickly, and exhausted were these unexampled heroes, each of them aged by a decade in three long years of hardship. They were offered food, were invited into the houses, were begged to tell the story of their adventures and sufferings. But they refused. That would be for later. Now they must fulfil their first duty, must discharge the vow they had taken in the utmost need; must march in penitent procession to the churches of Santa María de la Victoria and Santa María Antigua. In solemn silence the pious onlookers, forming in two lines on either side of the procession, watched these eighteen survivors walking barefoot and wearing white shrouds, each holding a lighted candle, marching to thank the Almighty, at the place whence they had departed, for the unexpected grace of being delivered from so many perils and allowed to return home in safety. Once again the organ sounded; once again, in the darkness of the church, the priest held the monstrance above the kneeling men as if it had been a small but radiant sun. Having thanked God and the Saints for their own rescue, it is probable that they breathed a prayer for the souls of the brethren and comrades with whom they had joined in prayer three years earlier. For what had become of them, those who on that occasion had looked upon Magellan, their admiral, as he unfurled the damask banner given him by the King and blessed by the priest? Drowned in the sea, murdered by savages, dead from hunger and thirst, rotted by scurvy, lost, or in prison. None but these eighteen had been spared by the unsearchable decree of Fate, chosen to receive the triumph, hallowed by God's grace. Gently, they murmured prayers for the dead, for the leader who had fallen at Mactan and for the more than two hundred lost comrades.

Meanwhile the news of the fortunate return of the eighteen spread like wildfire across Europe, rousing immeasurable astonishment and admiration. Since the voyage of Columbus no event had so stirred the contemporary world. Uncertainty had been put to rest for ever. Doubt, the fiercest foe of human knowledge, had been vanquished in the geographical field. Since a ship had set sail from the port of Seville, and, sailing continually westward, had returned to the port of Seville, it had been irrefutably proved that the earth was a globe surrounded by a continuous ocean. At length the cosmography of the Hellenes and the Romans had been transcended, in defiance of the veto of the Church and foolish fables concerning the men of the Antipodes who must walk upon their heads. Established once and for all had been the circumference of the earth, the measure of the cosmos. Other bold discoverers could and would fill in numerous details in the world-picture, but the basic form of our planet had been ascertained by Magellan, and persists for all time to come. The world was a restricted region which man had conquered. This day famous in history had firmly established the pride of the Spanish nation. Under the flag of Spain, Columbus began the work of modern discovery, and under the same flag Magellan completed it. Thirty years had taught more about the place of man's habitation than had thousands and thousands of years before. Though half unwittingly, the generation which had had this intoxicating, this stupendous experience, realized that a new age, the modern age, had begun.

Widespread was the enthusiasm aroused by the immense intellectual acquisitions resulting from this journey. Even the men of business who had equipped the fleet, the Casa de Contratación and Christopher de Haro, had good reason to be pleased. They had written off as a dead loss the eight million maravedis disbursed for the equipment of the five ships, when the return of this sole survivor gave ample compensation. The five hundred and twenty quintals (about twenty-six tons) of spices brought back from the Moluccas as freight by the "Victoria" produced a net surplus of about fifteen hundred gold ducats. The cargo of this one bottom more than repaid the loss of the other four—the death of two hundred men not figuring in the accounts.

Only about a dozen persons in the whole world were seized with panic when the news came that one of Magellan's armada had got home safely after circumnavigating the globe. They were the mutinous captains and their pilots who had deserted with the "San Antonio" and had got back to Seville more than a year before. What was joyful news to others sounded like a knell to them, since they had long cherished the hope that these dangerous witnesses and accusers would never make their way back to Spain, openly expressing this in their testimony ("al juicio y parecer que han venido no volverá a Castilla el dielo Magellanes"). Such certainty had they felt that ships and crew were long since in the depths of the sea, that they had not hesitated, before the Royal Commission of Inquiry, to describe their rebellion as a patriotic act. It need hardly be said that they were silent as to the fact that Magellan had already discovered the strait at the very time when they deserted. They spoke only of a "bay" which they had entered ("entraron en una bahía"), and declared that the way sought by Magellan was useless and futile ("inútil y sin prorecho"). On the other hand they were lavish in their charges against the man whose return they never anticipated. He had violated the King's confidence, intending to hand over the fleet to the Portuguese; and they themselves had only been able to save this one ship by seizing Mesquita, whom his cousin Magellan had wrongfully placed in authority.

It was true that the Royal Commission of Inquiry did not wholly believe the mutineers' assertions, and, with remarkable impartiality, declared the conduct of both sides to have been suspicious. The mutineers and their pilots were imprisoned, as well as the loyal Mesquita; and at the same time Magellan's wife (who did not yet know that she was his widow) was forbidden to quit the town. Let us wait, decided the Commission, until the other ships and the admiral return as witnesses. It was natural, therefore, that the salute of bombards which announced the return of one of Magellan's ships should sound deadly to the mutineers. They were lost men. Magellan had succeeded, and would take terrible vengeance upon those who, violating their oaths and the law of the high seas, had deserted him and had thrown his captain into chains.

They breathed more freely when they heard that Magellan was dead. The chief accuser was dumb. Still safer did they feel when they were informed that del Cano had captained the "Victoria" home. Del Cano was their accomplice, had taken part with them in the mutiny at Port San Julian. He would never accuse them of a crime in which he had himself participated. He would bear witness for them, not against them. Magellan's death was a signal boon, and so would be del Cano's testimony. They were right in so thinking. True, Mesquita was released from prison, and rewarded. But they themselves, thanks to del Cano's aid, escaped punishment for mutiny and desertion, and were forgotten amid the general rejoicing.

Del Cano's messenger brought news of safe return hot-foot to Valladolid. Emperor Charles was just back from Germany, having come from one historic moment to another. At the Diet of Worms he had seen Luther's resolute hand destroy the spiritual unity of the Church. Now, back in Spain, he was to learn that simultaneously another innovator had refashioned the picture of the world, and at the cost of his own life had proved its spatial unity. Impatient to hear more about the adventure (for he had personally collaborated to promote this achievement, which was perhaps the greatest and most enduring triumph of his life), the same day he sent command

to del Cano, who was to come instantly to court, accompanied by two of the most trustworthy and intelligent from
among the crew ("los más cuerdos y de mejor razón"), and to
bring with him all the documents that bore upon the journey.
The two whom Sebastian del Cano was to take with him to
Valladolid were easy to choose, the two "most trustworthy
and intelligent" men being obviously Pigafetta and the pilot
Alvo; but the captain's behaviour with regard to the Emper-
or's other wish, that all papers relating to the voyage should
be handed over, seems to have been more ambiguous. Some
suspicion, unfortunately, attaches to his attitude, for not a
line penned by Magellan's hand did del Cano take with him.
(The only extant document written by Magellan during the
voyage was preserved by the Portuguese, being found on the
"Trinidad" when that ship was seized by them.) Now it is
certain that Magellan, being a stickler for duty, must, as admiral of the fleet and aware of the importance of his mission,
have kept a diary, which can have been destroyed only from
jealousy. It probably seemed inexpedient to those who had
mutinied against Magellan during the voyage that the Emperor should learn too much about that affair; and the result
was that after the leader's death every line of his handwriting
mysteriously disappeared. No less remarkable was the vanish-
ing of the great diary which Pigafetta had kept, and whose
holograph original he gave personally to Charles V on the
occasion of this visit. ("Fra le altre cose li detti uno libro,
scritto di mia mano, de tutte le cose passate de giorno in giorno nel viaggio nostro.") This original diary cannot possibly
have been identical with Pigafetta's subsequently penned narrative, which was manifestly no more than an epitome of the

aforesaid journal. Besides, a report by the Mantuan ambassador can be quoted in support of the contention that the two
books were entirely distinct. On October 21, the ambassador
expressly refers to an extended diary by Pigafetta ("libro
molto bello che de zorno in zorno li e scritto el viagio e paese
che anno ricercato"), to promise three weeks later a compen-
dium of the same ("un breve estratto o sommario del libro
che hano portato quelli de le Indie")—precisely what is extant today as Pigafetta's report of the expedition, which has
been very inadequately supplemented by the notes of the
various pilots, the letter of Peter Martyr, and that of Maximilian Transylvanus. We can guess easily enough why Pigafetta's diary was destroyed; because it was thought expedient
to make away with any reports of the resistance which the
Spanish officers put up against Magellan the Portuguese, that
the triumph of del Cano, the Basque nobleman, should stand
out more clearly. We gather that this thrusting of Magellan
into the background was most annoying to the loyal Pigafetta. He felt that false weights were being used. It is the in-
variable tendency of the world to reward the man who has
the luck to finish a job, and forget those whose preliminary
expenditure of blood and of mental labour prepared it and
rendered it possible. On this occasion the distribution of honours and rewards was peculiarly unjust. The very man who
wanted to hinder Magellan's deed at the decisive moment, the
sometime mutineer Sebastian del Cano, annexed all the glory,
all the honours, all the dignities. An earlier offence (to escape
the penalty for which he enrolled himself as a member of
Magellan's fleet), that of having sold a ship to a foreigner,
was washed out by a formal act of exoneration, and he was

granted a pension of five hundred gold ducats. The Emperor raised him to the knighthood and presented him with a coat of arms, wherein del Cano is symbolically represented as being the doer of the immortal deed. Two crossed cinnamon staves with nutmegs and cloves occupy the inner shield. Above stands a helmet, bearing the globe, and the proud inscription "Primus circumdedisti me" encircle this globe. All the glory of Magellan's work is assigned to the man who, during the journey, tried to hinder it.

Pigafetta held his tongue, but thought the more. For the first time in his life this touchingly faithful young man became aware of the eternal injustice that prevails in our world. He got away as quickly as he could. ("Me ne partii de lì al meglio potei.") The courtiers might have nothing to say of Magellan's exploits, unworthy persons might snatch at Magellan's credit, but Pigafetta knew whose idea, whose work, whose service had made the famous deed possible. Here at court he could not venture to speak, but for the sake of justice he determined to establish the dead man's glory before the eyes of posterity. In his travel records he would not mention del Cano's name during his account of the homeward voyage, saying merely: "We sailed," "We determined," to indicate that del Cano achieved no more than anyone else. Let the court reward this intruder, though in a critical hour he had done everything he could to hinder the deed; the deed itself was imperishable, and the fame of it rightly accrued to the man who was beyond the reach of rewards and of honours. With wonderful fidelity, Pigafetta took the side of the vanquished, and eloquently defended the rights of him whose tongue was stilled in death. Dedicating his book to the Grand

ALLEGORICAL REPRESENTATION OF MAGELLAN

Copper engraving from de Bry's Travel Book (1594)

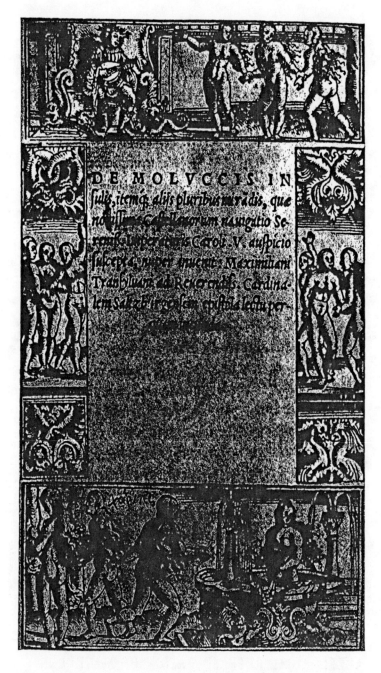

DE MOLVCCIS IN
sulis, itemꝗ, alijs pluribus mirãdis, que
nobilissima Castellanorum nauigatio Se-
renißim per ao ia Caroli V. auspicio
suscepta, nuper inuenit: Maximiliani
Transyluani ad Reuerenitß, Cardina-
lem Salzburgensem epistola lectu per

TITLE PAGE OF MAXIMILIAN TRANSYLVANUS'S ACCOUNT
OF MAGELLAN'S VOYAGE (COLOGNE, 1523)

Master of Rhodes, Pigafetta writes: "I hope that the renown of so high-spirited a captain will never be forgotten. Among the many other virtues which adorned him, one was especially remarkable, that he always remained exceptionally steadfast even amid the greatest misfortune. He bore the pangs of hunger more patiently than did any of us. There was no man alive who understood more than he about the sciences of cartography and navigation. The truth of this is proved by the way in which he brought to light things that no one before him had ventured to see or to discover."

But Magellan, the man who had really done the work, was not on hand in the hour of triumph. It is always death which first reveals the last mystery. Not until this moment, when his idea had been victoriously fulfilled, was disclosed the tragedy of the lonely man who had throughout life been allowed only to bear the burdens and never to enjoy the fruits of success. From among millions upon millions, Destiny had selected for a great deed this obscure, taciturn, reserved navigator who was ready to stake all his earthly possessions and his life on behalf of an idea. His mission called him to labour, not to joy, sending him forth like a journeyman, without gratitude or grace. Others received the credit for his work, others snatched the gain, others were acclaimed at festivals; for strict as he himself had been throughout, Destiny was even stricter to the hard-bitten soldier. It was only because he willed it with all the powers of his spirit that he was enabled to find his way around the world. But he was not permitted to finish his course. He could only look on, could only stretch out his hand towards the garland of victory; for when he wished to place it on his brow, Fate said: "Enough," and struck down the extended hand.

No more was accorded to him than the doing of the deed; he was denied its golden shadow, triumph and temporal fame. Nothing can impress us more painfully, therefore, than to read Magellan's last will and testament once more, after we know what happened when the time came for it to take effect. The homecoming denied him what he had prayed for in the hour of departure. None of the rewards he had struggled for on his own behalf and that of his dear ones was to accrue. Not so much as one of the dispositions among all those he had so thoughtfully specified in his testament was carried out by his successors after his heroic death. Pitilessly even the purest, the most pious wishes were refused. Magellan stated his desire to be interred in a Catholic cathedral; but his body fell to corruption on a foreign strand. Thirty masses were to be read over his coffin; instead, the hordes of Silapulapu exulted round his shamelessly mutilated corpse. Three of the poor were to be clothed and fed on the day of the funeral, but no one received a cloak of grey stuff, a cap, a shirt, and a pair of shoes, that he might pray to God for Magellan's soul. The silver that he bequeathed to the Holy Crusade, the alms that he devoted to prisoners, the sums that he wished to pay to monasteries and infirmaries, were none of them disbursed. For there was no one on hand able to see to the fulfilment of his last will and testament; and, had his comrades managed to bring home his body, there would not have been a maravedi available to buy him a shroud.

But were not Magellan's heirs wealthy? Did not the con-

tract assign to them one-fifth of all profits of the venture?
Was not his widow one of the richest women in Seville? Was
it not provided that his grandchildren and great-grandchildren
were to be adelantados, hereditary governors, of the newly
discovered islands? No, Magellan had no heirs, for there was
no one to get the will enforced. Indeed, there was no one to
profit by its provisions. Within a year his widow Beatriz and
his only son Rodrigo passed away—before the "Victoria"
got back to Seville. (As regards the expected second child,
we are told that Beatriz miscarried.) With one blow, his race
was extinguished. No one was on hand to wear his coat of
arms; no one, no one, no one; vain had been the precautions
of the nobleman, vain those of the husband and father; vain
the pious wishes of a good Christian. Diego Barbosa, indeed,
his father-in-law, lived on, but must have cursed the day
when this unlucky guest, this "Flying Dutchman," crossed
the threshold of his house. The newcomer had married his
daughter, and she was dead; had taken Duarte Barbosa, his
only son, with him on the voyage, and Duarte had never returned. Disastrous had been the atmosphere of misfortune
diffused by Magellan. Whoever befriended him and helped
him, became involved in his dark career; whoever trusted him
paid heavily for the trust. This great and dangerous deed had,
like a vampire, destroyed the welfare of its promoters, and
snatched the lives of most of them. Faleiro, Magellan's partner, having returned to Portugal, was imprisoned; Aranda,
who had smoothed Magellan's path, was subjected to a
shameful inquiry and lost his money. Enrique, whose freedom Magellan had promised, was treated as a slave immedi-

ately after his master's death; Mesquita, his cousin, was thrice put in irons for having been loyal to him; Duarte Barbosa and João Serrão were both murdered in Cebu within a few days of their leader's death. But the man who had opposed him, Sebastian del Cano, was able to grasp all the glory and all the profit which should have gone to the faithful and to the dead.

Something yet more tragic happened. The very deed to which Magellan offered his life and his all, seemed to have been futile. Wishing to gain the Spice Islands for Spain, Magellan did so at the cost of his life. Then, what had begun as a heroic enterprise ended as a petty mercantile transaction. For three hundred and fifty thousand ducats, Emperor Charles sold the islands to Portugal. The path Magellan had found was left almost unused, and thus proved of little advantage to anybody. Even after his death, danger dogged the footsteps of those who tried to follow his example. So many of the ships that wanted to sail through the Strait of Magellan came to grief in the attempt, that navigators for decades avoided this perilous passage and preferred to get their goods into the Pacific or out of it by the laborious land route across the Isthmus of Panama. So sedulously, in the end, was the strait shunned because of its risk, the strait whose discovery had been hailed by the world with jubilation, that within a generation it was almost forgotten, and had become a myth once more. Some forty years after Magellan's traverse, the famous poem *La Araucana* bluntly declared that the Strait of Magellan no longer existed, that it was undiscoverable and unnavigable, either because a mountain had blocked it by

falling into it or because an island had thrust itself up as a
barrier to the channel.

> Esta secreta senda descubierta
> Quedó para nosotros escondida
> Ora sea yerro de la altura cierta,
> Ora que alguna isleta removida
> Del tempestuoso mar y viento airado
> Encallando en la boca la ha cerrado.

So legendary had become the Strait of Magellan that fifty-
eight years after its discovery the bold marauder Francis
Drake was able to use it for a surprise descent upon the Spanish colonies on the west coast of South America, and for the
plundering of the silver-freighted argosies of Spain. Thereupon the Spaniards hastily built a fortress, to hinder the passage of other filibusters. The fleet which, in pursuance of the
Spanish monarch's orders, sailed into the strait, was pitifully
shipwrecked; and the name of Puerto Hambre, Port Famine,
recorded the starvation of the Spanish colonists of Patagonia.
Since then none but occasional whalers and other rare ships
have traversed the route which Magellan had expected to
become the main channel of intercourse between Europe
and the South Seas. When, in the autumn of 1913, President
Wilson, by turning a switch in Washington, opened the
sluices of the Panama Canal which the Americans had cut
between the Atlantic and the Pacific, the Strait of Magellan
was rendered superfluous. The decree of Destiny was that
henceforward it would remain of purely historical or purely
geographical interest. The long-desired "paso" was not to

be the route for thousands upon thousands of ships every year; Spain was to be no richer because of it, nor Europe mightier; it was never to be used as the nearest and most convenient way to the Indies. The result is that of all regions in the habitable world, the coasts of southern Patagonia and those of Tierra del Fuego remain the most forsaken and desolate.

But never in history does temporal utility decide the moral value of an achievement. He only can permanently increase the wealth of mankind who increases man's knowledge of himself and intensifies his creative impulses. In this sense, what Magellan did excelled the deeds of his contemporaries. Perhaps the most valid of his titles to renown is this, that he did not (like most leaders) sacrifice the lives of myriads on behalf of an idea, but mainly his own. Ever memorable, therefore, will be the heroic self-sacrifice of the Pioneer of the Pacific, and the splendid venture of these five poor little lonely ships that set forth on their voyage to play their part in the hallowed war of mankind against the unknown, and of which only one got back victorious after having circumnavigated the world. Nor will he ever be forgotten, the man who conceived this boldest of thoughts, and who, thanks to the mysterious transformation of energy which goes on in the human brain, was able to realize his dream in the world of fact. For by learning, after many years' fruitless search, the true dimensions of our globe, man for the first time discovered his own true dimensions, became aware of his own greatness with renewed pleasure and fortified courage. This deed of Magellan has shown for all time that an idea, winged by genius and sturdily energized by passion, proves stronger than the elements of nature, and that a thing which a hundred generations have regarded as no more than a wish-dream can by one man in his short lifetime be translated into the realm of reality and become an imperishable truth.

CHRONOLOGICAL TABLE

Birth of Magellan	1480
War service in the East Indies	1505–1512
" " in Africa	1513
Received in audience by King Emanuel and dismissed from Portuguese service	1515
Having renounced Portuguese nationality, he arrives in Seville	October 20, 1517
He signs the agreement with the King of Spain	March 22, 1518
The fleet leaves Seville for San Lucar	August 10, 1519
" " sails from San Lucar	September 20, 1519
" " reaches Tenerife	September 26, 1519
" " leaves Tenerife	October 3, 1519
" " arrives at Rio de Janeiro	December 13, 1519
" " leaves Rio de Janeiro	December 26, 1519
" " reaches Rio de la Plata	January 10, 1520
" " leaves Rio de la Plata	February 2, 1520
" " reaches Port San Julian	March 31, 1520
Mutiny in Port San Julian	April 2, 1520
Condemnation and execution of Quesada	April 7, 1520
Loss of the "Santiago"	May 22, 1520
Departure from Port San Julian	August 24, 1520
" " Santa Cruz	October 18, 1520
Reaches entrance of Strait of Magellan	October 21, 1520
The fleet enters Strait of Magellan	October 25, 1520
Desertion of the "San Antonio"	November 1520
The fleet enters the Pacific	November 28, 1520
" " passes St. Paul's Island	January 24, 1521
" " " the Tiburones	February 4, 1521
" " reaches the Ladrones	March 6, 1521
" " " Suluan in the Philippines	March 16, 1521
" " " Mazzava in the Philippines	March 28, 1521
" " " Cebu in the Philippines	April 7, 1521

Magellan killed in the battle of Mactan	April 27, 1521
Death of João Serrão and Duarte Barbosa	May 1, 1521
The survivors burn the "Concepción"	May 1521
The "San Antonio" reaches Seville	May 6, 1521
The "Victoria" and the "Trinidad" reach the Moluccas	November 8, 1521
The "Trinidad" proves unseaworthy	December 18, 1521
The "Victoria" leaves Tidore on the homeward voyage	December 21, 1521
The "Victoria" leaves Ombaya	January 25, 1522
"　　"　　" Timor	February 13, 1522
"　　" rounds the Cape of Good Hope	May 18, 1522
The "Victoria" reaches the Cape Verde Islands	July 9, 1522
"　　" at San Lucar	September 6, 1522
"　　" anchors at Seville (after a voyage of three years, all but twelve days)	September 8, 1522

APPENDIXES

APPENDIX I

COPIA DER NEWEN ZEYTUNG
AUSS PRESILLG LANDT *

Item wist das auff den Zwelfften tag des Monadts Octobers Ein Schiff aufs Presillg landt hye an ist kummen vmb geprech der Victualia, So dan Nono vñ Christoffel de Haro vnd andere gearmirt oder gerüst haben. Der Schiff sein Zway, durch des konigs von Portugal erlaubnuss vmb das Presilglandt zu beschreiben oder zu erfaren Vnd haben das Lanndt in Sechs oder Syben hundert meyll weyt deschribiert, dann man das vor wissen hat gehabt. Vnnd da sie kommen sein ad Capo de bona sperantza, das ist ein spitz oder ort so in das meer get, gleich der Nort Assril, vnd noch ein grad höher oder weyter. Vñ do sie in solche Clima oder gegent kommen sein Nemlich in Viertzig grad hoch, Haben sie das Presill mit ainem Capo, das ist die spitz oder ein ort, so in das mer get, funden. Vn haben den selbigen Capo vmbseylet oder vmbfaren, vñ gefundē, das der selb Calfo gleich ist gangen wie Europa leyt mit dem Syt ponente leuante, das ist gelegēheyt zwischen dem auffgangk oder Ost, vnd nyderganngk oder West, Dann sie haben auff der anndern seyten auch die landt gesehen, Als sie bey Sechtzig meyllen vmb den Capo kommē sein, zu geleicher weyss als wen ainer in Leuanten fert, vnd die skritta (!) de gibilterra passiert, das ist, furfert, oder hyndurch einfarn, vnd das landt von Barbaria sicht. Vnd als sie umb den Capo kūmen sein, wie gemelt ist, vnd gegen vns Nordwestwertz geseylet oder gefaren haben. Do ist vngewitter so gross worden, auch windt gewesen, das sie nicht weyter haben kunnen saylen, oder faren. Do haben sie durch Tramotana, das ist Nort, oder mitternacht, wider her vmb auff die annder seyten vnd

---

* This pamphlet, published in 1507 simultaneously by Erhart Öglin in Augsburg and by an anonymous printer, contains the erroneous account of an earlier discovery of the Strait of Magellan by a Portuguese expedition (c. 1502–1503). The beginning of the Swabian text here reprinted follows the copy in the

Costa, das ist landt, von Presill müssen faren. Der Piloto, das ist der schiffuerer, oder Schiflayter, So mit dysem Schiff gefaren ist, ist mein fast güt frewndt. Ist auch der berümbtest so in der konig von Portugal hat. Ist auch etlich Rayss in India gewesen, der sagt mir vnd vermayndt, das von sollichem Cabo dye Presill, das ist ein anfangk des Presill landt, vber Sechshundert meyl gen Malaqua nit sey. Vermayndt auch in kurtzer zeyt durch solichen Viagio, das ist weg oder rayss, von Lisibona gen Malaqua zufaren vnd widerumb kumen, das dem kunig von Portugal mit der Specerey ein grosse hilff wirdt pringen. Sie finden auch das das landt vō Presill hynumb get byss gen Malaqua. . .

APPENDIX II

CONTRACT CONCERNING THE DISCOVERY OF THE
SPICE ISLANDS ENTERED INTO BY HIS
MAJESTY WITH MAGELLAN
AND FALEIRO *

In the books which I, Francisco de los Cobos, possess on the decrees relative to the contracts with India and the spice agreements, there is a contract which His Majesty had drawn up with Ferdinand Magellan and Ruy Faleiro. Its contents are, verbatim, as follows: You, Ruy Faleiro and Ferdinand Magellan, knights of Portugal, have informed me that, with the help of God, you wish to undertake a voyage to discover unknown lands and to place them under Our rule, as is set forth in greater detail in the contract whose contents are as follows: Since you, Ruy Faleiro and Ferdinand Magellan, knights of Portugal, wish to enter My service, I commission you to seek, in that part of the ocean which is under Our suzerainty, islands, mainlands, spices, and other things by means of which We shall be advantaged and which will benefit Our land. Therefore do I enter with you into the following contract:

You shall with good fortune voyage upon the ocean and go in search of discoveries within Our demarcation. Since it would be unjust that others should cross your path, and since you take the labours of this undertaking upon yourselves, it is therefore My will and I promise that, during the next ten years, I will give no one permission to go in quest of discoveries on the same route and in the same regions as yourselves. Should anyone desire to go upon such an undertaking and come to Us for Our permission, We will, before We bestow it, inform you of it, so that you may be able to assume charge of it. If you are able to carry out the enterprise within the time proposed by

---

* Taken from the fourth volume of the *Colección de los viages y descubrimientos* by D. Martín Fernández de Navarrete, Madrid, 1837.

yourselves, you may then assume charge of it, if you are well equipped and have as many ships in good condition, and as well manned, as the others who wish to undertake the discovery. It is understood, however, that if We send out other expeditions, or wish to give Our permission to others for the purpose of discovering islands and mainlands, We may do so if their intention is to seek discoveries in that unexplored part of the South Seas beyond the island of San Miguel. Furthermore, if the Viceroy, or the persons who do now, or in the future will, abide there by Our command, or others of Our subjects or vassals, wish to set forth on discoveries in the South Seas and to send ships thereto for the purposes of discovery, then they may do so without hindrance from what is stated above or from any clause of this agreement. If, however, you wish to go in search of discoveries in one of these regions, you may do so, provided it is not in undiscovered and unknown territory.

You must so conduct this voyage of discovery that you do not encroach upon the demarcation and boundaries of the King of Portugal, My dear uncle and brother, or otherwise prejudice his interests. I prize the resolve that has moved you to undertake this voyage of discovery in Our service. For the services which you render Us, for the aggrandizement of the royal power, for the labours and dangers which you assume, you shall receive as reward the twentieth part of the proceeds and gains from all the lands and islands that you will have discovered, and shall besides receive the title of Viceroys of these lands and islands for your sons and heirs for all time. You shall furthermore be recompensed by Our giving you the permission and opportunity from this day henceforth to send yearly, in your own ships, or in whatever ships you may choose, the equivalent of 1000 ducats to and from these lands and islands, invested in such form and manner as may seem to you best. You may there sell and invest whatever you wish and pay unto Us as a royalty a twentieth part, without being obliged to render the other usual taxes, including even those which shall hereafter be imposed. This shall enter into force when you will have returned from this first voyage and shall not apply so long as you are still under way.

That you may be still further recompensed, it is moreover Our command that of the islands which you will have discovered, after 6 of them have been selected for Us, you may choose 2 from the remainder, of whose income and profit you shall have a fifth part, after deduction of costs.

To demonstrate Our favour, it is Our will, inasmuch as We recognize the great expenditure of money and labour which this voyage will entail upon you and since We wish to recompense you therefore, that of the net profits which you bring Us you shall have a fifth part, after deduction of the costs of the fleet. And so that you may the better be able to consummate the above-mentioned project and the enterprise have the needed certainty of success, I declare that I promise to outfit for you 5 ships: 2 each of 130 tons, 2 each of 90 tons, and 1 of 60 tons; equipped with crew, food, and weapons for 2 years, including 234 men, with the captains, able seamen, and ordinary seamen necessary for the operation of the fleet, and with whatever other persons are needed, in accordance with the memorandum. We shall at once decree that Our functionaries who officiate in the House of Commercial Law for the Trade with India (la Casa de Contratación) in Seville set this business promptly afoot.

And because it is Our will that what is stated above be secured to you and fulfilled, We desire that, if one of you should die, all the above-mentioned benefits shall accrue to the one left living as though both were alive.

And so that confidence and order and the necessary certainty be maintained, We must and shall name a factor, a treasurer, and an accountant for the above-mentioned ships, to keep all the accounts.

This I promise you and I give you My royal word that I shall protect you according to the above, and to this end I give you this signature of My name in Valladolid on March 22, 1518—the King—by order of the King: Francisco de los Cobos.

So that this contract may remain in force and be fulfilled in all its terms, you have prayed for the favour that it be confirmed and ratified and, whenever necessary, renewed. We appreciate the usefulness of yourselves, and of whatever you may discover, to Our realm, as well as the services which you, as I hope, will render Us and Our royal crown, and your ability, and the pains that the voyage and the discoveries will cause you. And to the end that an eternal memorial of yourselves and your services shall be set up, so that these services may be rewarded and others be encouraged to serve Us equally well, We do voluntarily vouch for, confirm, and approve this contract and its contents with full knowledge of the facts and with absolute royal power, and do decree that it shall be executed and maintained, fulfilled in every particular, now and for all time, in accordance with its terms. Through this writing, or through a copy signed by a royal scribe, I enjoin the Infante Fernando, Our dear and beloved son and brother, the princes, prelates, dukes, counts, marquis, the nobility, the masters of the Orders, their commanders and knights, the governors of castles, the members of Our privy council, the judges, the bailiffs, and all authorities and officials of the cities and market towns of Our kingdom, not only those now living but also those who will in the future come to be, that they shall according to their duty recognize and execute the above contract, and shall in no way act contrary to the contract or to any part of the same, no matter what laws and sanctions may be directed against it.

And if you wish Our letter on the matter of Our writing and the above-mentioned contract, We authorize Our treasurers and their representatives to deliver it to you whenever you need it and apply for it. We have commissioned Our chancellor, the notaries, and other officials to execute, present, and confirm it, and not to cause you any difficulties in so doing, upon pain of a fine of 10,000 maravedis to be paid into Our revenues. Moreover, I enjoin the man who will produce this writing, or his copy of it signed by a State scribe, to summon you to appear at Our court, wherever We may at that time be residing, within the first 300 days; otherwise he shall suffer the above penalty, and he must bring Us corroborated proof that he has shown it to you so that We may know how Our instructions are being carried out.

In the city of Valladolid, March 22, 1518.

The King.   Francisco de los Cobos.

I had this decree taken down from the above-mentioned books, by order of the Lord of the royal council, and I do hereby confirm the fact that it has been fully and exactly transcribed.

Valladolid, January 24, 1523.   Francisco de los Cobos.

APPENDIX III

ACCOUNT OF THE COSTS OF
MAGELLAN'S FLEET *

SHIPS AND SHIPS' GEAR

228,750 Ms. is the value of the ship "Concepción," 90 tons, including its gear and its boat.

300,000 Ms. is the value of the ship "Victoria," of approximately 95 tons, with its gear and its boat.

330,000 Ms. was the cost of the ship named "San Antonio," 120 tons, with its gear and its boat.

270,000 Ms. is the value of the ship named "Trinidad," 110 tons, with its gear and its boat.

187,500 Ms. was the cost of the ship "Santiago," 75 tons, with its gear and its boat.

24,188 Ms. includes the expenditure of 20,438 Ms. for bringing the ships from Cadiz and San Lucar to Seville and 3750 Ms., which the factor Juan de Aranda laid out when he went from Seville to Cadiz in order to buy the ships.

13,482 Ms. was expended for day labour to launch the ships from the stocks.

104,244 Ms. was the labour cost of the carpentry work on the five ships.

129,539 Ms. was the labour cost for the caulking of the ships.

6,790 Ms. was the labour cost for the woodworkers who sawed the planks for the above-mentioned ships.

175,098 Ms. was the cost of the wood for the beams and planks as well as for the smaller pieces of wood that were bought for repairs on the ships.

142,532½ Ms. was expended for the metalwork on the ships' bottoms.

31,670 Ms. for the oakum bought to caulk the ships.

72,267½ Ms. for pitch, tar, and oil for greasing and caulking the ships.

53,852 Ms. for tallow to rub into the ships.

149,076 Ms. was the cost of 173 pieces of sailcloth which were bought as reserve stock for the voyage.

32,825 Ms. for thread and needles for sewing the sails, as well as for the labour costs of those who sewed these sails.

37,437 Ms. was the cost of the spars and yards for the ships.

3,937 Ms. was the cost of a small boat for the ship "Trinidad."

---

* Taken from the fourth volume of the *Colección de los viages y descubrimientos* by D. Martín Fernández de Navarrete, Madrid, 1837. "Ms." stands for maravedis.

15,475 Ms. was the cost of the ships' pumps, spikes, and nails.

6,563 Ms. for the ships' helms.

9,364 Ms. was the cost of the sacks, shafts, and leather for the pumps.

1,285½ Ms. for six rolls of sinew.

3,687½ Ms. for thick twine.

4,204 Ms. was the cost of 8 pulley blocks for launching the ships from the stocks.

34,672½ Ms. was the cost of the tackle of the fleet as well as of the tackle required to rig them.

511 Ms. was the cost of 3 ladles for the pitch.

1,962 Ms. was the cost of 13 consignments of ballast.

807 Ms. was the cost of 32 ells of cloth for making sandbags and other things necessary to ballast the ships.

438,335½ Ms. was paid as wages and board for the ships' companies while they outfitted the ships for the voyage.

42,042 Ms. was the cost of 13 anchors bought for the ships.

1,008 Ms. was the cost of 8 large and small saws for the ships.

1,762 Ms. was the cost of assorted augers and drills for the fleet.

663 Ms. was the cost of 6 grappling irons for drawing the ships from the stocks at the launching.

2,495 Ms. was the cost of 76 skin bags for tarring and greasing the ships, and for storage purposes on the voyage.

4,277 Ms. was the cost of wood fuel needed in caulking the ships.

1,054½ Ms. was paid to the pilots who brought the ships from San Lucar to Seville.

324,170½ Ms. was the cost of 221 hundredweight of cables, splices, and buoy lines as well as 1000 *arrobas* of hemp from which were made ropes needed by the ships. Included are the 38,972 Ms. for the labour and 14,066 Ms. which was the cost of the anchor lines, buoy ropes, and seam roping.

25,029 Ms. was the cost of 80 flags, together with their painted decoration, and a royal standard of taffeta.

49,584 Ms. was the cost of the brigantine which was built.

84,144 Ms., of which Duarte Barbosa spent 7500 Ms. in traveling from Seville to Bilbao; and of which Anton Semeño expended 3750 Ms. in bringing the money to Bilbao; and of which 24,390 Ms. was paid for the loading of the ship which came from Bilbao. The remainder, 48,504 Ms., was spent on miscellaneous items for the ships and carriages.

ORDNANCE, POWDER, AND INCIDENTALS

160,135 Ms. was the cost of 58 fieldpieces, 7 falconets, 3 large bombards, 3 *pasamuros*. These all came from Bilbao in addition to the ordnance that the ships already had.

109,028 Ms., of which 104,200 Ms. was for 50 hundredweight of powder, and 4828 Ms. for the freight charges from Fuenterrabia.

5,477 Ms. was the cost of 165 pounds of powder bought in Bilbao for the training of the men.

11,633 [sic!] Ms. was the cost of the iron and stone projectiles and balls for the ordnance of the fleet.

3,850 Ms. was the cost of the moulds for making cannonballs for the falconets, *pasamuros*, and fieldpieces.

39,890 Ms. was the cost of 221 *arrobas* and 7 pounds of lead, of which 84 *arrobas* was for caulking and the remainder for cannonballs.

3,276 Ms. was expended for burnishing the ordnance.

8,790 Ms., of which 4290 Ms. was spent for the board of the soldiers, who were given a definite sum daily. The remainder, 4500 Ms., was paid out to them for premiums and incidentals.

CROSSBOWS, ARQUEBUSES, ARMOUR, AND OTHER WEAPONS

110,910 Ms. was the cost of 100 suits of armour, with arm and shoulder pieces and helmets, and 100 breastplates.

33,495 Ms. was the cost of 60 catapults and 360 dozen arrows from Bilbao.

10,500 Ms. was the cost of 50 guns from Vizcaya.

6,375 Ms. was the cost of the harness and 2 complete suits of armour for the captain.

6,800 Ms. was the cost of 200 round shields from Bilbao.

680 Ms. was the cost of 6 sabres from Bilbao which the captain received.

44,185 Ms. was the cost of 95 dozen spears, 10 dozen javelins, 1000 lances, 200 pikes, 6 spearheads, and 6 lance shafts from Bilbao.

2,499 Ms. was the cost of 120 balls of thread and 7 scoops for grain.

3,553 Ms. was expended to put the weapons in good condition as well as for leather and 6 pounds of emery for cleaning them, and for 3000 nails and 200 extra buckles.

5,611 Ms. was the cost of 50 powder horns for the ordnance and of 150 ells of wick.

PROVISIONS FOR THE FLEET AND THE EXPENSES FOR THE SAME

372,510 Ms. was expended for biscuit, of which 363,480 Ms. was the cost of 2138 quintals and 3 pounds of biscuit at 170 Ms. per quintal, and 6375 Ms. was the cost of the biscuit which the ship "Santiago Bretona" purchased, and 2655 Ms. was laid out for the loan of the sacks and the shipment of the biscuit.

590,000 Ms. for wine from Jerez: 508 bottles at the price of 511,347 Ms. 78,653 Ms. was expended for the following: 37,870 Ms. for the freight charges; 18,428 Ms. for the importation; 6324 Ms. received by Gonzalo Díaz while traveling 93 days purchasing it. 3320 Ms. for the hoisting of 420 casks. 6115 Ms. was the cost of the cork and the tarpaulin nails, as well as of the couriers sent from Seville to Jerez on the business of this wine. 4790 Ms. was spent by Juan Nicolás while he purchased the wine; and 1806 Ms. went to the people who guarded him while he loaded in Jerez and unloaded in Seville.

23,037 Ms. was the cost of 50 *hanegas* of beans, 90 *hanegas* of chick-peas, and 2 *hanegas* of lentils.

58,425 Ms. was the cost of 47 hundredweight and 5 *arrobas* of edible oil bought for the fleet.

62,879 Ms. was the cost of 200 small casks of anchovies and 166 dozen dried fish and sturgeon, as well as 9 dozen of dentex and 63 dozen of *corundillos*. There were 17 hundredweight and 23 pounds of dried fish besides.

43,908 Ms. was the cost of 57 quintals and 12 pounds of salt pork, purchased at various prices.

17,735 Ms., of which 7 cows bought in San Lucar cost 14,000 Ms. and 3 pigs 1180 Ms., and of which 2560 Ms. was spent in San Lucar for meat.

26,434 Ms. was the cost of 984 cheeses, which weighed 112 hundredweight and 6 pounds, and which were purchased at various prices.

393,623 Ms. was expended, including 230,017 Ms. for 417 hogsheads, 253 butts, and 45 tuns at various prices.

FOOD AND OTHER MATERIALS FOR PROVISIONING THE FLEET

15,451 Ms. was the cost of 21 *arrobas* and 9 pounds of sugar, bought at 720 Ms. per *arroba*.

3,655 Ms. was the cost of 200 hundredweight of vinegar brought from Moguer and delivered in the ships' stores at this price.

2,198 Ms. was the cost of 250 strings of garlic and 100 bundles of onions.

5,997 Ms. was the cost of 18 hundredweight of raisins.

1,130 Ms. was the cost of 16 quarter-casks of figs.

2,922 Ms. was the cost of 12 *hanegas* of almonds in the shell, inclusive of the freight cost.

8,980 Ms. was the cost of 54 hundredweight and 2 pounds of honey, inclusive of the freight cost.

750 Ms. was the cost of 2 hundredweight of currants.

1,554 Ms. was the cost of 3 jars of capers.

1,768 Ms. was the cost of the salt.

1,575 Ms. was the cost of 3 hundredweight and 22 pounds of rice.

380 Ms. was the cost of 1 *hanega* of mustard.

5,779 Ms. was the cost of the quince-paste for the fleet.

13,027 Ms. was the cost of the medicaments, salves, and various ointments, and the distilled water for the fleet.

5,927 Ms. was the cost of 5 pipes of flour, of which each ship in the fleet had its own.

COPPERWARE AND OTHER MISCELLANEOUS OBJECTS FOR THE FLEET

21,515 Ms. was the cost of the copperware of the fleet, of which 6165 Ms. was for 5 great cooking pots of copper which weighed 280 pounds; 3700 Ms. was for 5 copper kettles which weighed 132 pounds; 7695 Ms. was for 2 copper bake ovens with a weight of 171 pounds; 1215 Ms. was the cost of a copper kettle with a weight of 27 pounds; 2200 Ms. was the cost of a large kettle for cooking pitch weighing 55 pounds. The coppersmith Cabrera received 540 Ms. for putting a bottom in one of the kettles and 11 pounds of copper besides.

884 Ms. was the cost of 10 large knives for the ships.

516 Ms. was the cost of 42 wooden measures for the rationing of wine and water.

3,440 Ms. was the cost of 8 hundredweight of candles and the 42 hundredweight of candles made of the tallow bought for the ships; also 20 pounds of wool waste which they took along to make candles in case of need.

1,430 Ms. was the cost of 89 lanterns which the ships received.

495 Ms. was the cost of 9½ pounds of ornamented wax candles which were provided for the blessing of the ships.

8,860 Ms. was the cost of 40 wagonloads of wood which were bought for the fleet.

1,280 Ms. for 40 ells of canvas, of which each ship received 8 ells for table cloths.

476 Ms. was the cost of 14 pans.

158 Ms. was the cost of a chain for the kettle.

256 Ms. was the cost of 12 pairs of bellows with their iron pipes.

1,530 Ms. was the cost of 22½ pounds of wax which the ships received for waxing the thread for sewing sails and armour-harness.

768 Ms. was the cost of 12 large knives for the pantries of the ships.

204 Ms. was the cost of 5 large iron spoons.

5,834 Ms. was the cost of 160 platters, 200 soup plates, 100 carving knives, 66 wooden platters, all of which came from Bilbao.

240 Ms. was the cost of 20 compass lanterns.

330 Ms. was the cost of 12 funnels, 6 large and 6 small.

125 Ms. was the cost of 5 hammers.

995 Ms. was the cost of 18 pans over and above the 14 before mentioned.

653 Ms. was the cost of a mortar and pestle for the pharmacy.

3,622 Ms. was the cost of 35 padlocks which the stewards of the ships received.

2,891 Ms. was the cost of the leg-irons, manacles, and chains of the fleet.

200 Ms. was the cost of 8 pieces of iron for sheathing.

240 Ms. was the cost of 20 pounds of steel for reinforcing the picks and other tools.

297 Ms. for a hundredweight of tested weights of iron for the purpose of weighing the weights and other objects in discovered countries.

2,400 Ms. was the cost of 50 mattocks and hoes.

1,600 Ms. was the cost of 20 iron bars and levers for the ships.

2,531 Ms. was the cost of 56 iron bars and hammers, and 2 large iron sledges.

1,200 Ms. was the cost of 2 iron lanterns.

360 Ms. was the cost of 8 pairs of tongs which the stewards received.

1,224 Ms. was the cost of 12 borers, 6 awls, 5 boat hooks, all of which came from Bilbao.

24,938 Ms. was the cost of 19 hundredweight and 12 pounds of iron in small pieces which the stewards received.

10,639 Ms. was the cost of the matting and baskets for the fleet, of which 9290 Ms. was the cost of 128 mats for the *pajoles* and 1349 Ms. was the cost of 87 baskets for holding the ships' biscuit and 22 fig baskets for the weapons.

30,254 Ms. was the cost of the fishing tackle divided up as follows: 8500 Ms. for 2 draw-nets; 125 Ms. for 6 angling rods; 425 Ms. was the cost of the cork for the draw-nets; 8663 Ms. was the cost of the flax and cord for fishing; 8715 Ms. was the cost of the harpoons and fishing forks from Vizcaya; 3826 Ms. was the cost of 10,500 fishing hooks.

ENUMERATION OF MANY THINGS THAT WERE NECESSARY FOR THE FLEET

9,147 Ms., including 3000 Ms. for a smithy which was bought with its entire equipment, and 6147 Ms. for some large bellows, an anvil, and blast pipes, which came from Vizcaya.

1,211 Ms. was the cost of 15 blank books, in 5 of which the expenses of the fleet were to be kept and the other 10 were given to the officers (officials) for keeping accounts.

2,635 Ms. went to the stevedores who loaded the ships.

2,125 Ms. was the cost of 2 hones and a whetstone for the two barbers who went with the fleet.

2,895 Ms. was the cost of 5 drums and 20 tambourines for the diversion of the crew of the fleet.

16,513 Ms. was the cost of the church decorations together with everything necessary for the priests of the fleet to read masses.

5,735 Ms. went to the pilots, 3700 to those who brought the fleet from Seville to San Lucar, and 1985 to those who took the ships out of the harbour of San Lucar.

11,250 Ms. went to Rodrigo de Garay for his services to the fleet from the time that it was equipped until it left Seville.

7,500 Ms. went to Juan de la Cueva for his services during this time.

12,014 Ms. was paid for quicksilver and cinnabar, rush ropes, dressed leather, and copper.

5,625 Ms. was received by the man who was sent to the court from Portugal, to pay his expenses.

45,000 Ms. was paid to the couriers of the royal court and to Juan de Cartagena.

6,750 Ms. was given to the caravel and toward the maintenance of the man who brought letters to the Canary Islands.

15,000 Ms. was received by Luis de Mendoza, the treasurer of the fleet, in 40 ducats for the things that had to be bought on the Canary Islands.

THE WARES CARRIED BY THE FLEET AND THE WAGES PAID FOR THE MANNING OF THE FLEET

1,154,504 Ms. was paid in wages to the 237 persons of the fleet as an advance for 4 months.

1,679,769 Ms. was the value of the wares which the fleet took along for purposes of trade and of the silk and cloth garments and other things which were to be given away.

CHARTS, QUADRANTS, THEODOLITES, MAGNETIC NEEDLES, AND TIMEPIECES FOR THE FLEET

68,182 Ms. was expended for sea charts and quadrants, as follows:

    1,125 Ms. went to Nuño García for buying parchment for the charts.

    900 Ms. for a dozen parchment skins.

    864 Ms. for still another dozen.

    13,125 Ms. for 7 sea charts.

    11,250 Ms. for 11 sea charts.

    13,500 Ms. for 6 sea charts.

    1,121 Ms. for 6 wooden quadrants.

    750 Ms. for 1 wooden theodolite.

    4,500 Ms. was paid by Magellan for a globe.

    4,500 Ms. was paid to Magellan for 6 metal theodolites.

    4,080 Ms. was paid to him for 15 magnetic needles.

1,875 Ms. was paid to him for 15 quadrants of wood and bronze.

476 Ms. for some gilded compasses with boxes which he sent to His Majesty with the map.

340 Ms. for a leather box for the globe.

612 Ms. for 12 hour glasses.

750 Ms. for 2 magnetic needles.

600 Ms. for 6 compasses.

750 Ms. was paid to Nuño García for 2 magnetic needles.

136 Ms. was paid for the repair of a spoiled magnetic needle.

884 Ms. was the cost of 4 large boxes for 4 compasses.

6,094 Ms. for 16 magnetic needles and 6 timepieces which Bernaldino del Castillo sent from Cadiz.

SUMMARY OF THE EXPENDITURES FOR THE FLEET

3,912,241 Ms.[1] was the cost of the 5 ships of the fleet with their gear and armaments, powder, armour, and lances.

415,060 Ms.[2] was paid for copper, fishing tackle, couriers' pay; also for sea charts, quadrants, theodolites, compasses, timepieces, and other things.

1,589,551 Ms. was the cost of the biscuit, wine, oil, fish, meat, cheese, and vegetables; also of the casks and bottles for the wine and water.

1,154,504 Ms. was paid out in wages for 4 months to 237 persons, including the captain and officers.

1,679,769 Ms. was the cost of the trade goods and of the silk and cloth clothing and other things to be presented as gifts.

Thus the expenditures for the fleet amount to 8,751,125 Ms.

From which is to be deducted 416,790 Ms. for the things which remained over from the fleet and were stored in Seville.

8,334,335 Ms. remains as expenditures.

6,454,209 Ms. was contributed by His Majesty.

1,880,126 Ms. was contributed by Christopher de Haro.

---

[1] As given above these items actually add up to 3,912,971 Ms.

[2] As given above these items actually add up to 414,565 Ms.

INDEX

INDEX